accelerating performance

performance

**powerful new techniques
to develop people**

SUNNY STOUT ROSTRON

**KOGAN
PAGE**

First published in 2002

Kogan Page Limited
120 Pentonville Road
London N1 9JN
UK

Stylus Publishing Inc
22883 Quicksilver Drive
Sterling VA 20166-2012
USA

British Library Cataloguing in Publication Data

A CIP record for this book is available from the British Library.

ISBN 0 7494 3642 5

Typeset by Saxon Graphics Ltd, Derby
Printed and bound in Great Britain by Clays Ltd, St Ives plc

To my parents, Cliff and Lila

Contents

Acknowledgements

I am very grateful to a number of colleagues for their generous help with this book. For their time, talent and insights, I would like to thank Rita Morris, Ivan Midderigh, Myrna Wajsman, Jenny Greenwood, my sister Deborah Barnett, Karen Miller, Robin Price and Jana Husek. And I cannot say enough for my two editors: my husband Bryan Rostron, and friend and colleague Catharine Browne, for their expertise, energy and vision.

I am deeply appreciative of the trainers, facilitators and performance consultants with whom I have worked over the years. Sharing and working with them has been a pleasure. It is one of the themes of this book that we should give each other the gifts of our own expertise. I hope that some of what I have learned from the following colleagues will be evident in these pages: Steve Blower, Eve Brock, Mary Colletti, Jacqueline Connelly, Susan Dellinger, Robert Paul Denton, Joyce Dufala, David Fishel, John Frazer-Robinson, Judy Fuggle, Michelle Gilder, Jacqueline Guthrie, Celia Kemsley, Bernard le Roux, Jess Levant, Sue Lupton, Jose Menendez, Ian McDermott, Min McLoughlin, Ros Palmer, Mark Rittenberg, Julian Simmonds, David Stone and John Townsend.

Finally, I would like to say a special thank you to Jo Larbie, for her friendship, guidance and total support.

Sunny Stout Rostron

Introduction: What's different about this book?

Everything. It's for you if you're looking for a new way to develop people. If you want to link learning with building performance, it's for you. If you want to be passionate about your job and adopt a new role as a performance consultant, it's for you. Or if you want to become a cutting-edge, world-class facilitator, this book is for you.

It's a participative, fun, fast-track journey for the new guard in performance development. This book is about how to develop people, accelerating their performance and that of the organization. It will help you to be instructor-led but participant-driven. *Accelerating Performance* gives you a mental tool kit to combine the how to's of the last 10 years, known as the 'decade of the brain'. It examines how to create a link between the mind and the body, because the way we think affects our physiology and our behaviour.

How can you, and why should you, incorporate creativity, storytelling, theatre techniques, music, drawing, rapport, relaxation and deep democracy into your workshops? *Accelerating Performance* combines the principles of brain-based learning and emotional competence. It explores how and why using multiple intelligences increases learning, retention and performance – enhancing your own development and flexibility as a performance consultant.

It teaches you to design creative seminars using the essential tools of the actor's trade: voice, body, breath, imagination and presence. Using the powerful tools and techniques of the theatre, you will explore possibilities to stretch your own limits as a performance coach and those of your participants.

You'll learn the principles of deep democracy, which honour the majority voice in decision making, but include the wisdom of the minority voice. Decision making and diffusing conflict play a big part in any performance workshop. The fundamentals of deep democracy enable you to facilitate change, resolve conflict and manage challenges easily and effectively.

This book is a breakthrough and a how-to, breaking through your own limitations to achieve your peak potential. Whether you are a veteran trainer, performance consultant or career coach looking for a wider vision, or you're new to the profession, this book is for you. It will transform your style, performance and delivery. It will help you to structure seminars, workshops and lectures that open up an exponential world of learning and creativity. It's a very different, imaginative and fascinating journey into the facilitation of learning and performance development.

To illustrate these innovative and powerful techniques, I give examples from my own workshops in the corporate, legal and education fields. These are fun and immensely effective tools. It's new. It's innovative. I do it. It works. Enjoy the ride.

1

Reach for the stars

Performance developers are eclectic. That's their job. Constantly seeking new ideas, techniques and tools of the trade – that's how they break through to accelerate performance and develop people. This book is about training, facilitation and performance development: how it can be effective and fun. I hope to communicate simply, clearly and through personal examples from my own work, to demonstrate how I have put together all these tools to tremendous effect.

Whether you want to learn new training techniques, explore creative ways to enhance your facilitation skills, or push beyond your individual limits to develop your own and your participants' performance, these techniques will take you into a new realm. From start to finish, your style of facilitating and your workshops will be transformed; from breaking the ice at the beginning of a session, to the use of motivation and innovative thinking. In this book, I introduce the acting techniques of the theatre world, the exciting use of brain-based learning and the application of deep democracy.

To accelerate performance and become part of the new guard requires a mastery of facilitation techniques. Here we explore creative problem solving, handling conflict, and designing new ways to motivate your learners and enhance their performance. Whether you want new ideas, new structure or a new job, *Accelerating Performance* will help you break through and open up the exponential world of learning, discovery, creativity and fun. When you reach for the stars, you may not hold their light and brilliance in your hand, but you and your ideas will always be illuminated.

Revolutionizing training

What's it all about?

Accelerating performance is more than just continually learning how to do what you do in new ways. It is ongoing: learning new ways to deliver, present and structure your workshops – and designing creative exercises to involve your participants in as many ways as possible. Flexibility and innovation are your best friends as a facilitator. If you continue to do what you have always done, you will soon be out of work in today's competitive, fast-changing workplace.

This book offers you a spectrum of fresh ideas, development methods and techniques to choose from. I have included guides to other books, tapes and performance consultants. This is for you to continue on your own road, breaking through your own barriers and self-imposed limitations. All performance developers need to learn from their participants and each other. That is how they move forward.

This book is a route map. It's a journey and an adventure, for you to explore what you already do well. Add ingredients to your own 'training recipes', which will help you bake a new cake, create a new taste. Improve every time you step onto the stage, or in front of an audience. Have fun. Read the book all the way through, or dip into each chapter as and when you feel the need to tune up your skills or spice up your development programmes.

Please use this manual as a practical new way to design and deliver development sessions. It is structured to help you align your own programmes to the learning needs of participants, and to your teaching and communication preferences.

Remember, you are always your own best model for excellence. You are just adding more flexibility, creativity and sheer enjoyment to how you do what you do.

Who is this book for?

Accelerating Performance is for you if your role or function includes any of the following, or if you directly or indirectly manage any of these positions:

- trainer (technical, sales, management, performance development...)
- training coordinator
- training manager
- training specialist
- career coach
- career developer
- career planner
- change agent
- consultant
- facilitator
- human resources developer
- human resources manager
- personal coach
- professional coach

- performance development
- professional development

In this book I use the terms *performance developer*, *performance consultant* and *performance coach*. These roles include those of trainer, coach and facilitator. Why? Someone in the role of performance coach focuses on what people must do to achieve results. This is different from the traditional training process of focusing on what people must learn.

Traditionally, trainers have identified and addressed the learning needs of people. We have moved on with the development of training's new guard, whose job is to develop people and performance. The role of the performance consultant is to identify and address people's performance needs. The training function is often viewed as a cost rather than an investment, and training programmes are sometimes seen to have a limited link to organizational goals. On the other hand, the function of the performance consultant is to produce measurable results (such as improve how people do things, help them work more efficiently), and to link performance to the goals of the organization.

If your job is to develop people, change behaviour, improve performance and get results, for the individual and the organization – then read on!

Building performance

Learning from failure

Life is short. Do what you love and do it with passion. To do so requires a certain willingness to let go of the concept of failure. In fact, there really is no such thing as failure – there are only results and feedback. Here's an example.

CASE STUDY: CLARIFYING OBJECTIVES

I once facilitated a weekend workshop for a major UK sports and leisure organization which wanted a 'motivational day' on marketing. I came highly recommended, and my seminar was to be the last day of a weekend workshop. I wasn't very happy about the brief I received by telephone. The conference organizers didn't seem clear about their goals, which meant their goals weren't clear to me. I decided to get on with the preparation despite unclear objectives on both sides. I set myself up for 'failure' before I had even begun.

I prepared a one-day workshop on the essentials of marketing, with lots of interactive exercises to creatively identify how to market within their sector. It wasn't what they had in mind. Once I started speaking, all became clear. They needed a facilitator to help them to identify marketing training needs, and to identify who within the organization could mentor others. Despite my attempt to save the day, only about 50 per cent of the audience really benefited. A second lesson was that many of the audience had been up all night at their gala dinner, so a large percentage hadn't had any sleep.

Although it felt like failure, it was only feedback. I hadn't failed; I reached 50 per cent of the audience, and I learnt the first lesson any facilitator needs to know: find out the specific aims, goals and objectives of your client.

Learning from Lincoln

The story of Abraham Lincoln illustrates that there is no such thing as failure, only feedback. I heard it many years ago at a Tony Robbins seminar. It has become an anecdotal tale repeated by performance consultants round the world. Abraham Lincoln, America's 16th president, failed at business at the age of 23. He was defeated in the same year for the state legislature; failed again at business at age 24; lost his sweetheart who died when he was 26. He had a nervous breakdown at 27 and lost a congressional election at 34. At 46 he lost a bid for the Senate. At 47 he lost a nomination for Vice President of the USA. At age 50 he lost another Senate race. At the age of 51, Abraham Lincoln became President of the United States.

He learnt from every experience; he never saw his losses as failures. Lincoln learnt how to change his approach where necessary, and saw his losses as feedback and results. They were not necessarily the results he wanted, so he adjusted and fine-tuned his approach to every election – until he finally won the highest honour in his country.

Allowing risks and mistakes

Letting go of the fear of mistakes takes courage. This is primarily because we all fear rejection. But there are no right answers in many situations, and to let go of the fear of mistakes is the best way to learn. Think about how you have learnt all your most valuable lessons. This is exactly how I learnt to value the clarity of objectives prior to facilitating any workshop or speaking on any topic.

It's also about belief. All human behaviour is organized around belief. Whenever someone says something is important or not important to do, it's because they have a belief about it. If you have a belief that there is no such thing as failure, it will free you to take risks, to be imaginative, innovative and creative. You can't possibly fail. You'll only learn from your results, your achievements and feedback from others about what works, what doesn't work and what needs work.

One of the primary lessons for a performance developer is that you cannot please everyone. No matter what the style, content or format of a learning programme, the personal style of the facilitator sets the tone for the learning process.

You always succeed in producing a result. If it's not the approach you want, then learn from your mistakes and change your approach.

High-performance psychology

Performance development needs to engage the whole person: attitudes, skills and the ability to think critically. This is so participants can learn concepts to apply to new situations, and to solve more complex problems. It's important, therefore, for performance developers to understand adult learning styles, and how to accelerate performance through the principles of performance psychology.

Learning from failure is the first premise of high-performance psychology. Michael Gaffney, president of Onexus University in Ottawa, says, 'Failure is a valuable commodity. It creates ongoing learning by pointing to what should have been. Failure increases the chance that your next effort will be a success.'

Gaffney failed to make a success of an internet company in 1985, eight years ahead of its time. Gaffney's belief in the power of positive thinking stems from his experience as an athlete and a coach. He coached the Canadian Olympic diving team for 11 years. He advocates applying the principles of high-performance sports psychology to the workplace, especially mental preparation and goal setting.

I work with sports professionals, primarily in the golfing arena. One of the areas we constantly work with is setting goals – or, more importantly, identifying the process of achieving those goals. Be prepared to take one step further, to continually learn from your mistakes. By paying attention to the path we tread, we learn continually from what works, and what doesn't work.

High-performance sports psychology is all about mental preparation. The first step when setting goals is to identify what drives you: what are your values, what really turns you on, what are you passionate about? Then you can set specific, well-formed goals.

1. State your goal in positive, active terms.
2. Where are you now in relation to your goal?
   Where are you in your present life?
3. When you achieve your goal, what will you be experiencing?
   What will it feel like, look like, sound like?
   Can you visualize it, is it compelling?
   Describe this goal as you see yourself achieving it in the future.
4. How will you know when you have achieved your goal?
   What will you feel like, what will it look like, what will it sound like?

5. What will you be able to do once you've achieved your goal?
   What will change?
6. What steps do you need to take to achieve this goal?
   Write them down and put specific timings to them.
7. Who else is involved in achieving this goal with you?
   What is important to them in achieving this goal?
   How can they help you to achieve it?
   Where, when, how and with whom do you want this goal?
8. What resources or skills do you need to achieve this goal?
   What resources do you already have (physical, mental, psychological) that will help you to achieve your goal?
   How did you achieve a similar goal before?
9. Why do you want this goal?
   What will you gain or lose once you achieve it?
   What will happen if you get it?
   What will happen if you don't get it?
   What won't happen if you don't get it?

High-performance psychology is based on individuals' mental maps: how we organize our thinking. A positive mental map is revealed in a famous story about Thomas Edison, inventor of the light bulb. It's said he tried 9,999 times to create a working light bulb. When asked why he continued after failing so many times, Edison replied: 'I've only learnt 9,999 ways that don't work.'

The great golf champion Gary Player was once asked, 'You sure are lucky aren't you?' To which he replied, with a twinkle in his eye, 'You're right, I am lucky. And the funny thing is, the more I practise, the luckier I get!'

Shoes off

Creative collaboration

Is your training locked into old ways of thinking? If so, it's important to jump-start your creativity. Here are a few ways to move in a different direction from your standard style of facilitating or training.

- *Brainstorm*. Have regular brainstorming sessions with your team. Prior to any workshop, brainstorm the key ideas you want to get across. Draw a brainstorm map to illustrate those ideas clearly. If several of you are team teaching, you may prefer to first create, then compare, your individual brainstorm maps. See Chapter 6 for detail on how to draw brainstorm maps.

- *Creative coaching*. Ask other performance coaches to sit in on one of your workshops, to observe your style and method. Listen to their constructive comments and identify what you could do differently. It's difficult to let go of ego and accept their constructive criticism, but it's worth it for the learning. In return, sit in on one of their workshops to coach them, offering constructive comments at the end of their session. Sharing styles and ideas with other performance developers helps you to grow, giving you ideas about how to do things differently.
- *Role model*. Choose several trainers, facilitators or speakers you admire. Tape them, or sit in on their sessions and identify three things you could adapt. Whenever possible, video a role model, review the video and identify their patterns of excellence.
- *Borrow ideas*. Identify icebreakers, creative ideas, interactive exercises and different ways of creating dialogue that other facilitators use. Adapt those methods for yourself. We learn a great deal from the excellence of others.
- *Training and development*. Once a quarter, identify areas where you need to improve. Attend a training workshop that will satisfy a performance need or stretch you. It may be topic-oriented, or it may be focused on facilitation techniques, presentation, delivery or creative thinking.
- *Creative thinking tools*. Adopt creative tools when planning your sessions. A useful creative thinking tool is Edward de Bono's 'six thinking hats'. Apply each hat colour to factors you need to consider when designing a workshop. These questions will help you to think expansively about the seminar, speech or programme you are planning – giving you the big picture, but also examining the detail. See the brain fitness and motivation chapters for more techniques to incorporate new thinking into your workshops and your individual client coaching.

Pushing beyond your limits

Think of yourself as a pioneer, opening up new routes for learners. What have you done lately to brush up on your skills, to learn something new, to push beyond your skills and your comfort zone in the learning environment?

Let's face it: in most organizations, the reason for training is to achieve organizational objectives. Your role as a performance consultant is to achieve organizational objectives and help people develop at the same time. But people cannot achieve organizational objectives if their personal objectives are not in alignment with those of the organization.

Your learners look to you to blaze the way: to give them guidance, to lead them. If you are going to enable your participants to learn, then you are also expected to be continually learning yourself. Here are some of the roles you will be expected to embody:

- administrator and supervisor
- authority on methodology
- coach and counsellor
- consultant and advisor
- creator and designer
- facilitator and assistant
- leader and role model
- manager of people
- motivator and instigator
- planner and organizer
- subject expert
- technical expert
- trainer

How can you fulfil all of these roles unless you are continually learning? Whatever your role, flexibility and the ability to be proactive are essential at all times. Clarify the role of performance consultant within your organization. If you work for yourself, clarify your role with clients. Continually update your skills as:

- *Facilitator.* Your role is to facilitate learning. A facilitator lets the group become responsible for its aims and outcomes, and manages that group process. In Chapter 9 we explore cutting-edge facilitation skills to help you achieve excellence. The facilitator also provides feedback to management as to how performance objectives can be met.
- *Designer and provider.* You design, structure and provide training. Your role is proactive, with responsibility to undertake a training needs analysis and to identify overall performance-development objectives. Do you (or your team) design and deliver training in a ritualized, standard format? What could you do differently? What do you need to do to implement new techniques?
- *Consultant.* Your role is to analyse current problems within the organization that involve personnel, and to recommend performance-development solutions to achieve results. What consulting skills do you need to develop to fulfil this role?
- *Manager.* Performance-development consultants may also be managers, responsible for the development, delivery and evaluation of all performance-development activities. They may also recruit and train trainers, and are responsible for the control of the development budget. What new responsibilities can you take on in this area?
- *Innovator.* As innovator you provide solutions to effect change and to solve performance problems. This requires working closely with senior management on organizational issues. It also requires creative thinking to effect change.

What new techniques could you bring into your workshops? (See Chapters 4, 5, 6 and 7 for innovative training tools and ideas.)

- *Coach*. As a coach you assess where employees are now in terms of their ability and productivity. You help to determine individual goals and expectations, developing a plan to achieve those goals, evaluating performance on the job and giving feedback. What coaching skills do you possess? Have you completed a coaching course or certificate? Do you have a psychology background? Are you a practitioner in neuro-linguistic programming? What can you do to incorporate new coaching skills and techniques into your work?

- *Trainer*. The trainer is primarily concerned with using a variety of methods to deliver training. The trainer can act as a facilitator, provider, consultant, manager and innovator, providing training solutions to effect change and to solve performance problems. What is the role of trainers and the training team in your organization? Have you developed a structured approach to training?

Exercise: What is your role? (1 hour)

If you can, try to do this exercise with fellow performance developers; if not, spend an hour brainstorming on your own.

1.   Performance-consultant roles

Whether you work for yourself or an organization, you need to play a proactive role. What are the key roles you play as a developer of performance in the organization? Why are they needed?

2.   Skills, knowledge and attitude

Performance developers require a number of skills and a certain amount of knowledge. If you are going to push beyond your boundaries and take up the role of pioneer, what are the key skills and knowledge you and your development team require to be effective? When we discuss metaskills in Chapter 9 we will look at the attitude you bring to the learning environment. Attitude is one of your most important assets as a performance consultant. How do you develop compassion, neutrality and detachment?

3.   Core values and beliefs

In this book we'll look at the importance of values in relation to motivation and peak performance. Values and beliefs govern all human behaviour. Throughout history, they have been the justification for prejudice and strife. Values and positive beliefs are important for you as a performance developer if you are to bring about relevant, positive changes in behaviour in the workplace. What values and beliefs are useful for you to be effective as a performance consultant in the organization?

Here are a few powerful beliefs and values:

- There is no failure, only feedback.
- There are no resistant participants, only inflexible communicators.
- Resistance in a delegate is a sign of a lack of rapport.
- There are no unresourceful people, only unresourceful states.
- Whatever you think you are, you are always more than that.
- People are doing the best they can with the resources they have.
- The mind and body affect each other.
- It's important to respect everyone's model of the world.
- You are in charge of your mind, and therefore your results.
- You have the flexibility to draw it out of them.
- You as a facilitator can enable their potential.
- Fun helps learning to take place.
- Anything is possible.

4.   Where to now?

Now that you have begun to identify roles, skills, and positive beliefs that drive you, draw up a list of strengths and ways to improve in each area. Create an action plan to develop yourself in areas where you need to improve, new skills and talents you are passionate to learn. Identify ideas that will challenge your thinking and habitual facilitation and training practices. Set specific timelines for each goal.

Building your career power

Only you can do it. Only you can set your goals, specific to your own role, whether as trainer, coach, consultant, facilitator or manager. The way forward is through creative, innovative, continual learning that is fun, relevant and specific. This should also fit your beliefs – and you should be passionate about it. If you are not passionate to build your career, what are you passionate about? Are you in the right job?

Specific skills for you to consider are:

- ability to incorporate brain-based learning;
- active listening skills;
- adapting content and style to participant needs;
- applying adult learning theory to course design;
- audiovisual support that enhances learning;
- innovative learning techniques (drawing, music, theatre);

- dealing with difficult delegates;
- designing memorable interactive exercises;
- empathy;
- facilitating debate and discussion;
- facilitation metaskills;
- group-process monitoring;
- participative active learning;
- performance and delivery skills;
- rapport skills.

Getting started

How to read this book

Over the years, I've had many requests from trainers, coaches and facilitators for one comprehensive manual with new performance tools and techniques they can adapt for their own sessions. Now that you have begun to consider your strengths and weakness, beliefs, values and passions, go on to read the first page outlining each chapter. Then flip through the book, simply reading the headings, to give you some content details. When you reach the end of the book, go back and explore those chapters most relevant to your immediate needs.

Chapter 2: Acquiring personal mastery

How can you become a master of your craft, an expert who achieves peak potential? The secret is learning and anticipating change; in short, developing a success habit. Reach for the stars. Set your goals high so they are worth the achievement. Develop total belief in your ability to learn. How can you embark on your own creative renaissance? Invest in professional mastery and start today. Add zest to your work. Make it more personal for your learners.

Chapter 3: Icebreaking

You may want new ideas to begin your workshops; if so, the chapter on icebreakers is for you. The first step on meeting your delegates is to let them know they are walking into the kingdom of possibility – where dreams come true and anything is possible in the realm of learning.

It's your chance to set the tone of comfort, safety, fun, energy, relaxation: whatever message you want to convey. How can you give the gift of your name, and teach them to do the same? Collect concerns and let participants speak out about their needs. Engage your learners. Bring together hearts and minds to explore, team build, enhance creativity, problem solve and develop resourcefulness.

Chapter 4: Think like a star, act like a performer

Shakespeare got it right: all the world's a stage. Performance consultants play many roles, many characters: we can learn so much from the acting world. To develop the performance of your learners, discover theatre-based exercises that are active, dynamic, purposeful, challenging and team building. They incorporate meaning into learning, improve overall communication, rapport, creative thinking skills, and develop mental as well as emotional flexibility. This creates understanding of other points of view: not to be missed if you want to explore learning that is fun. Exploit your entertainment value; engage learning that lasts long past the return to the workplace.

Chapter 5: Brain fitness: your mental tool kit

Is your goal to understand more about the brain? How does it work? How can you introduce whole-brain thinking into your sessions? This chapter looks at exercises to expand the thinking powers of your learners, to accelerate performance and achieve potential. The essentials of brain-based learning are to help participants make connections between new learning and their existing experience and expertise.

Brain research highlights the importance of emotional intelligence: how can you incorporate this into your sessions? Why should you? Pressures and insecurities drive the workplace today. The learning strategies of brain fitness will improve confidence and self-esteem, and accelerate performance. Explore the array of brain fitness tools available to you.

Chapter 6: Real magic: motivation and innovation

When did you last harness the magic of enthusiasm, sparking new ideas that created the will to achieve? Adults learn best when motivated. This chapter will help you harness your group's imagination, motivation and creative performance. Learn how to assess the psycho-geometrics (personality styles and preferred work styles) of your team.

Introduce brainstorming, memory mapping, contradictory thinking, reframing, six-hat thinking and flipside questions. Use storytelling techniques, metaphoric thinking, drawing and journalling to free up the creative bent of your teams. Are you a squiggle or a square? Read on to find out.

Chapter 7: Music: the beat goes on

Many performance developers use music in their training seminars, but how strategic are they in their use of it? Do you know what music works best for creating energy? Or to stimulate thinking, change the mood, develop creative thinking skills or generate outstanding links to learning? How does Mozart make us smarter? Which pieces of music work best?

How can you use classical music and rock'n'roll for learning? What legal parameters must you consider? Do we dare integrate singing and learning, something children learn early? Music is a powerful tool for learning, retention and improved performance. Music inspires. Learn how.

Chapter 8: Doing the dance: rapport and communication or stress?

Rapport is a naturally occurring dance that happens when people communicate. How can you harmonize the energies and natural rhythms of your learners to enhance relationships, build teams and increase your effectiveness as a facilitator? How can you teach learners to agree and disagree and stay in rapport? What is appropriate language to match teaching to learner styles?

What specific skills can you develop to enhance rapport with your learners? How can stress break rapport and communication? Your delivery skills are crucial, so how can you let go of the fear of mistakes, and use adrenaline and nerves to positive effect? Learn how to lead this dance!

Chapter 9: Facilitation metaskills and deep democracy

This chapter explores facilitation, metaskills and the principles of deep democracy. Metaskills are the attitudes and beliefs that a facilitator conveys to a group. They cannot be learnt in the same way we learn technical skills. Learn to work with neutrality, compassion, detachment, congruence, patience and humility.

One of your most powerful tools when managing any group process is the concept of deep democracy, a highly effective way to facilitate group decision making, and to gain the wisdom of the minority voice. Revolutionary deep democracy is a crucial skill for the 21st-century facilitator and performance coach.

Chapter 10: Synchronicity: putting it all together

In this last chapter we look at how to combine all the cutting-edge tools and techniques explored so far: how to incorporate music, strategic icebreakers, facilitate with metaskills, so setting your training programmes apart. With the introduction of brain-based learning and innovative techniques such as metaphoric thinking, storytelling, music and theatre exercises – the rest is up to you.

It seems to me that you are the final chapter of this book ... and the first chapter of your own. You are just beginning. Enjoy the journey.

Where to go for more

At the end of every chapter I list an array of books, journals and web sites available in that specific topic for you to explore further.

Books

Buzan, Tony (1998) *The Mind Map Book: Radiant thinking*, BBC Books, London (beautiful examples, illustrating note taking, structuring information, enhancing memory)

Campbell, Don (1987) *The Mozart Effect*, Hodder and Stoughton, London

de Bono, Edward (1985) *Six Thinking Hats*, Penguin Books, London (an easy explanation of the six different thinking styles)

Dellinger, Susan (1990) *Psycho-Geometrics: Communicating beyond our differences*, Prentice-Hall, Englewood Cliffs, New Jersey

Edwards, Betty (2000) *The New Drawing On The Right Side Of The Brain*, Souvenir Press, London

Goleman, Daniel (1996) *Emotional Intelligence: Why it can matter more than IQ*, Bloomsbury, London

Jensen, Eric (2000) *Music With the Brain In Mind*, Brain Store, San Diego, California

Rose, Colin with Nicholl, Malcolm J (1997) *Accelerated Learning for the 21st Century*, Dell, New York

Stout, Sunny (1993) *Managing Training*, Kogan Page, London

Journals

Belton, Erline (2000) Truth or consequences, *Training and Development* (May) pp 36–37

Flacks, Niki (1994) Don't go out there alone, performance tips for trainers, *Training and Development* (June) pp 19–23

Gaffney, Michael (2000) Diving into online education, *Training and Development* (May) pp 38–39

Galagan, Patricia A and Salopek, Jennifer J (2000) Training's new guard, take this job and love it, *Training and Development* (May) pp 35, 56

Muir, Tom (2000) You gotta know what you don't know, *Training and Development* (May) pp 44–45

Salopek, Jennifer J (1998) Train your brain, an interview with Daniel Goleman, *Training and Development* (October) pp 27–33

Wajsman, Myrna and Lewis, Greg (1999) Path to empowerment, *CAmagazine* (Jan/Feb) (Toronto, Canada) pp 45–51

Weiss, Ruth Palombo (2000) Brain-based learning, *Training and Development* (July) pp 21–24

Audiocassettes

Robbins, Anthony (1986) *Unlimited Power*, Nightingale Conant, Niles, Illinois, USA

Web sites

Thomas Edison, Good quotations by famous people, Dr Gabriel Robins, University of Virginia: http://www.cs.virginia.edu/robins/quotes.html

Abraham Lincoln, The History Place presents Abraham Lincoln: http://www.history-place.com/lincoln/index.html

2

Acquiring personal mastery

The magic is in the learning

Personal mastery is all about learning. It's about growing, developing awareness and challenging your assumptions. This chapter looks at the tools you need to develop your own capabilities, and those of others. Develop powerful, positive beliefs; become a master learner. Drive performance through learning.

The path to personal mastery is the renewal of your spirit. We'll look at the African spirit hierarchy to identify the dominant energies and cultural values in the workplace, and to better manage ourselves and the organization. But personal mastery requires vision. Where are you now? Where are you going? How will you get there? Renew your vision and you renew your spirit.

As a performance consultant, your job is to put people in touch with their own power. You enable people, helping them to develop enquiring minds. Before you can understand others, however, you must first understand yourself.

The teacher always has the most to learn. Richard Carlson, in *Don't Sweat The Small Stuff*, talks about achieving success magically. Although I love the concept, acquiring expertise is a life-long process. The magic is in the journey. My approach is:

M   Have the right *mindset*
A   *Attitude* leads the way
G   *Get* up and *go* ... just do it
I   *Innovation* and *imagination* allow people to dream
C   *Creativity* sparks enthusiasm and motivation
A   *Achievement* means believing in you
L   *Learning* is the key

The secret is learning, anticipating change and developing a success habit. What are your opportunities? How can you harness them, discovering your own resources, gifts and strengths? It's all in the learning: that's the magic.

Defining personal mastery

To enhance performance, teach an appreciation for constant learning. This is the path to personal mastery. Becoming a *master of your craft* is the art of collecting new ideas in order to improve your expertise. Learn all you can. Share your knowledge and expertise with others. Teach them to do the same.

Take up an interest in new topics, in new areas of performance development. Move outside your box. Developing people requires passion in your own development, dedication to theirs. Add zest to your work. Learn from audiotapes, reading, your delegates, other performance consultants and life experiences. Make learning more personal for your participants. Have them share their expertise, their stories, their anecdotes.

Peter Senge, in *The Fifth Discipline Fieldbook*, defines personal mastery as one of the five learning disciplines. He writes: 'Personal mastery is learning to expand our personal capacity to create the results we most desire.' He defines learning as a two-part activity: the first, to study; the second, to practise constantly. Ultimately, this means that learning is mastering self-improvement.

Affirm positive beliefs

Recently I spoke to one of my clients who is facing self-doubt. He is a brilliant international sportsman. However, like all of us, when he doesn't play well he becomes despondent and feels he will never play well again.

Focus on what you can control

One of the things I asked him was: Where are your thoughts taking you? What are you thinking? My advice: get curious, focus on what you can control. You can control your own thinking, visualizing your own excellence. Whenever you are full of doubt, become curious. What has just happened? What can you learn from it? Identify another time when you faced a similar situation and successfully pulled yourself out of it. What did you do? How can you model that?

Focus on excellence

How did you successfully recover from a similar situation? Focus on your belief in yourself; belief is powerful. Create a new list of positive beliefs. If you think you can, you're right. Look back at the times you have achieved excellence. Pick an event similar to this one. Identify what you did that time to reach your goal. Look at what you are doing now: how is that different?

For example, on that particular day my client was focusing on a shot he had played badly. He spent ten minutes fuming about why it had happened. It's better to get curious, better to ask: when did this happen before, and how did I get out of it? Focus on a similar event when you spectacularly turned adversity into success. Get into that previous state of mind. Visualize yourself having turned around a similar event, hear your own voice coaching you, feel your physiology focusing on the result you want.

A lovely illustration is the movie *The Legend of Bagger Vance*. One of the champion golfers steps out of the crowd onto the green and goes into a trance-like state. He focuses only on his goal; the crowd vanishes. You can visibly see his physiology change as he focuses all of his senses on driving the ball. The result? Success.

Reach for the stars

Never affirm limiting beliefs. If you do, it will be impossible to set out your stepping stones to success. If you plan to reach for the stars, begin by believing in yourself. Start there. What positive beliefs will help you to achieve your dreams?

Engage all of you: your beliefs, attitudes, skills, achievements, everything you have learnt from your mistakes. Set positive goals. Write them in active, present tense (I am, I can, I see myself). Visualize your result:

- What will it look like, sound like, feel like?
- Is it compelling?
- When have you achieved something like this before?
- What did you do to achieve it?
- Break it down step by step.

Get into that frame of mind. What were you feeling, thinking, seeing and hearing when you achieved something similar before? Feel yourself in that state. What can you do differently that will help you to achieve this goal once more?

Learn from mistakes and learn from your own excellence. Understand how you do what you do. Model your own excellence. Write down:

- When have you done it brilliantly before?
- How did you do it?
- How can you practise that?

Bust through your fears

Reaffirm your successes, reaffirm your belief in yourself. Often we focus on what we fear, what we are afraid of. Stop focusing on what is out of your control. If necessary, identify your fears. Turn them into positives. Make them work for you, not against you.

CASE STUDY: FEAR OF PUBLIC SPEAKING

I had a colleague who was to speak at a conference in front of a large audience for the very first time. She was used to speaking only in front of small groups. The thought of facing more than a hundred people set the butterflies in her stomach flying out of formation. To help her, we made a list of her positive beliefs, then a list of her fears. These we turned into a positive action list.

Her positive beliefs:

- I'm really good at what I do.
- I don't have to know everything.
- My audience is a resource centre to tap into.
- I'm good at handling a challenge.
- I'm good at learning new things.

Her fears:

- I've never done this before.
- What if I fail?
- What if they don't like me?
- I'll forget what I'm going to say.
- How will I handle difficult questions?

We turned her negatives into positives:

- I've spoken many times to audiences.
- I can focus on small groups in the audience.
- When I speak, my voice is strong and clear.
- They are looking for my expertise.
- I handle questions well.
- I'll do my voice and breathing exercises.

If you bust through your own fears, you're on the road to excellence – to achieving peak performance and to reaching your potential.

Challenge your most cherished beliefs

We have talked about empowering, positive beliefs, but it's important to be clear about your entire belief system. What beliefs do you hold that stop you, that prevent you from going in a new direction? Write them down. Evaluate them. Be clear about what stops you from going that extra mile. There's no traffic jam on the extra mile.

Exercise: Catch the cynic's voice

We often hear people say, 'I know I can achieve anything I want.' But sometimes that little voice in the background says, 'Hah!' When it happens to you, catch it, hear it, pull it out and begin to question it. Play devil's advocate with that voice. Sit down and have a conversation between these two voices: the believer and the cynic need to talk. What can you learn? The cynic is testing you. What can you learn from this?

Having a conversation

For example, I know I am good at what I do. But sometimes, just before a very difficult session, a little voice in my head says, 'What if you don't do it well tomorrow, then what?' I sit down, and literally have a conversation between those two voices. I set out two chairs, and even put labels on the two chairs: cynic and expert. The two voices have a conversation, and I switch chairs as I adopt each voice. I carry on until the two voices are working together and I have restored my self-belief. This usually means identifying the importance of:

- being prepared;
- not having to be perfect;
- being willing to learn from others;
- being willing to go with the group's issues;
- throwing out the need for ego reinforcement;
- remembering when I've done it well before;
- visualizing doing it well tomorrow.

Invest heavily in professional mastery

Your personal and professional development is your own responsibility. What are you doing to invest in yourself? When was the last time you wrote down and reviewed your life and career goals? Hopefully in the next chapter of this book! What is your development plan for the next 12 months? Have you written it down?

A colleague I work with says that I 'make her jump'. When I asked what she meant, she said, 'You always suggest going the next step – constantly learning, gaining self-awareness.' I'm not suggesting we should make people jump. I'm advocating that we need to have a plan to achieve our potential, to reach for the stars. Goethe once said, 'If there is something that you think you can do, even dream that you can – begin it! Boldness has mystery and power and magic in it.'

Wrestle with your demons

When coaching clients, we first identify values and their key roles, personal and professional. We set goals for each role, aligning them with their values. Conflict emerges when personal values are not in alignment with those of the organization.

There are two types of demon we wrestle with. Demons are those nagging thoughts in our head that speak to us day in and day out. The first is self-doubt. The other is internal conflict, when our values do not match those of the culture within which we work.

For example, I spoke with a group of international women lawyers who had set up their own training and development forum. Their conflict was with senior management, who did not believe this forum was necessary. No budget, and no time, was made available for the professional development of this group. Internal conflict was set up, within the firm and within the minds of the women lawyers. Without professional support these women began to question the validity of their forum, but they also began to question how much the firm valued them and their perspective.

Your personal development work will be infused with your values. Perhaps your values are honesty, integrity and continual learning. If you work in an organization that is hesitant to invest money in developing people, your demons (self-doubt and internal conflict) are going to sit heavily on your shoulder, whispering in your ear. The organization will be questioning the validity of your role.

Why arm wrestle with yourself? Remember to do the job you love, and do it with passion. Therein lies success. Therein lies the achievement of your dreams – and the achievement of individual and organizational dreams.

Identifying your professional coach

Do you have a coach or a mentor with whom you work at least several times a year? Someone with whom you can share your fears, hopes and burdens? The job of a coach is to ask questions, to help you think through your crises and dilemmas. Coaching has become the new buzz word in the workplace for good reason; coaches help us to think out loud and to problem solve.

Coaching, suddenly, is a fast-growing phenomenon. Coaches help people to improve performance. We know that: it's what we do for others. But if you don't have one ... why not? Someone with a different set of thinking styles will bring you enlightenment, different expertise and questions to help you think things through.

It can be difficult to find the appropriate or the affordable personal or career coach. One way around this is to co-coach or co-mentor a colleague or partner. I have several professional friends, and the joy of working together is also the joy in counselling each other. Our skills lie in different areas. When we face difficulties, we arrange an informal telephone (or face-to-face) session to talk things through. A coach can be affordable in terms of money and time. Who can you work with? What are the benefits?

A mentoring programme

Do you have a mentoring programme at work? If not, could you be the one to set it up? Personal and professional development is like learning: it requires constancy. I'm asking many questions here for good reason: it's what you should be doing! Development always starts with a question. The wisdom of Socrates: asking questions opens the mind.

In the 1980s I worked in the newspaper industry. We had created a training and development programme for my staff of about 250 people. The only one not included in this programme was myself. I tried to attend a few workshops to enhance my management skills. My boss was clearly unhappy that I should do so. In one instance, he spoke to me several times during a workshop, and nearly ruined any possibility of learning. His view was, Why was I not at work? Why did I need development? It was my job to develop others!

Aiming for 96

There's more to life than just work. Where is the balance? When setting your goals, how do you balance your job, career and personal life? When setting goals, I like to tell clients a vision I have for my 96th year. It's actually a little joke between myself and a childhood friend. I once said to her, 'I'm thinking of sitting in my rocking chair, looking back on my life when I'm 92.' She replied, 'Don't you know? We're heading for 96.' So 96 it is. Now I have a vision of sitting peacefully in my rocking chair, sharing my wisdom with others – and learning from them. There will always be something new to learn.

Your career is up to you

Develop total belief

The vision of the road ahead is crucial: for yourself, your team and your organization. Without vision, how will you know where you are headed?

- Where are you going?
- How will you get there?
- What are the obstacles?
- How are you stopping yourself?
- What needs to change?
- What's working?
- What's not working?

Exercise in belief (15 minutes)

Take about 15 minutes out of your day to reflect. I would suggest doing this exercise in a time of quiet, when you will not be interrupted. Do this even on a non-work day. Put on a piece of beautiful music, and let your thoughts wander with the music. As you reflect, think about the following questions:

- What have you accomplished this week?
- What did you accomplish that you are proud of in the last month?
- What have you done in the last year that relates to your goals?
- What do you need to recognize in yourself in terms of accomplishments?
- What random acts of kindness have you afforded others?
- What kindness have you afforded yourself?
- What can you learn from this?
- How can it help you at work, and in your personal life?
- What does it tell you about your belief in yourself?

Once you have thought about this, start jotting down the positive beliefs that have helped you with your achievements. What other beliefs would help you in the next week, in the next month, in the next 12 months?

Having completed this exercise, think about how to incorporate it into your performance-development sessions at work. How will it help your team to develop positive beliefs and improve performance?

Your six-step plan

Learning creates possibility. Developing others creates possibility. Setting goals creates possibility. Vision creates possibility. Dreams create possibility. So what is your dream? This is a quick-step strategy to acquiring personal mastery.

1. Write down your short-term and long-term goals every year.

I sit down with clients twice yearly to set and review goals. In the first session we identify values, roles and goals. We agree the client's top ten goals, and create the first month's action plan. Within that session we set new, empowering beliefs. At the half-year we review what has been accomplished, where they are now, how to stay on track – or what to change.

2. Identify values: what really drives you?

This is vital: for yourself, and your work with clients. Values are all about what motivates you, what drives you. Our values underpin all of our behaviour, and give us the motivation to achieve. One of my clients identified:

- aesthetics;
- being in control;
- belonging;
- challenge of doing a good job;
- financial security;
- laughing and sharing;
- physical safety;
- sense of purpose.

CASE STUDY

A little story: My husband goes off once or twice a year on a wilderness safari with some friends. They camp in tents on the outskirts of the Kruger National Park in the north-eastern corner of South Africa. It's pretty adventurous in my mind, as they walk about four hours a day with binoculars and water for companions, to sight elephant, lion, buffalo, leopard and rhinoceros.

Each time my husband returns he talks about the tracker who leads their way through the bush. The tracker gives them tips: what this footprint means, how to use a specific herb for medicine, which plants provide water, what can be eaten, what is poisonous. The tracker never tells them how to be in the bush. He provides guidance, asks questions to get them to think, and they model him.

They have learnt how to walk quietly, how to sharpen their senses, be observant, how to deal with danger, how to learn from nature. That is one good performance coach. His values? Respect for people, animals and nature.

The point of the story? This trekking into the wilderness is built into my husband's annual timetable. It gives him a chance to rejuvenate, relax and think creatively. For him, it's time out. How many of you take time out? An annual adventure, a class in pruning roses, a cookery course, a language programme? It doesn't matter what it is. What matters is taking time to renew your vision, to renew your spirit.

3.   Review goals monthly

Setting goals is a worthless activity if you don't take the time to evaluate what you have achieved and whether you are still on track. I speak with most of my clients on a monthly basis, even if just on the phone. It's a chance to check in, to think about their approach. Is it working, and if not why not?

Your job as a performance coach is to ask the right questions – not to tell them what to do. Our questions help clients to figure out their own path. We are simply guides. We ask the questions; we help them find their own solutions.

4.   Check your achievements weekly

Life rushes past. The weeks go by and we think, 'What was that goal I was trying to achieve? When was that deadline?' Keep a list of your monthly and top 10 goals in your diary. Review them once a week.

- What have you done this week that moves you one step closer to achieving your monthly, short-term goals?
- What else do you need to do to move you one step closer to achieving your long-term, annual goals?
- What are you doing on a weekly basis to achieve your job, career and personal goals?
- Where is time built in for you – to relax, recover and reflect?

5.   Set time limits

It's important to set deadlines for each goal. They can be reviewed! You cannot achieve a dream if it's got no time limit. A colleague started to dream about buying a second house abroad; it was a dream with no deadline. All of a sudden, the perfect house arrived on the market. Very quickly she had to assess:

- Was it the right thing?
- Did it fit into her career planning?
- How would it fit into her personal life?
- Could she afford it?
- How could she afford it?

The end result: she bought it and her life has been transformed, but it nearly didn't happen. It's very hard to take that risk, to step outside the box, to go for that dream. Give yourself the chance.

6.   Dream big

What's a goal, it is often asked, but a dream with a deadline?

Several years ago, I realized that I needed more counselling skills if I was to be more effective in helping my clients to dream. Looking at the options, I set out to study neuro-linguistic programming for a number of years. This led to the discovery of process-oriented psychology and the principles of deep democracy.

This learning has been fascinating. It has, however, not always been easy. But I wouldn't have missed this journey for anything. In Chapter 9, I mention the importance of doing inner work – work on yourself. Your ability to guide your clients is dependent on how much work you have done on yourself. Lead the way.

What needs further work? Your learning will open new doors, new routes, new opportunities. Keep opening the door. Let in the light.

New light through old windows

What can you learn from past experiences? How can you look at the past from a different perspective, from a perspective of learning? This exercise is to develop performance. It helps participants see something they have experienced in the past that they were unhappy with or that has remained unresolved. 'New light through old windows' offers a new way of seeing.

Use this strategy to obtain new learning from a past experience. It's brilliant for use when coaching or training. Do not, however, use this exercise for an experience that was traumatic, or caused great pain or sadness to the person. That experience would require counselling.

Exercise: New light

1. *Think of an experience that holds negative connotations for you, but not something that is traumatic.* Ask your clients to really get in touch with that experience. They may wish to close their eyes.

    When I first did this exercise, I thought of the day I was made redundant from a very prestigious management position. I was unaware I was going to be dismissed, and I was shocked at the insensitive way it was handled.
2. *Check they are associated.* Have a look at their face, hands, feet. Are they physiologically in tune with that past experience?

When I think of this experience, my body goes into a kind of automatic shock. My jaw tenses, my body tenses. I can't think clearly. My feelings are raw. The situation seems surreal.

3. *Making a movie.* Ask your clients to see a movie, in their mind's eye, of that experience. Suggest that they put up a cinema screen (in their mind's eye) in front of them, perhaps 20 feet away. Suggest they start the memory reels rolling. Have them view the movie, from start to finish, of that experience. It's important that you tell them to 'See yourself in the film, as if you are looking at it back there, then.' Ask them to 'Have a look at your younger self, back there, then.' This helps them to keep their distance between where they are now, in their present life, and back there at a younger them, in a past experience. Give them time.

When I do this, I turn my head to the left, look up and slightly to the left. I put up a movie screen and run the movie, from the beginning right until the end of that experience. I see myself looking understandably distraught and frustrated.

4. *What is the learning?* Say to them, 'As you stay with me here, today, look back on that experience. What learning can you gain from watching yourself back there, then?' Once they have acknowledged that they know, ask them to slowly become conscious of themselves back in the room, with you.

When I see this movie, it occurs to me, each time, to be prepared for anything. The biggest learning is that there is no such thing as failure. I wasn't made redundant because I was a failure. In fact, I had done very well. I just didn't fit the mould with that management. My learning came later. At the time, though, the experience was shocking. In fact, they were trying to get me to go on a pretence, which did not set well with my values. Fortunately I handled it well. I have grown since that event, which I now feel has enhanced my skills and expertise.

5. *Future vision.* It's important to take this learning into a future experience, where it may be useful. Ask your clients to think of a future event where this learning may be useful, given the knowledge that they can now behave differently.

For me, I learnt the lesson well. I use this to envision working with clients. It helps me to remember that I am good at what I do, but not every contract will be right for me. It also reminds me to learn from every experience, positive and negative.

Your path to renewal

In essence, your path to personal mastery is the renewal of your spirit. *Webster's Dictionary* defines spirit (amongst many definitions) as 'the principle of conscious life; the attitude or principle that inspires, animates or pervades thought, feeling or action; the soul or heart as the seat of feelings or sentiments, or as prompting to action'.

Dana Zohar, author of *Spiritual Intelligence*, believes spiritual intelligence to be one of the three main intelligences built into the brain. She defines rational intelligence (IQ) as our logical, linear intelligence. Emotional intelligence (EQ) is what we use to read each other's feelings. EQ is what we use to adapt to situations in which we find ourselves. According to Zohar, spiritual intelligence (SQ) is the intelligence we use to imagine how things could be better. SQ is what we use to transform situations, to look for meaning in our lives, to find a sense of purpose.

The African spirit model

In a trade publication, *Training and Development*, I read Lovemore Mbigi's ideas on the African spirit model with fascination. Mbigi wrote that modern management is weak in managing the spiritual and emotional resources of its people, and yet these determine the values of the organization.

The African spirit model is a metaphor. In this ancient hierarchy, the spirits represent our ultimate real self, our way of being in the world, our total consciousness. This hierarchy of the spirits can serve, not only as a model for management, but for self-management – to help us attain personal mastery.

The metaphor uses a pyramid, not unlike American psychologist Abraham Maslow's hierarchy of needs (physiological, safety, belonging, esteem and self-actualization). Maslow's hierarchy follows the life cycle. His theory is that people are motivated by unsatisfied needs, and that certain lower needs must be satisfied before higher ones can be met. The African model identifies how to dispel negative spirits, or negative energies, from the workplace. The point? To create a positive climate where learning can flourish.

Learning from the African spirit model

At any given time in the workplace, there are two or more dominant energies that determine the spirit of the organization. These energies determine the outcomes, consciousness and culture that flourish within the organization. Use this particular metaphor to identify your dominant culture and values at work. For a positive climate to flourish, it's important to dispel negative energy. If the organization cannot let go of negatives when embarking on a path of renewal, the working atmosphere will be oppressive.

For example, in the valley where I live, near Cape Town, we have been working on a partnership project to rebuild a school within a poor, disadvantaged local community. It has been necessary to renew various partners at different times to keep up the momentum and the energy of the project. The Trust has brought in fundraisers, project managers, legal advisors and trainers. At times there have been conflict and negative energies within the project community. This happens in all organizations. If we use the African spirit model, it is important to move away from destructive energies within the group, bringing in new partners to move the spirit of the project up the ladder through cynicism, innovation, survival, performance and relationship building.

This model can be used to audit the dominant energies, cultural values and concerns within your organization. Let me share the model with you, moving from top to bottom.

1. **Rainmaker spirit – relationship spirit.** The rainmaker represents truth, morality, balance and human dignity. It is concerned about relationships with clients, colleagues and the people within the organization. The rainmaker is the conscience of the organization, balancing ecological, social, political, economic and spiritual needs.

   Are your people motivated to go to work to support business goals? Do they have the information they need to do their job? Do they have the tools and resources they need? Are they supported, rewarded? Does their working environment nourish them?

   People are the essence of your organization; relationships lead to excellence. It is also in 'relationships' that we need to clarify the role of 'leadership' within the organization.

2. **Hunter spirit – restless spirit.** The hunter is the spirit of performance, enterprise and entrepreneurship. The hunter has an eye for opportunities and deal making. This is the quest for pragmatic and creative solutions to compete and survive in the marketplace. Is there a place for new ventures, new endeavours in

Figure 2.1   African spirit hierarchy and values

your workplace? What about you – what new ventures have you launched in the last year? What entrepreneurial skills do you need to achieve greater success?

3. **Truth spirit – divination spirit or sangoma.** The truth spirit knows the truth and is not open to other views. This level is occupied by experts, specialists and traditionalists. In South Africa, the sangoma is the healer, the local doctor, often psychic. The opportunity for learning is reduced at this level. To counteract this, bring in mavericks, non-experts and different thinking styles. Develop whole-brain thinking teams who can introduce new views, new opinions and new expertise.

4. **War spirit – spirit of personal power and conflict.** The war spirit embodies personal power, conflict and gamesmanship. It helps us to understand power cultures and influences within the organization. The war spirit gives rise to political structures within the organization. What are the political power structures and areas of conflict in your team, in your organization? To use this spirit positively, develop your personal power and empower others.

5. **Clan/family spirit.** The clan spirit ensures the survival of its group. You have encountered this in the workplace before: those who want to go, those who don't want to go and those who should go. Interested in the survival of its group, this energy enhances group solidarity through rituals, activities, ceremonies and symbols. Hence we create 'employee of the month' and customer care programmes. At this level, it's important to build teams that interact. This encompasses the creation of teams, the mourning of change or loss of a team member, and building new teams to ensure the work goes on.

6. **Wandering spirit – innovative spirit.** This spirit is concerned with its unique creative ability. It is a weak spirit in many organizations. This is because innovation is often not rewarded. Too often only lip service is paid to this quality. To enhance the innovative spirit, bring in creativity from the outside, enhance it on the inside. Creativity, if not cultivated, is elusive. Think about how to reward innovation in the workplace, to encourage people to take risks with new ideas.

7. **Avenging spirit – spirit of revenge.** This spirit is both passive and aggressive. It embodies bitterness, anger and revenge. It can be quiet, then explode in an unforeseen moment. Develop a new vision in the organization if this spirit is alive and well. We see the spirit of revenge in marginalized groups, who sabotage learning and the creative process. This spirit can represent groups who have been treated unjustly. It's important to look at behaviour and understand all points of view. You could introduce the principles of deep democracy here, bringing in the wisdom of the minority voice (see Chapter 9).

8. **Witch spirit – spirit of destruction.** This spirit represents cynicism, negativity and destruction. It will actively sabotage and devour the organization's energy. It is dominant in sluggish, bureaucratic organizations with complex reporting hierarchies. Although conflict is needed to generate creative thinking,

it should be participative and tolerant of other views. Too much conflict can result in unproductive arguments that stifle creativity and can inhibit change. Identify this energy and turn its negativity to positive use.

Embark on a creative renaissance

The African spirit hierarchy has lessons that can be applied to managing an organizational culture. It promotes the importance of values as tools for self-empowerment and increased performance.

What is the predominant spirit, or energy, in your workplace? Are two or more energies in conflict with each other? An organization's spirit determines its performance outcomes, consciousness and ethos. Use this model to gauge your dominant organizational values and culture. Embark on a behavioural renaissance that involves:

- open communication;
- deep democracy;
- visioning;
- storytelling;
- brainstorming;
- music and creativity;
- whole-brain thinking teams;
- the spirit ladder.

Organizations are made up of people, and people embody certain attitudes, beliefs and capabilities. The hierarchy of values in the African spirit model helps us to identify an organization's emotional and spiritual resources, and what needs to change.

1. **The cynic must go.** Negativity is destructive. To move out of the role of the cynic (even the saboteur), begin to question everything. Where are you now, where to next, how to get there? Never ask why; ask how.
2. **Let go of powerlessness**. Negative emotions such as bitterness, anger and resentment will leave you feeling powerless. Awareness, compassion and understanding will help you to stay grounded within yourself. When you feel you are losing your self-esteem or confidence, recognize it, do something about it. As a performance coach, your ultimate aim is to empower others. That isn't possible if you are angry or resentful. Negative emotions take away your energy and power.
3. **Be innovative.** What have you done lately that is imaginative, creative, innovative, different? What did it feel like? Can you do more of it? How can you empower others to do the same? Without development, the creative ability in each of us is weak. How can you develop it in yourself and others?
4. **Survival or revival?** Are you barely surviving in the workplace, in your job, in your career? Sit down and take a creative look at what needs to change, and

how to change. How can your community help you? Talk to someone in your community at work, at home, in your church, in your social life. Or find yourself that mentor you have been promising yourself for ages. We all know people who are so busy being busy that they miss the opportunities to move on, to develop themselves. Sometimes they wait too long.

5. **Develop personal power**. Understanding conflict within yourself, and in others, will help you to manage your own power. Going to war with others takes energy, particularly negative energy. How can you empower yourself, yet empower others along the way? That's the essence of performance and organizational development. It's worth absorbing the essence of some of the martial arts. When energy comes at you, rather than putting up a blocking force, take in that energy and continue to roll with it.

6. **Ain't it the truth?** Sometimes we develop ourselves to such an extent that we think we are in the right. We forget there is no right. Our expertise today could be a redundant skill tomorrow. If there is a truth, it is continual learning and development. That is the way forward. It allows you to change, to grow, to move. You also enable others to do the same.

7. **Perform with vision.** That's what it's about: positive, energetic, dynamic performance. But it takes vision: for yourself, your team, your organization, the future. It's a quest: for whole-brain teams, creative solutions, thinking outside of the box, taking a risk, doing something different – with each activity aligned to values and goals.

8. **Collaborate and celebrate**. This is the rainmaker, the relationship spirit. Values at this level are integrity, dignity, morality. We can't make it without other people: engaging others, having respect for others. But to have a relationship means first having a relationship with yourself. Oscar Wilde once said, 'To love oneself is the beginning of a lifelong romance.' Do you love yourself, cherish yourself, have your best interests at heart? Only then can you do the same for others. The rainmaker creates rain. Rain is water, water is nourishment. How can you nourish yourself and nourish others? The best way is through collaboration, cooperation and support.

Drive performance through learning

How can you drive your own performance and that of others? The answer lies in the learning factor. Create an environment for learning within your organization. Develop mental fitness: for yourself, your team, the organization as a whole. Drive performance through learning rather than being driven by performance. Leap over your own obstacles, your own barriers to performance. Here's how.

- **Rekindle your passion for learning.** Develop an off-the-job passion. Maybe you've always wanted to learn how to sail, sing, play golf, learn a new language; go for it. I read about a woman who decided to take up juggling as a hobby, and another who took up the role of drummer in a local band on weekends. It takes you outside your sphere of work, and rekindles your passion for learning, your zest for life and your ability to take risks.

- **Sing your praises**. Think about past successes. Make a list of them right through the years. Often we focus on obstacles, or failures. Keep a file on things that have gone right. For most performance consultants, it's useful to keep a file of testimonials from clients who have sung their praises. When reviewing your goals, acknowledge your successes. Keep them on file for your next performance appraisal, or to negotiate a promotion.

- **Look back at history**. Look at your progress from a historical perspective. Remember that learning is gradual and takes practice, whether you are practising new skills or trying to master a new topic. Where were you ten years ago, five years ago, one year ago, six months ago, one month ago? What have you achieved since then? Remember to include long-term planning whenever you review your values and goals. Write it down! That is the only way to keep track.

- **Look for new ways to diversify**. Increase your learning curve. Remember, an unused brain goes stale. New challenges are energizing; they keep you motivated. I recall a client who decided to leave her powerful job in a government ministry to create a new niche market, exporting organic produce. She had enormous expertise in the field of agriculture, but her new business was quite a challenge. I'll always remember her saying, 'I'm forever looking for new ways to grow and diversify.'

- **Collaborate and cooperate**. Stay connected to others. What can you achieve with another colleague? What can you share and do together? The profession of performance development is perfect for collaboration and cooperation. Professional camaraderie is powerful. Join a number of networks to connect you to others in similar positions. It can get lonely out there. Connect with others. Share your passion; learn from theirs. Camaraderie is a big motivator.

- **Cross-train your brain**. The body thrives on exercise, and so does the brain. Do some of the creative exercises in Chapter 5 to stimulate right- and left-brain thinking. Stretch yourself, take on new activities that use different thinking styles. Become a whole-brain thinker. Activate your creative side, which is essential to fulfilment and motivation. Use music to enhance performance. Try journalling, painting, gardening. What can you do today to get started?

- **Bungee-jump your skills**. A touch of anxiety does you good. Do something you've never done. Pick a new challenge to bungee-jump your skills. It may be speaking at a trade show, training your staff, writing an article, serving on a board in the local community, lobbying for your industry, spearheading a task force. Push out the boat a little, enter deeper water. But wear a life jacket – get support from others.

One of the challenges my husband and I have taken on in the last few years has been to move from the northern to the southern hemisphere, from the developed world to the developing one. It has pushed us and stretched us. For me it has been a terrific learning curve. If we had known the deep waters we were wading into, we might have thought twice. I'm glad we didn't. Taking risks creates a new kind of magic.

- **Nourish your career**. A career is like a relationship. If you don't nourish it, it will flounder. If you're tired of it, or if you've lost your passion – find a new passion. Perhaps it's time to think about a new job or a new career. Look for something, a project or activity, that is deeply connected to your values. Perhaps you're a lawyer and you've always wanted to work for Lawyers for Human Rights. Or, like one of my students, are about to enter medical school, who volunteered to work for 'Doctors Without Borders'.
- **Recognize the stop signs**. It's okay to slow down, whether you roller blade with your kids on weekends, play golf or build a car from scratch. Whatever it is, do it. Take the time out. Balancing work and relaxation is critical to maintain spirit, energy and motivation. Balance is also critical to maintain good health. You can only push so far, for so long. Stop, give yourself a break. Breathe, let go. A colleague recently took two weeks out of her hectic schedule to work on her new house. She went back to work rejuvenated, with a mind free of clutter. Know when to stop, then do it.
- **Manage your resources, renew your spirit**. Renew your spirit, your energy. Balancing your positive and negative energies requires awareness. It demands consciousness: where you are in your organization, where you are in your life. Ultimately, managing your emotional, mental, cultural and spiritual resources is the road to mastery. Your spirit is made up of your values and your personal essence. Who are you? Take time out to find out. Go on a development workshop, a meditation retreat, take a holiday, or even a sabbatical.

Be the architect of your future

What is your commitment to yourself, your team, your organization? Are you a risk taker? Do you constantly expose yourself to new experiences? Do you learn from your mistakes?

Personal mastery takes energy, passion and motivation. Embark on your own renaissance, your own path to renewal. Break free of your personal obstacles.

Be a role model for others. Empower them, too.

Personal mastery seeks, through learning, to become everything you are capable of becoming – there's *your* magic.

Where to go for more

Books

Carlson, Richard (1998) *Don't Sweat The Small Stuff: Simple ways to minimize stress and conflict while bringing out the best in yourself and others*, Hyperion, New York

Maslow, A (1968) *Toward a Psychology of Being*, John Wiley, New York

Maslow, A (1970) *Motivation and Personality*, 2nd edn, Harper and Row, New York

Senge, Peter M et al (1994) *The Fifth Discipline Fieldbook: Strategies and tools for building a learning organization*, Nicholas Brealey, London

Senge, Peter M et al (1999) *The Dance of Change: The challenges of sustaining momentum in learning organizations*, Doubleday, New York

Zohar, Dana and Marshall, Ian (2001) *Spiritual Intelligence: The ultimate intelligence*, Bloomsbury, London

Journals

Calvert, G, Mobley, S and Marshall, L (1994) Grasping the learning organization, *Training and Development* (June) pp 38–43

Koonce, Richard (1998) I'm so glad we had this time together, *Training and Development* (December) p 16

Mbigi, Lovemore (2000) Managing social capital, *Training and Development* (January) p 15

Radio

Radio National (10 October 2001) Spiritual Intelligence with Dana Zohar, The Religion Report, Radio National, Australian Broadcasting Corporation (http://www.abc.net.au)

Audiocassettes

Carlson, Richard (1999) *Don't Sweat The Small Stuff: Simple ways to minimize stress and conflict while bringing out the best in yourself and others*, Simon and Schuster, New York

Web sites

Use any search engine to search for 'personal mastery'

Abraham Maslow: http://www.maslow.com

McGraw-Hill, organizational behaviour: http://www.dushkin.com

Peter Senge: http://www.fieldbook.com

Good quotations by famous people: http://www.cs.virginia.edu

3

Icebreaking

Icebreakers create an element of safety in the room, whether you are training, facilitating, coaching or speaking. Icebreaking helps people make choices about who they are and how they want to be – within the organization and in the training environment. They also discover that there are powerful and positive results to making their own choices.

Icebreaking allows participants to affirm who they are, outlining their goals and choosing the group's norms. Part of performance development is to help participants look at their organization and themselves, discovering who they are and what roles they want to play.

Breaking the ice means opening the door to self-discovery in performance – and discovery of others. We all have individual beliefs and values that coexist alongside those of the organization. In the learning environment, icebreaking helps the group to set the behaviours, values, goals and structure of the workshop, whatever the norm of the organization. Icebreakers break down individual barriers to learning in order to create change. This leads to identifying strengths, areas for improvement and learning needs.

Icebreaking helps participants integrate what they know with what they need to know. It is a way to build trust and understanding, balancing that with the need to be self-confident and safe in a potentially vulnerable environment. Icebreaking doesn't just break the ice. It helps people bring their hearts, minds and passion for learning back into the workplace. Icebreakers create the understanding that we can work together, play together, disagree together – and still believe in our own potential.

The crucial job of icebreaking is to open the door to opportunity. This may involve risk. Your job as a performance developer is to create an atmosphere of safety and trust that allows risk-taking, creativity and problem solving to happen. A well-chosen icebreaker can create that spark, welcoming everyone to the magical kingdom of learning.

Begin before the beginning

Trust building

I was alerted to the importance of building trust with my participants when I noticed comments on happy sheets handed back to me at the end of conferences and training seminars. There were comments that said:

> She made me feel so welcome. I was nervous about attending this workshop by myself, but the facilitator welcomed me, and seemed genuinely interested in putting me at my ease and hearing about me.

Or comments like:

> I've always thought that trainers were only interested in getting us through the topic. The trainer spent more than half an hour prior to the workshop walking round the foyer to personally meet with and talk to all the delegates before starting the course. It made me feel confident in her style.

Or:

> When I approached the registration table, not only was there someone to sign me in, it was the facilitator who personally greeted me, and asked who I was and why was I there. It made me think that the programme was going to be worthwhile and tailored to me after all.

If you take the time to meet your audience or your participants – whether you're facilitating a team brainstorm within an organization, speaking to a large audience at a conference or presenting a seminar with attendees from numerous organizations – they will feel that you have taken a personal interest in them, their organization, their issues. You will have started your first icebreaker.

Giving the gift of your name

The most important word in anyone's language is their name. One of the first things I do to create dialogue with delegates is to give them the gift of my name. What do I mean by that?

The first part of any icebreaker is to find out the name of every delegate, and to ask if that is the name they prefer to be called. Often colleagues give nicknames to fellow workers, without even asking permission! I ran a seminar recently for a small, entrepreneurial company in Cape Town. As we went round the circle sharing names and their wishes for the day, I asked each person to say something about the origin of their name. Two people wanted to be called something different than their current name at work. It was very important to them, as no one had ever before asked which of their two names they preferred to be called. It was an 'aha' moment and an insight for their co-workers.

If you have a very large group of people, say, more than 40, you may feel you cannot take the time to learn all of their names, or have them introduce themselves individually. In that case, ask them to work in small groups of three or four. Do this exercise standing as it creates more energy. Have them each share the origin of their name in their small groups. When you come back into the larger group, ask for a couple of contributions as to what they learnt about each other.

Networking names

This is a technique to use in a networking situation, when you are trying to start up a conversation with someone you have never met. We all have a strong, passionate connection with our name. I discover every time I run a workshop that at least one person wants to revert to a previous name, nickname or birth name. Working on the African continent for the last few years, I've discovered people have a variety of names for a variety of occasions. They often express a desire to be called a mother-tongue name not necessarily known to all their colleagues.

In one workshop I had an Andi who wanted to be called Andrea, in another a Florence who wanted to be called Thuliswe, and a Frank who wanted to be known as Themba. Names are important. They express a person's identity, crucial in an environment where learning new skills can test self-confidence.

Giving the gift of your name to the group, and encouraging them to do the same, is a quick way to build trust and camaraderie, breaking the ice. My name, Sunny, is a nickname of a nickname, and when people discover my original name they are curious to hear the story – it gives them a personal connection. People, as you know, relate to people.

Exercise: Gift of your name (15–30 minutes)

Giving the gift of your name can be done in a number of different ways. To start the session, ask delegates to stand up and work in pairs. Clap after two minutes to indicate they should switch and find a new partner. Continue until everyone has met most of the people in the room. Or have people chat in threes if your group is larger than 25.

After they have worked in threes, ask the group to come back into one large group. Each individual introduces one person in their trio, and says something interesting they learnt about that person with reference to their name. I recommend giving them about 30 seconds each. As facilitator, you will not forget anyone's name in your group!

Establishing a learning environment

Exercise: Strengths and weaknesses (15–30 minutes)

Icebreakers are an excellent way to establish a climate for learning. To do so, either ask delegates to present themselves to the entire group, or have delegates work in small groups of three or four. They are to think of three areas of strength they bring to the group, three areas where they need to improve and what specifically they would like to do differently as a result of the workshop. From the start, although they need new skills to accelerate performance at work, you acknowledge their existing skills and competence.

Performance development should engage the whole person: his or her attitudes, skills, beliefs, values and ability to think critically. If you can establish a learning environment from the beginning, delegates are more willing to absorb new concepts. They will be motivated to learn how to solve complex problems they are faced with at work. It's not enough for you to teach new information. Learners need to first be motivated, then willing to apply that information.

Icebreakers establish a learning environment:

1. Use actual examples

The icebreaker is the time for meaningful and practical information rather than theory. Share who you are and what you bring to the group – your expertise, experience and knowledge. Tell a story that illustrates something about you; perhaps why you are working with them. It's important they don't think you are perfect, because no one can live up to perfection. It puts you on a pedestal from which they will want to pull you down.

Once you have introduced yourself, participants will feel more comfortable sharing personal details about themselves. Ask them to share safe information, such as their names, their work experience, their strengths and what areas need work, relative to this particular session.

If you share one small story that tells something about you, ask them to think of a little story to share that highlights something about them and why they are here. I often tell the story of how I became involved in training, and how it started with a fall down a set of stairs on live television.

2. Adults learn best by hearing, seeing, doing and reflecting

Your icebreaker should use a variety of approaches to help reinforce concepts and participant abilities. We retain 90 per cent of what we learn – if we see, hear, say and do it. Build visual images and colour into your icebreaker. Use slides, over-heads, flipcharts and whiteboards. Bring in auditory imagery with verbal presentations, circle discussions, videos and presentations. Use kinesthetic imagery with hands-on, experiential, interactive exercises.

3. Adults learn differently

Use your icebreaker to explore participants' backgrounds and individual characteristics such as life stage, language, culture, work experience and work needs. Every single individual brings expertise and knowledge that can be shared with the group. Find out how they prefer to learn new information. Do they prefer lectures, discussion, debate, role plays, case studies? Or interactive group work, individual work or working in teams? They won't believe you have asked them. Participants will be delighted and flattered to be consulted. Explain that you will try to include everyone's preferred learning method during the session, detailing which methods may not be relevant to the topic or time available.

4. Adult learners want skills to be more effective at work

Use your icebreaker to motivate and to build curiosity. There may be ideas, concepts or skills your delegates had never considered learning. Subsequent to the group introductions, I write up two flipchart pages. One page lists specific skills, strengths and talents that were highlighted by the group during the icebreaker. The second sheet lists specific areas individuals wish to improve. In this way, participants discover synchronicity and similar needs among themselves.

5. Call on their intelligence and experience

Ask participants to introduce themselves by sharing how much experience they have had with a particular problem. Reassure them that they have all the resources they need to apply new knowledge – and that you will help them to do so as you proceed with the programme. You can even add up the number of years of experience the group has. This demonstrates their cumulative skills and how they will learn from each other.

6. Empower them by bringing in their attitudes, skills and abilities

Empower them by asking questions. Assure them that they, not you, will discover a myriad of potential answers to their complex issues. Let them know that you have many answers, but you don't have them all. Among everyone in the group resides an infinite variety of possible answers.

7. Establish a physically safe, psychologically comfortable and supportive learning environment

If you create a relaxed and comfortable atmosphere, adult learners will feel a degree of control and will be more willing to ask questions. A safe environment will help them to learn from each other let go of the fear of making mistakes.

8. Be flexible and show respect for your learners

During the icebreaker, focus on how you give feedback. Acknowledge any requests, observations or worries. I have coached trainers who, during the icebreaker, say things like, 'No, we're not doing that today,' dismissing outright a request or indication of a need from a delegate.

To create a learning environment, you must love learning yourself. If you love to learn, that will be communicated to your learners. Your own continual learning motivates you to constantly improve your skills – and will inspire your participants to adopt a similar mindset. Enthusiasm is contagious. Even if a delegate requests something not included on the agenda, be flexible enough to figure out where it can be slotted in (if it's relevant) – either now, later or in a future programme. Show respect and acknowledge their needs.

In a recent workshop for a poor, disadvantaged school in Cape Town, I was asked for help in dealing with negativity, hostility and conflict among staff, teachers and the governing body. I explained that we really needed a day. However, to immediately assist with the problem, I suggested we pick a few real issues and learn how to deal with them. I taught a quick three-step method in handling conflict by separating out and acknowledging emotion and fact. We applied it to a particular incident that happened that day and role-played how to handle similar situations in the future. The sidestep took an hour, not a day. What they learnt was how to be flexible, because I role-modelled flexibility by allowing time for a very important issue. The sidestep was not planned, but it was important to the cohesiveness of the group. This taught them a new skill that could be related back to the workplace.

Building a climate of possibility

Important clues are generated during the icebreaker. You learn what flexibility is needed (on your part) for your programme to work, and how much time you may need for each section of the session.

Asking questions opens the floor to ideas from everyone, and quickly establishes a climate of 'anything is possible'. When I started to facilitate learning 20 years ago, I thought I had to prepare topics perfectly – as if I had all the answers! I understood the need to build in experiential exercises, but I didn't realize in the early years that those exercises introduced the sense of possibility – showing there are many ways to solve a problem and to present a topic. Over the years, I have learnt to be well prepared, but to be willing to listen for what may have to change. Your first clues often appear during the icebreaker.

Socrates and sleuthing

Socrates should help you during the icebreaker. Socrates was famous for asking questions. The icebreaker provides the ideal time to clarify delegate needs. Questions establish a climate of learning, possibility, enquiry, interest and curiosity. Find out why your delegates are there, what they need from the programme, what they need from you – and what you can provide, based on your expertise and the brief you have received. The icebreaker gives you a chance to establish what skills, talents, strengths and room for improvement your group encompasses.

As a facilitator, your job isn't to just answer questions: it's to use Socratic direction, asking questions to break the ice and to discover what needs lie under the surface. Your sleuthing begins the moment your first delegate walks into your lecture hall, meeting or training room.

Bonding and team building

Creating a climate of trust

As people arrive, assume the role of host. If you exhibit host behaviour, people will begin to feel comfortable around you. Give them your name, ask theirs, introduce participants to each other as new ones arrive. Once the seminar begins, continue in your role as host.

Creating a climate of trust means giving something of yourself: your name, who you are, your credentials and why you are there. At the annual Legal Education and Training Conference in the UK several years ago, I was rapidly reminded that I had too quickly launched into the topic for the day, How to Evaluate Training, without totally satisfying delegates' curiosity about my credentials. Why was I there if I wasn't a lawyer? Several individuals wanted to ask me questions. They were lawyers after all. They felt I had not given them enough information, and were not willing to proceed until they were satisfied that I was exactly the right person for them. If I had not taken the time to do so, the seminar would not have continued. That was a big lesson. Who is your audience, what do they expect of you, what do they need to know from you? It's important for you to give them what they need before they feel they can trust you.

I relearnt this recently working with a large media marketing firm in South Africa. I had introduced the topic, and had launched too quickly into how their organization was perceived in the market place – before giving them enough information about myself to satisfy them. Again, someone asked if I would say something more about who I was before proceeding.

I have learnt that your participants need something first from you before they are willing to give something of themselves. Be willing to take the risk first, to show your credentials. But watch your ego. I have worked with trainers who want only to boast about how wonderful they are. That is not the point. Delegates want a few minutes to decide if they trust you, to see if they are willing to spend an hour, a day, an entire week with you. They want to know who you are, why you are there, who gave you the right to facilitate a session for them and what are your credentials in their sector.

Be careful. Speak briefly, concisely and give what's needed. It's their seminar, not yours. It's they who are important, not you. They, quite simply, need to have an answer to the question: 'Why have we got you for the day, for this programme?' Even though I'm Californian, in a recent Training the Trainer seminar in Silicon Valley where I grew up, I was careful to say that I'm away so much, it may mean that they will need to teach me a few things!

Questions learners want you to answer:

- Who are you?
- What are your credentials?
- How did you come to be there?
- What do you want from them?
- What can they expect from you?
- What's the agenda for the day?
- Who decided the agenda?
- Can you change it?

Letting learners speak

The icebreaker is important for one simple reason: it is the first moment when learners give something of themselves. It establishes that this is to be their workshop, their programme, their conference, their seminar. If participants are encouraged to speak out from the beginning, the ice begins to thaw. You dissipate the discomfort that exists between people who have never met before, or who are nervous in a new environment.

Get your learners to speak right from the beginning of the day. You create a climate of trust, comfort and a sense that the programme is tailor-made for them. It will quickly underline problem areas, issues and people.

Dealing with learner anxiety

Ten creative icebreakers (30–60 minutes each)

Anxiety and stress interfere with your participants' ability to learn. (See Chapter 5 for stress and its effect on the brain.) Many delegates feel they are not capable of learning quickly, particularly if they haven't been in a learning environment for many years. This anxiety can create a huge sense of risk and a fear of failure. Your icebreakers can relieve learner concerns. Below are ten icebreakers that create an atmosphere of fun, learning and creativity, helping to break down barriers and relieve learner worries.

Icebreaker 1: Your best resource is you

We all have what we need to learn new skills and to apply that learning in our jobs. When facilitating, I emphasize that, as a team, if we put our resources together, our potential is unlimited. I suggest we find out a little bit about ourselves and what resources we have among us. Ask people to work in pairs and then present their colleague to the group. (Allow eight minutes per pair, and one minute per presentation.)

Each person is to ask the other the following questions, and to listen actively. People don't take notes, just concentrate on what their partner says. When presenting their partner to the group, have them conclude with something they have in common. They are to simply ask of each other:

- Who are you?
- How did you come to be here?
- What do you want from today?

Icebreaker 2: Synchronicity is in the cards

This icebreaker helps to relieve anxiety about learning and taking part in a learning programme. Pass out blank index cards (A5 or $3'' \times 5''$). Ask each individual to write down:

- how many years they have been out of full-time learning
- their greatest fear about taking part in a training programme
- what they hope to gain from the workshop

Tell them their answers will remain anonymous. Have one of the participants collect and shuffle the cards, then hand them out again. If they are fewer than 15, have them work as one large group. If they are more, have them work in small groups, and deal the cards out evenly to each group.

Each group creates a brainstorm map to reflect the information on their cards (allow five minutes). Give them colours, symbols, pictures, anything to help them with their brainstorming (see Chapter 6). Give each group one minute to present their map. It's a good way to help participants realize what they feel in common.

Wrap up the session by asking what activities they engage in where they have to learn new skills: for example, do-it-yourself in their home, rebuilding a car engine, trying out a new recipe, going on holiday to a new country, learning how to play bridge, bringing up their first child. It's amazing what new skills we continue to learn as adults.

Icebreaker 3: Learning from failure
Ask participants to work in pairs or threes and to share:

- What do they consider to be the biggest failure in their working life?
  - How did they overcome it?
- What is their best success?
  - What enabled them to achieve that success?
  - What did they learn as a result?

Give them 15 minutes to share, then ask each pair/trio to present three things they learnt by doing the exercise. This icebreaker creates the idea that there is no such thing as failure – only feedback, emphasizing continual learning, particularly from mistakes.

Icebreaker 4: The cloverleaf
This is my favourite icebreaker. Draw a four-leaf clover on a flipchart, put it up on a slide or hand out a piece of paper with a four-leaf clover and a circle in the middle of it. In large groups, have participants work in threes or fours. In small groups, they introduce themselves individually to the entire group using the cloverleaf format. No matter what size of group, demonstrate how you want them to do this, prior to thinking about their cloverleaf. Usually I allow groups two minutes to prepare their cloverleaf, then limit presentations to two minutes each. The size of the group determines your flexibility.

- **Centre circle: origin of your name.** For this icebreaker, first use the cloverleaf to introduce yourself. In this way you give the gift of your name. I tell a story to explain the origin of my name.
- **Top cloverleaf: one word that describes you**. I often use the word ENERGY, telling people how I was given that nickname by a friend. Sometimes I use the word PIONEER, explaining that I see myself as a pioneer of learning, someone who's always pushing beyond personal boundaries,

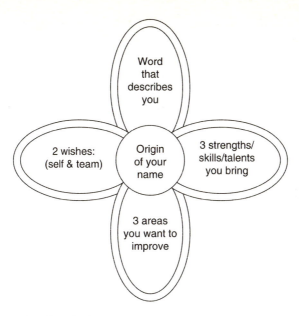

Figure 3.1   The cloverleaf

venturing beyond what is known and safe – and how that metaphor influenced my American childhood.

- **Right cloverleaf: three key strengths**. Ask participants to describe three key strengths they bring to the organization, the team or the learning group. They must relate their strengths to the topic at hand. What three strengths do you bring to them as facilitator, trainer or speaker?

- **Bottom cloverleaf: three areas to improve**. Each person describes three areas where they need to improve, relating them to the seminar topic. Some facilitators find this difficult. Some believe you should never reveal a 'weakness'. However, no person on earth is perfect, and if you set yourself up for perfection, you'll set yourself up to fall. Find what's relevant to your group and your topic. We all have areas where we need to improve. If you set the tone that you have room for improvement, it gives your participants permission to do the same. If you set yourself too high, they will not feel they can identify with or learn from you. They need to feel that it's possible to learn. They will often model themselves on your behaviour.

- **Left-hand cloverleaf: T-shirt slogan, theme song, blockbuster film, wish for today**. There are a number of choices here. Sometimes I ask them to think of a T-shirt slogan relevant to them and the topic (for a negotiation skills workshop mine is: Plan your destination, but travel creatively). Or think of the name of their own blockbuster movie (my example is *You Can't Fly High*

Enough). Or their theme song if they have one – and they can choose one already recorded. Examples are *It's Gonna Be Good* by Wilson Pickett, *You've Got What It Takes* by Marv Johnson, *We Are The Champions* by Queen, *The Sky's The Limit* by Fleetwood Mac, *Ain't No Mountain High Enough* by Diana Ross.

The topic I prefer for this left cloverleaf is 'What are two wishes for today – one for yourself and one for the group?' This helps to identify their own specific need, and it identifies areas within the team that need work.

This exercise can stand as an icebreaker on its own. What do they wish for themselves for the day, and what is their second wish for the team? Ask the group to map or write on a flipchart two lists: Strengths and Areas For Improvement (one flip page) and Individual Wishes and Team Wishes (a second page). This exercise identifies topics to be covered during the programme, and also identifies future training needs. Allow an additional five minutes to draw their map.

Icebreaker 5: Collecting concerns

A lovely way to create a climate of trust and learning is to ask participants to list their concerns or questions about the workshop at the beginning of the session. To start with, say something like this (the topic being selling):

> I'd like each of you, as you introduce yourself, to say something about the need to learn professional consultative selling. This can be something you are unclear about, are concerned about, don't like, a question you have or an idea you would like to share. I'll record your concerns and questions on the flipchart so we can begin to address them.

As facilitator, you'll gain valuable information about the individuals in the group and about the current issues in the organization. The individuals will also begin to voice the things that bind them together. Remember: you don't need to answer all of their questions. Your skill as a facilitator is to field their questions, to see if someone else can answer them; or even to ask a question back to identify who else can answer the question. In this way, you open the floor to dialogue and discussion.

Icebreaker 6: When's your birthday?

I learnt this from a colleague, Jo Larbie, who also trains lawyers. It works particularly well when you want to highlight communication, team-building or management skills. Once you have introduced the session, ask your group to stand, and brief them. In this exercise, they cannot speak or write notes to each other. They can communicate in any other way.

Ask them, as quickly as they can, to group themselves in order of their birthdays. I typically use month and birth day only – getting into which year can be embarrassing for some. You will see some interesting results: leadership, frustration, sense of fun, competition, team work and negotiation skills. Once they are grouped, check verbally what month and what day their actual birthdays are to ascertain how they did. Ask what they learnt from the exercise. It's a quick way to break down barriers, ensuring everyone is at the same level. (Allow 10 minutes.)

Icebreaker 7: What's your story?

This is a wonderful exercise. Ask participants to introduce themselves by telling a story: a story about who they are, why they're here and what they're hoping to learn. However, they must use a parable, anecdote or metaphor to tell their story. I usually give a few examples using simple fairy tales, or even current films, to demonstrate. Allow one minute for thinking time and two minutes for presentations.

Ask them to use different voices to emphasize feelings they had prior to coming to the workshop, and a voice to emphasize how they hope to feel when they leave. This exercise brings fun and energy into the icebreaking session, and has the advantage of generating ideas. It's important to get across the need to talk with feeling and passion – it identifies what they want from the session.

Icebreaker 8: The global village

I adapted this from a fellow trainer, John Townsend, many years ago at his Master Trainer Institute in France. In the first few minutes of a five-day workshop, John asked all 20 of us to stand in front of a world map pinned to the wall. We each had to point out where we came from, where we live now and to give a few more details about ourselves. Each presentation takes about a minute.

I sometimes use a globe that can be spun for this exercise, or a map to indicate where you started out as individuals on a programme and how you have come together into your own global village by the end. I complete the workshop with everyone standing once again in front of the map or globe. I ask individuals to identify what they have learnt, what they'll do differently and how it has altered their map of the world.

Icebreaker 9: What's your route map?

I talk a lot about the route map for any session, whether I'm speaking for an hour, a day or a week. But it's important that everyone identifies their own route map. How did they get here? Now that they are here, what do they want?

Hand out a piece of flipchart paper and coloured marker pens to each individual. Give them five minutes to draw the route they have travelled:

- where they started (in life, in work, in attitude);
- where they are now (in their job, within the organization, in their life);
- where they are going (in their job, in their career, in their life).

Ask them to use as many symbols and graphics as they can to represent ideas. I start with American, British and South African flag's in the middle of the page. I draw spokes out from the centre with pictures to represent various jobs, major learning experiences: a picture that represents what I'm doing here, today, with them; finally, a symbol to represent my future dreams.

Their objective is to tell their story: who are they, how did they get here, what do they need from this session? Depending on the size of the group, I suggest about two to three minutes per presentation. The fewer your numbers, the longer the presentations can be. This exercise brings out humour, fun, energy and the motivating factors that bind the group together.

Icebreaker 10: Soap opera

People want to know other people. They want to know their hopes, their fears, and whether they are like themselves. Most of all, other people can be inspirational. The world of work is complicated, stressful, full of politics and sometimes even mundane. Just like a soap opera! Here are a few questions to add to your icebreaker introductions. They add a bit of creative thinking, personal information and fun.

Participants can do this exercise in pairs, switching partners several times after three minutes, or present to the entire group. It creates energy and fun, and breaks the ice.

- What was your first job?
- What books are on your nightstand right now?
- Which TV programme is most like your workplace?
- What are you passionate about?
- What drives you crazy?
- What is one dream you have yet to fulfil?

Learners connect

Icebreakers help you and your participants to identify quite a number of things.

- What do they do well?
- Where do they fall down?
- What don't they know that would help them to enjoy their jobs more?
- What learning will help them fill the gap?
- What are their fears and anxieties?
- What are their hopes and dreams?
- What do they share in common?

- Where are they today?
- Where do they want to be tomorrow?

Your icebreaker sets the tone for learning and makes it safe to take risks. It helps participants to connect with you and with each other. It also motivates them to pursue their learning goals, becoming responsible for their own growth and development.

Cut through the clutter

The learning journey

Icebreakers start your session off with a bang. They help you tap into the abilities of each individual, and remind you that your group brings diverse skills, talents and expertise. Icebreakers set the tone. They create the route map for development. Icebreakers begin the learning journey. They establish an appropriate learning climate, demonstrate respect for your learners and help you to motivate by example. Your ability to build relationships with your participants (from the moment they arrive) will engage and relax them.

Finally, and most importantly, icebreakers help you as facilitator to understand the diverse wishes and skills your participants bring to the workshop. Your icebreaker attempts to create an understanding of where they are now, where they are going and how you and they plan to get there.

Full circle

Icebreakers are not necessarily just for introductions. Use them as energizers, skill-builders and to enhance group dynamics. Also use them to end the day – summarizing what was gained, and what individuals and the group will do differently based on the learning route taken.

Once you have arrived at your destination, the end of the route, start at the beginning. What icebreaker began your day, and how can you adapt it to close the day?

- Where are they now?
- What did they gain?
- What do they have in common?
- What will they do differently?
- How can they take what they have learnt back to the workplace?

You have come full circle. What story or metaphor can they now tell to share their learning journey?

Bringing our hearts back to work

Icebreakers introduce individual skills and talents, bringing in an element of ourselves: our hearts and minds. If you, as the facilitator, are willing to share something of yourself, it sets the tone for the entire workshop. It's crucial that you love learning, and that you love helping others to learn.

If you are inspired to continually improve your skills, this will be transmitted to the participants, inspiring them to learn, and to take a deeper interest in their job and career. Your enthusiasm, passion, humour and willingness to engage your learners will encourage them to bring passion, interest and critical-thinking skills to the complex issues they face at work.

Engage and captivate the learner

Learning needs to engage the whole person – attitudes, values, beliefs, skills, self-esteem, and mental and emotional flexibility. In this way participants can learn new concepts, solve complex problems and deal enthusiastically with real issues. It's not enough to teach information and theory.

As performance developers, we must capture our participants' interest. If you use real examples, helping participants to transfer learning to the workplace, they will be motivated and empowered. Stir their interest with icebreakers that start your session with a bang, moving into group activities and discussion that provoke questions, reflection and new learning.

Where to go for more

Books

Caroselli, Marlene (1998) *Great Session Openers, Closers and Energisers: Quick activities for warming up your audience and ending on a high note*, McGraw-Hill, New York

Jones, Ken (1995) *Icebreakers: A sourcebook of games, exercises and simulations*, ringbound, Kogan Page, London

Luvmaur, Sambhava and Luvmaur, Josette (1990) *Everyone Wins! Cooperative games and activities*, New Society, Santa Cruz

Nilson, Carolyn (1993) *Team Games For Trainers*, McGraw-Hill, New York

Scannell, Edward E (1983) *More Games Trainers Play*, McGraw-Hill, New York

Sheely, Steve (1998) *Ice-Breakers and Heart-Warmers: 101 ways to kick off and end meetings*, Serendipity House, Littleton, Colorado

West, Edie (1996) *201 Icebreakers*, McGraw-Hill, New York

West, Edie (1999) *The Big Book Of Icebreakers: Quick, fun activities for energizing meetings and workshops*, McGraw-Hill, New York

Journals

Caudron, Shari (2000) Learners speak out, *Training and Development* (April) pp 52–57

Caudron, Shari (2000) Lights, camera, makeup! *Training and Development* (May) pp 14–15

Fisher, Tom (1998) High anxiety: preparing trainees to learn, *Training and Development* (December) pp 14–15

Flacks, Niki (1994) Don't go out there alone, performance tips for trainers, *Training and Development* (June) pp 23–24

Web sites

Use any search engine to search for icebreakers + trainers (try www.yahoo.com or www.google.com)

http://adulted.about.com (suggested icebreaker publications to order)

htttp://www.flora.org/mike/poped/icebreakers.html (for large groups)

http://home.earthlink.net (download suggested icebreakers online)

4

Think like a star, act like a performer

'All the world's a stage'
Shakespeare

As performance consultants, we can learn a lot from the acting world. Engaging an audience, holding their attention, projecting an image, staying focused – communicating a key message. The skills I have found most useful in the last few years are theatre-based techniques. In almost all of my workshops and seminars, I include some type of 'dramatic' exercise.

More and more people are discovering that the rules of theatre also apply dramatically well to the business and professional world. Theatre schools teach focus, communication, team work, motivation, spontaneity and imagination. Increasingly, performance coaches are taking one-day acting classes to learn about the skills of an actor.

Experiential exercises taken from the acting world help develop performance. They are active and dynamic. Your learners learn by doing. The exercises actors use will challenge you, and stretch you to your limits. In this chapter, you can experiment with storytelling, role playing, dynamic circle exercises, voice work, music, metaphor and films. This doesn't mean you need to include all of them – pick one or two that will engage your learners and communicate your message more effectively.

Theatre-based exercises will help you build team work within the group: to actively listen and remain focused on others; to improve overall storytelling and creative thinking skills; to develop mental and emotional flexibility on your feet; and to increase appreciation for varying points of view. Whether you want to act it out, sing it out, tell stories or bring in the movies – these techniques will help you to think like a star, act like a performer.

Entertainers or trainers

Trainers are performers. They need to entertain, motivate, teach – and make it fun. Metaphor, storytelling and the movies are often used by facilitators to bring in the element of fun and to create an experiential learning environment. Using the skills of the actor makes it easier to educate, train and motivate.

Trainers are presenters as well as performers. They have to embrace stage fright, get into the role of facilitator, teach visualizing skills to achieve goals, accentuate the positive, convince their audience and use powerful imagery to get across their message. Trainers need to learn to modulate their voices, take appropriate pauses and be more emphatic in making their points. Most adult learners, if exposed to hours of lecture-based training or too many speakers, begin to dream, fidget and lose interest.

Using theatre-based exercises encourages participant-centred training and contributes to near-total recall. Theatre-based exercises help learners to overcome inhibition, project confidence and improve their communication skills. The rules of the theatre teach communication, spontaneity and imagination, and build team work.

Making the link

Before introducing theatre-based exercises for participant-driven learning, it's crucial to make the link between learning and the dramatic arts. I had this drummed into me when I was trained in theatre-based learning with Corporate Scenes (Berkeley, California). In subsequent workshops of my own, I learnt to spend at least an hour making the link. You can do this in any number of ways. A key exercise that I use, no matter what topic of training, is to link the world of theatre with the theme of the seminar, or alternatively with participants' professions. Choose from any of the following three exercises.

Exercise 1: Parallels (15 minutes)
The generic question is, 'How is your profession similar to that of the theatre or dramatic arts?' You can make it more specific. For example:

How are each of these professions similar to that of the theatre or dramatic arts?

- teaching?
- law?
- sales?
- management?
- PR?

Typical answers – *our aim is to*:

- adopt roles successfully;
- change opinions;
- create change;
- educate;
- entertain;
- express/handle emotions;
- increase awareness of issues;
- involve others;
- inspire;
- manage;
- motivate others;
- organize;
- present other points of view;
- teach;
- transform our thinking.

Your job as a facilitator is to help participants see the parallels between the two worlds. In doing so, you will be able to use theatre-based exercises to introduce and practise new skills. I once made the mistake of not drawing the parallels, and in the middle of the second day several people began querying the value of the exercises we were doing. I then had to make the link, halfway through the workshop. Theatre-based exercises allow you to open doors to a fun, experiential way of learning. If you don't make the link, you risk losing the commitment of your participants.

Exercise 2: The actor's trade (15 minutes)

Immediately after your icebreaker and introductions, link the skills of an actor to learners' roles (as managers, team leaders, communicators, teachers, facilitators). This can be accomplished similarly to the first exercise. Put up two flipcharts with one of the following questions: What are the skills of an actor? or What are the skills an actor needs to communicate with an audience? You'll hear some typical answers such as:

- body language;
- breathing;
- communication skills;
- eye contact;
- pacing;
- role player;

- strong voice;
- timing;
- volume.

Encourage your group to dig deep for other skills such as:

- commitment (to the play, and to the theatre group);
- energy;
- passion;
- risk taking;
- team work (to work with other actors).

Try to draw up a list of over 25 skills. Ask what parallels there are with the skills required to fulfil the group's roles of manager, team leader, marketer, sales representative, consultant – whatever the role you want to relate to an actor's skills.

The skills they require will strongly parallel those required by an actor. Help your participants to think laterally about acting skills that don't immediately seem to relate to their profession. There will undoubtedly be a way to relate that skill back to the workplace; for example, to entertain. Entertainment is a key ingredient in most professions, and can often be linked to the need for fun and humour.

Exercise 3: Putting it all together (30 minutes)

To introduce the theme of the dramatic arts into your workshop, make a link between the skills of the actor and the skills you are trying to develop in your workshop, whether you are training managers, negotiators, communicators, teachers, trainers, visionaries, sales people or team leaders. In order to work with theatre skills, learners need to understand how and why the theatre can help. Here is another exercise that will help you make the link. Ask the group to brainstorm three questions:

- What is the role of storytelling in plays, film and community theatre?
- What skills does an actor need to communicate with an audience?
- What behaviour helps theatre/film troupes to work together successfully?

Divide your group into three small groups, and put each question up on a flipchart. Each group spends 5 to 10 minutes on the first, second, then third question. Move the groups round until all three groups have added ideas to the three flipcharts. Put the flipcharts onto the wall. Ask the group if anything is missing.

Review of question one

Cross out the word 'storytelling' and put in whichever theme you are emphasizing: communicating, managing, negotiating, teaching. Ask if there are any parallels between the role of storytelling and managing, negotiating, communicating, teaching. Almost every point will be relevant. Typical answers are:

- communicating;
- conveying a message;
- relating history;
- entertaining;
- teaching;
- motivating;
- creativity;
- relieving stress.

Review of question two

Cross out the word 'actor' and put in whichever role you are emphasizing: communicator, manager, negotiator, teacher. Ask if there are any parallels between the skills of an actor and the skills of a communicator, manager, negotiator or teacher. Again, you'll discover almost every point will be relevant. Typical answers are:

- being a role model;
- being influential;
- belief;
- concentrating;
- constructively critical;
- expressiveness;
- eye contact;
- flexibility;
- forgiveness;
- honesty;
- imagination;
- leading by example;
- letting go of mistakes;
- listening;
- memory;
- non-verbal skills;
- patience;
- passion;
- persuasion;
- practice;
- self-confidence;
- tolerance;

- trust;
- voice skills.

Review of question three

Cross out the word 'troupe' and put in 'team'. Ask if there are any parallels between the skills required by a drama group to work together successfully and those of a task force or project team. Typical answers might include:

- acknowledging each other's skills;
- can-do attitude;
- commitment;
- dependability;
- discipline;
- forgiveness;
- generosity;
- positive attitude;
- punctuality;
- reliability;
- respect;
- sharing goals;
- team work.

The link to the world of theatre

In this way you link the dramatic arts (theatre or film) and the skills of an actor to the commercial, corporate and professional worlds. You are now free to use the timeless art of storytelling and drama to drive home complex points about leadership, vision, team work and customer service.

The Marx Brothers and *Duck Soup*

The rules of theatre apply brilliantly to the business world – whether training in presentation skills, communication, conflict resolution, customer care, negotiation or sales, marketing, media relations, business planning, leadership and management.

I suggest hiring the Marx Brothers video *Duck Soup*, or even the Monty Python series with John Cleese's funny walk. These are exercises in taking on someone else's style. I use it as an exercise in mirroring, trying to walk someone else's walk, attempting to put yourself into their shoes. The mirror exercise, mimicking a partner as do the Marx Brothers in *Duck Soup*, can help your participants to become more attuned to others – such as clients, colleagues or your boss.

Many theatre schools use exercises such as this to teach you to see the world from the other's perspective.

The mirror walk

Ask your delegates to find a partner. Partner B will walk the walk of Partner A, following closely behind A. Tell the followers to move exactly as their leading partner moves: mirroring exactly their leg movements, step, arm swing, how the head and shoulders are positioned and move. Have the pairs switch roles. Partner B leads, Partner A follows and mirrors. Have them discuss and bring their observations back to the group. Ask what they learned about the other person, and what they noticed about how their partner engages with the world.

Exploiting stage fright

Do you know when to modulate your voice, take appropriate pauses, be silent, or be more emphatic in making your points? Whether you are giving a speech, chairing a meeting, presenting to a potential client or managing an exhibition stand at a trade fair, the rules of the theatre will help.

Voice exercises can be incorporated into training to relieve stress, emphasize the need for relaxation or to change the pace. They can also help teach participants how to manage adrenaline and warm up. Most important, they will show delegates how to vary voice volume for emphasis – to ensure their voice is heard.

Exercises in breathing, voice and dialogue

Here are a few breathing exercises to wake up delegates after a refreshment break. This exercise makes delegates alert by pumping oxygen into a stale brain. Breathing exercises are also useful for teaching stress relief. This is the best adrenaline management when nervous in front of others, and helps to give more mental power. Oxygen regenerates the brain. Just yawning allows oxygen into the brain. This releases the throat and mouth muscles, and dissolves tension in the diaphragm so that delegates can relax and project their voices.

Breathing from the belly: the relaxing breath (5 minutes)

Anyone who has taken a yoga or Pilates class will have learnt about the art of breathing from the belly: to centre yourself, generate full brain power and ensure you are relaxed. Here are a couple of fun exercises to emphasize breathing from the centre for focus and energy.

Ask delegates to sit comfortably in their chairs and to place their hands softly on the abdomen. It's important that you speak slowly and gently, asking them to breathe in and out, concentrating on the rising of the belly as they breathe in and the flattening of the belly as they breathe out. You can suggest that they close their eyes.

Ask them to breathe in slowly through the nose and gently out through the mouth. Do this exercise 5 to 10 times, as if filling a balloon as they inhale, letting the air out of the balloon as they exhale. Ask them to deepen their breathing and to gradually open their eyes.

Ask them to notice how differently they feel from five minutes before. Their energy will be relaxed, they will feel comfortable and confident.

The energizing 'HA' breath (5 minutes)

Ask delegates to stand, but demonstrate this exercise first. Placing your hands on your belly and slightly bending your knees, breathe in and then expel the air out in a series of loud ha's: HA, HA, HA, HA, HA, until all of your breath is expelled.

Ask participants to do it with you this time, expelling their breath in loud ha's. Repeat two more times, but stand up between each movement. Tense and release.

Do both these exercises with your delegates after a session break, when you want everyone to be relaxed and centred. Based on a yoga exercise, this activity is used by actors to create a sense of relaxation and to become aware of using 'all' of you when communicating.

Exercise 1 (5 minutes)

Either stand or be seated. Breathing in, begin to tighten the muscles in your toes, then your feet, calves, thighs, buttocks, abdomen, arms, chest, neck, face ... until every single muscle is as taut as you can make it. You will find yourself holding your breath once every muscle is tightened. Release all the muscles and your breath with a slow, long exhalation.

Exercise 2 (5 minutes)

Before a presentation, seated or standing, breathe out ... out ... out ... some more, pressing your lower tummy in (pushing navel to spine). Squeeze the air right out. Hold for a few seconds, then stop pressing the air out and air will rush in, right to the bottom of your lungs. You'll experience your lungs filling with air, your diaphragm fills out and you are once more in control.

Warn participants that if anyone is pregnant, it is important that she doesn't hold her breath. This exercise creates a sense of relaxation because holding the breath stops the oxygenation of the bloodstream; when you breathe in once more, oxygen floods back into the bloodstream and the brain.

Just voice

Speakers, presenters and actors warm up their voices prior to rehearsal and performance. They warm up their speech muscles as well as their physical muscles. Here are a few exercises to relax the voice and develop good vocal muscle.

Exercise 1: The moving alphabet (10 minutes)

- Demonstrate this exercise first while standing. Have the group face the widest wall in the room.
- The tutor demonstrates. Point one hand and forefinger at the left-hand corner of the ceiling, breathe in and say the alphabet in one breath, moving the pointed finger along the ceiling until you reach the right-hand corner.
- Ask the group to do this with you. Increase the number of times they say the alphabet on one breath – to twice, three times, maybe even four times.
- When finished, recover your breath! Then ask, What did we learn? How can we use this?

Exercise 2: Shakespeare I love you (20–30 minutes)

A wonderful exercise to develop vocal muscle and flexibility is one I learnt from a colleague, Ivan Midderigh, in an active-communicating master class many years ago. Ivan took a passage from a play by Shakespeare. We had to stand in a semi-circle, all 12 of us. First we practised saying each of the five lines in a soft voice, then in a medium-pitched voice, a deep deep voice, then a really loud voice. For each voice give your learners a benchmark. For example: a soft voice is whispering to your loved one; a medium voice is speaking conversationally on stage; a deep voice reverberates far down in the belly, like that of a bear emerging from a cave after a winter's hibernation; a really loud voice is losing your cool.

Finally, divide your group into three and run through the passage as if the group is singing in the round. Each group begins ots round with a different voice, one after the other, until it has run through every line of the verse. Suggested Shakespearean verses are listed below.

Developing voice

To develop the voice, you can use Shakespearean passages, fairy tales, poems or short stories. Have your participants vary:

Pitch: Making the voice pitch deep to squeaky.
Inflection: Emphasizing different parts of the word or line.

Volume: Strength of the softness or loudness of the voice.
Pace: The speed or slowness at which you speak.

Shakespeare verses are wonderful because of their resonance and poetry – and they are perfect for performing. Choose your own verse, or pick from one of my favourite passages and try it with your next workshop.

Passages From Shakespeare

1. **Miranda in** *The Tempest*:
    O wonder!
    How many goodly creatures are there here!
    How beauteous mankind is!
    O brave new world
    That has such people in 't!

2. **Puck in** *A Midsummer Night's Dream*:
    Up and down, up and down;
    I will lead them up and down:
    I am fear'd in field and town;
    Goblin, lead them up and down.

3. **Bottom in** *A Midsummer Night's Dream*:
    The raging rocks
    And shivering shocks
    Shall break the locks
    Of prison gates ...
    The foolish fates.

4. **Fairies' song in** *A Midsummer Night's Dream*:
    You spotted snakes, with double tongue
    Thorny hedge-hogs, be not seen;
    Newt, and blind-worms, do no wrong;
    Come not near our Fairy Queen.

Changing viewpoints

This is a very popular exercise in drama classes. It teaches mental and emotional flexibility and an appreciation for other viewpoints; it also encourages listening to others with active interest. It is a useful activity to learn how to turn negatives into positives, and to think problem solving rather than problem finding.

Exercise 1: State of mind (5 minutes)

To get your participants used to moving from one state of mind to another, ask them to walk around the room. Tell them to use their voices, arms, facial expressions and non-verbal body expression to indicate that it is a wonderful, happy, fulfilling, optimistic day. Clap after 10 seconds to indicate they are to change their verbal and non-verbal expressions to demonstrate a miserable, dreary, depressing day.

After about 10 seconds, clap again and switch them to expressing a wonderful day. Do this a few times as they get used to quickly switching between positive and negative, happy and sad, for and against. Finally, clap to finish the exercise. Ask them to walk around the room and find a partner to work with for the next exercise.

Exercise 2: Positive versus negative (30 minutes)

Have your participants work in pairs for this exercise. This is a lively exercise that develops creative thinking, mental flexibility, clarity and expressiveness in speaking. I first learned this exercise from Mark Rittenberg of Corporate Scenes.

Performers and directors

Thinking in theatrical terms, one person adopts the role of 'performer', the other takes on the role of 'director'. You as tutor indicate when the performers are to start and finish.

The job of a director is important. The director gives the performer a topic, and indicates the performer is to give the 'positive' argument and then the 'negative' one, for that topic. Topics need to be simple: things such as shopping, driving, travelling, eating, singing, playing cricket, baseball or football.

The director gives the performer a topic, then immediately clicks fingers and says 'Positives'. The performer begins to tell a story about the subject, giving 'positives' only. The director clicks after about 10 seconds, saying 'negatives'. The performer tries to move seamlessly into the 'negatives'. Ask delegates to use linking words such as 'and', 'although', 'however', 'also'. The director indicates two or three changes, and the performer attempts to move easily from 'positive' to 'negative'.

Work-related

Clap to indicate the end of the exercise for the entire group, then ask performers and directors to change roles. Once both partners in each pair have had a chance to enact the 'positives' and 'negatives' of a topic, ask everyone to find a new partner. Run through the exercise again with new partners. They can choose topics that are more complex. Topics can be work-related, for example, customer care, team work, promotions, telephone skills, e-mail etiquette, computer breakdown. Once both partners in each pair have spoken, change partners once or twice more. Change topics with each new level. Often I enlist topics they indicated in their wish list at the beginning of the day.

Group review

Once you have run this exercise three to four times, the group comes back into a circle to discuss:

- What skills were they working on?
- How do they relate to the workplace?
- What did they learn?
- How can they take this learning into the working environment?

Exercise 3: Cards, hats and colours (30 minutes)

This is a similar exercise to 'positive versus negative', using Edward de Bono's six thinking colours. Hand out six coloured cards to each pair, or six coloured baseball caps. Still working in pairs, the director gives a topic to the performer, then switches coloured cards about every 10 seconds to indicate moving from positive to negative, emotional to neutral, creative to control. The facilitator claps hands after one minute to indicate switching places. If you use baseball caps, the speaker dons one coloured cap, then another, to indicate a change of speaking style. This is a very energetic exercise, getting both mind and body moving!

Black	Negative, logical assessment; why something won't work.
White	Neutral, objective manner; uses facts and figures.
Yellow	Positive thinking; optimistic, constructive thinking.
Green	Creative, lateral thinking; concerned with creative and new ideas.
Red	Emotional; uses feelings and non-rational thinking.
Blue	Controls and monitors; defines the problem; step by step.

Group review

Once various pairs have run through the exercise three times, the group comes back into a circle to discuss:

- What skills were they working on?
- How do they relate to the workplace?

- What did they learn?
- How can they take this learning into the working environment?

On a role (30 minutes)

Before any role-playing exercise, first establish why role playing is useful and relevant. To determine the importance of role playing, break your participants into groups of three or four. Ask them to work on the following three questions. They can work in small groups on all three questions, or they can move between three flipcharts (each chart listing one of the questions). Each group adds their ideas in answer to each question.

- What roles do we play: at home, at work and in our social life? Ask group members to brainstorm and come up with as many roles as possible.
- What attitudes, behaviours and characteristics are required in all of these roles?
- How many roles do we play at any one time?

Group review

Individual groups present their findings, or you can pin up the three flipcharts and ask each group to sum up one of the questions. Facilitate any other points brought out during the large group review. Emphasize that adopting different roles is an essential skill we have fine-tuned since we were small children. Once you have facilitated the learning points, and the group agrees to the usefulness of role play, you can segue into determining parts for a role play, skit, pantomime or short play.

Act it out

A wonderful way to help participants solve problems, turn negatives into positives or begin to think creatively is to have them produce a skit, short play or pantomime on the subject.

Royal National Theatre, London

A few years ago, we did a year-long management development programme for the Royal National Theatre in London. For each team, one of the programme highlights was the final day. At the end of a five-day programme, participants were asked to put on a skit, very appropriate as they were working in the world of the theatre. They were given a morning to determine:

- what they had learnt from the programme overall;
- what they needed to do differently in future;
- how to communicate what they had learnt to other departments.

They had free rein. Some decided to create a fictional story with fictional roles, other teams enacted stories using generic job-title roles. The end result: a reinforcement of their ability to solve problems, think creatively, motivate each other and work as a team.

School play

I recently ran a workshop for Mvula School in one of the poor, informal settlements in Crossroads in Cape Town. On the second day, the staff prepared a surprise. They considered all the skills they had worked on the day before, and with their newly acquired skills put on a small play. They assigned roles to five people, and acted out how they should have organized the workshop they were attending. The organizing of the workshop had been a first for them, fraught with people problems from start to finish.

Their play showed the importance of identifying staff training needs, finding the right facilitator, researching affordable venues, organizing transport and food, and motivating sceptical staff to attend. It was brilliant – even more so for being staged in three languages! This not only illustrated their newly learnt motivational, team-building and communication skills, but demonstrated how they had learnt from mistakes and conflict.

The moral of the tale (45 minutes)

Another way to act out a situation is to take a problem. One team acts out the original handling of the problem, a second team enacts how it could be done differently and a third team acts out or tells the moral of the tale. I use this with handling difficult people, running meetings, negotiating, team working, client care – or any issues on participants' wish lists from the beginning of the day.

Role playing exercise (60 minutes)

It's often easier to pretend to be someone else than to be yourself. This exercise teaches focus, communication, spontaneity and imagination. It is designed to help learners project confidence and overcome inhibition.

Divide your participants into small teams of three or four. Each person takes the role of a historical figure – Napoleon, Lincoln, Churchill, Joan of Arc, Florence Nightingale – and acts out how to solve a problem, how to manage a crisis or how to negotiate between different interested parties, but in the guise of the historical character.

Discussion and review (30 minutes)

At the end of each role play, ask individual teams to discuss the following questions, flip their answers on a flipchart page and bring them back to the group to discuss.

- What happened?
- What did they learn?
- How could they do it differently next time?
- How can they apply their learning to the workplace?

Role play 1: Leadership crisis management

This exercise takes a crisis – a historical event that has been resolved within your industry or the world at large. It is useful for learning to practise the skills needed for leadership, communication, negotiation, conflict resolution, understanding other points of view and team building. Allow 30 to 45 minutes per role play. You need players to make up the two teams. One team would typically have a spokesperson, legal advisor, translator/interpreter and possibly a noted diplomat or politician.

USA and China

A US plane has been forced to land on Chinese soil. Both countries huff and puff in public, but neither side actually wants to escalate to a hostile standoff. How do they achieve a compromise where both sides save face? There are two elements at stake: the crew and the plane. These offer possible tradeoffs. How can they be used? For example: 'If you stop being so belligerent in public, we will offer this.' Do they want the crew back or the plane? What can they agree to in public, and what can be decided behind the scenes?

Role play 2: Making a global deal

This exercise takes a historical event that has been seen from many critical viewpoints. It offers useful learning in communication, negotiation, conflict resolution, leadership. Allow 30 to 45 minutes for the role play. You will require a minimum of three players: US President Roosevelt, Soviet leader Stalin, British Prime Minister Churchill. You may choose one or two observers who take notes and give feedback at the end of the role play.

Yalta

Churchill, Stalin and Roosevelt are at Yalta, ironing out the final details of a post-Second World War settlement. What do they need to take into consideration?

Remember: they have to go back and sell it to their respective people in Great Britain, the USSR and the USA.

Role play 3: Spin doctoring

This exercise takes a historical event where the role players experiment with different methods of approach. Skills to work on: crisis and conflict management, publicity management, communication, leadership and creative problem-solving skills.

Foot-and-mouth

The Prime Minister of Great Britain has to manage an unexpected bout of foot-and-mouth disease, which has hit the cloven-hoofed animals in the UK. How can he and his team manage the crisis? The role players are the Chief Vet, two editors of Britain's largest daily newspapers, the Prime Minister, the PM's spin doctor and the Farmers' Union's angry leader. How can they creatively manage and resolve the crisis? Brief your teams that they can change history here!

Role play 4: Reaching a compromise

This exercise takes an historical event that has already been resolved. It can be used for training in leadership, communication, negotiation, conflict resolution or team building. Allow 30 to 45 minutes for the role play. For this exercise, as few as three people can make up a team, which consists of two players plus an observer who comments at the end. Or you can expand it to include the two leaders plus key players in their back-up team. Here's an example.

Mandela and de Klerk

Nelson Mandela and F W de Klerk are negotiating the move to a full democracy in South Africa. They both want to avoid civil war. Both men have angry followers to placate and convince of any compromise they may achieve. They have to come to a middle agreement. How do they do it? Brief your role players that it is not just a deal the two leaders want to achieve. The agreement will have to be sold to the country, to their political supporters and to the world at large.

Role play 5: Football

This exercise takes a major championship event with a sport many people can relate to (football, known as soccer in some countries). This team negotiation is to manage a potential crisis that will have huge PR ramifications for the sport, the team, the club and possibly the country.

The FA Cup

Your team is about to play in the FA Cup final, but its members are threatening to go on strike if they do not receive double their annual salary if they win the Cup. How will you manage this crisis? The role players are:

- Football manager: picks and motivates the team. He sees his job as motivating the team to win. But he wants money left in the kitty to buy a sensational new Italian player for the next season.
- Team coach: wants to give them anything to make them win. His reputation depends on it.
- Club owner: says s/he can't afford to double their salaries.
- Two players. One wants to play regardless. A second player says, 'We are the club. Why shouldn't we be paid for results?'

Role play 6: Consumer affairs

This exercise involves a large supermarket. Your customers are upset to discover that your 'organic' eggs are from grain-fed chickens but are not 'free range'. You have received a lot of adverse publicity about your supposedly healthy, organic eggs, and you need to ensure the situation is resolved before you begin to lose customers and market share. The supermarket has set up a forum to resolve the issue.

Organic eggs

The supermarket manager wants to minimize adverse newspaper publicity as quickly as possible. The local Green campaigner, who is in the middle of a closely contested local election, wants to gain as much mileage as possible (in his favour) for resolving the crisis in the consumers' favour. Three consumers are on your panel; they will all report back to the local Consumers' Association. One is keen to sue the supermarket for misinformation; another is eager to resolve the problem as quietly as possible in the consumers' favour; the third is undecided. The final role player is the man who produces the eggs, whose argument is, 'Do you want to pay double?'

Role play 7: Film situation

You are making a documentary. The crew of a new yacht is in the middle of a transatlantic race from Cape Town to Brazil (or Portsmouth to New York). The yacht is in second place. Three-quarters of the way across the Atlantic, water begins to seep into the engine. Half the crew want to head for the nearest port. Half feel they can win if they keep going. How does the crew come to a decision when one half is about to mutiny?

Transatlantic race

Your film crew is to work out what the boat's captain decides and how the captain convinces the crew to unite behind a dramatic decision.

Circle exercises and team building

In this type of experiential learning, one of the most important aspects is to have delegates sit in a circle where they can look into the eyes of everyone in the group. It can be quite a challenge if you have more than 25 participants. I recommend keeping to this number or fewer, otherwise the exercises take too long.

Numbers, animals and alphabets

Exercise 1: Numbers

This circle exercise uses a simple numbering system, counting from one. It works on energy, focus, concentration and team building. Ask the participants to sit on the edges of their chairs, and to make sure they can see the eyes of each person in the circle. An option is to use numbers in a second language for fun, and more intense concentration.

As facilitator, start by saying the number 'one', with energy and with a clap, to the group. Get them to repeat with you – and don't let them get away with no energy, no commitment or no volume! Let them know you will now work round the group. Repeat number 'One' and a clap. Everyone, including you, looks at the person on your left, whose job is to lean forward and say 'Two' with a clap. The group repeats, always with a clap: 'One, two.' And so it continues until the entire group has taught their number to the group.

You carry on round the circle until you reach the last person. Then explain that you will go round the circle twice, all together counting with a clap, then round the circle twice backwards, all together counting and clapping. Fast!

The purpose of the exercise is to get the group to concentrate and focus, using voice and body. At the end of the exercise, have someone flip what skills you have been working on (e.g. team work, voice, eye contact, energy, concentration). Although it seems simple, it is amazing how difficult it is to synchronize focus, energy and team work. An option is to use numbers in a second language.

To sum up, you as facilitator lead the discussion. Ask:

1. What happened during the exercise?
2. Was it fun, did they make mistakes, was that okay?
3. What did they learn and what skills did they use?
4. What did they learn about team work?
5. How can the learning be applied to the workplace?

Exercise 2: Alphabet animals

This circle exercise uses animals, and as you go round the circle, participants voice the name of an animal to suit their letter of the alphabet. The facilitator goes first with the letter A, and could use aardvark. The person to the left of the facilitator will have the letter B, and could use bear; the third could use cheetah for C. The facilitator starts, teaching aardvark with a clap to the group. The group repeats together with the facilitator, 'Aardvark'.

The facilitator turns to the left, and the second person teaches 'bear' to the group. The group repeats, always with a clap: 'aardvark, bear'. The facilitator faces the third person, who teaches 'cheetah' to the group. The group repeats, 'Aardvark, bear, cheetah'. And so it continues until the entire group has taught an animal name to the group. The facilitator takes the group round the circle twice repeating each animal from A with a clap; then takes the group in reverse round the circle twice – a much tougher task.

The purpose of this exercise is to work on focus, concentration, team work, memory and energy. At the end of the exercise, have the team flip what skills they were working on, what worked and where they fell down.

To sum up, you as facilitator lead the discussion. Ask:

1. What happened during the exercise?
2. Was it fun, did they make mistakes, was that okay?
3. What did they learn and what skills did they use?
4. What did they learn about team work?
5. How can the learning be applied to the workplace?

Alternative exercise: Cities and countries

As an alternative to the above exercise, use capital city names such as Auckland, Buenos Aires, Cardiff, Delhi, or country names such as Australia, Bermuda, Canada, Denmark, Egypt.

The importance of metaphor

There was an old man who began an orchard upon his retirement. Everybody laughed at him. Why plant trees? They told him he would never live to see a

mature crop. He planted anyway and he has seen them blossom and has eaten their fruit. We all need that type of optimism.
(Deng Ming-Dao)

A metaphor is a picture word, and forms the basis of many stories. Metaphor can be one of the most useful tools for a trainer. To think like a performer, think how theatre and films use metaphor successfully to get across a message. In the learning environment, you can use metaphor in a number of ways to enforce learning points.

Metaphors help us to express ourselves more comprehensively than just a simple explanation. They take us out of our usual thinking box and give us a different perspective on the problems that surround us. Here are a few exercises that develop the use of metaphor and creative thinking in your workshops.

The story of Red Adair: a global view

Paul Neal 'Red' Adair is a well-known firefighter. He became world famous for pioneering techniques in fighting oil well fires and capping wild well fires. Most people remember him for his work in the Gulf War. I once heard a story about Red Adair early on when he was fighting fires somewhere in North America.

The story goes that he lost quite a few of his firefighters in a big fire because the wind changed. Red Adair was so upset that he personally went to visit the families. He was tempted to quit, but when he thought about what he had learnt, he knew he had to ensure a tragedy of this kind would never happen again. He bought a helicopter and trained several members of his team to keep watch from above so they had a global view.

The helicopter metaphor (45 minutes)

Whether this story is true or not, I do not know, even though it has been relayed to me several times. The purpose of the story is to illustrate the use of metaphor to get across a message, to show the importance of a global view, to balance rolling up one's sleeves and getting involved in a project at hands-on level. Ask your participants to think of a similar story to get across a message they need to communicate to their teams or customers. The main criterion is to use a metaphor. As in this story, the helicopter was the metaphor for the global view.

Give them about 30 minutes in a small group to come up with a story, rehearse it and present it to the larger group. It's important that it be related to their business and the training topic in some way.

The cheese metaphor (90 minutes)

The delightful story *Who Moved My Cheese?*, written by Dr Spencer Johnson, is a lovely example of how metaphor can be used in a work environment. The story is a parable about four characters who live in a maze and spend their days looking for cheese for both food and happiness. Cheese is a simple metaphor for everything you want in your life. The four imaginary characters are two mice, Sniff and Scurry, and the little people, Hem and Haw. The four represent the simple and the more complex parts of ourselves.

This simple parable reveals the most profound truths about achieving what we want in life, whether it is a successful career, our dream relationship, more money or good health. The story is about the maze where the four are searching for what they want. It is a wonderful metaphor about change, adapting to change, working together and being flexible – and how to achieve your best.

I use this story in a number of ways. Recently, I asked a group to read it overnight and to put on a skit the next day using the four characters. They were allowed to change the characters if they liked. They had 45 minutes to prepare and rehearse, then 15 minutes to present their skit with the key messages they thought the book had to share.

After the presentations, the group sat in a circle, discussing the key learning points and how they could apply them in the workplace. They worked with some of the key precepts in the book, looking at the cheese metaphor as an analogy about searching for what you want to have in your life:

- a good job;
- a loving relationship;
- more money;
- a particular possession;
- good health;
- spiritual peace of mind;
- what happens if you're not willing to change.

Their final analysis was, 'The quicker you learn to let go, the sooner you...' and 'Change happens, move with the ...'.

Metaphor and creative problem solving (30 minutes)

Metaphor takes us outside of a problem, and allows us to generate more creative solutions. Metaphor very powerfully gives us new ways of tackling issues and new ways to understand the world. At the heart of creative problem solving is the notion that being removed from your problem helps you to generate creative solutions.

To use metaphor to problem solve, have your delegates generate a metaphor for their problem and then brainstorm that metaphor in relation to their problem. Say the issue is 'how to move from number two to number one in the marketplace'. The metaphor could be: 'Our problem is like being in the last round of the World Cup Final and we're in second place.' Or, 'Our problem is similar to two finalists in the Wimbledon Tennis Championships. One will be the winner; the other, second.' Look for the way the soccer team or the tennis champion will generate solutions to win.

It can be difficult to find a metaphor that really represents your problem. Split your group into teams and have them brainstorm a series of metaphors that represent the issue they are working on. Then have them share their metaphors with the larger group. Each group generates ideas using the other teams' metaphors.

Metaphor and communication (1 hour)

One of the concepts I work with is that of the iceberg. You will read more about the iceberg metaphor in the chapter on deep democracy. Imagine an iceberg, with one-third of its physical mass above the level of the sea. Two-thirds of the iceberg lies underneath the surface of the water. If you think about daily conversation and dialogue between co-workers and team mates, most of their daily interaction takes place at the level of conscious awareness: that is, above the surface (one-third of the iceberg). However, to understand more about each other, we need to lower the level of the water – and dig a little deeper than surface level (uncover some of the hidden two-thirds of the iceberg).

The following creative exercises lower the water level, helping participants to discover a little more about other people's essence and what drives them. Ask participants to choose one other person to work with for about an hour.

Their brief is to have a conversation. I suggest Person A asks questions about Person B for about 30 minutes; then Person B asks questions about Person A. It's helpful if you give delegates a couple of key questions. For example:

- What one word would they use to describe themselves? (See cloverleaf exercise in Chapter 3.)
- What have they accomplished in the last 12 months that they are proud of?
- What are their key disappointments in the last 12 months?
- What are they passionate about in work? Outside of work?
- What are their key goals for the next 12 months?

When the participants come back into the larger group after an hour, give them about 10 minutes to think of a metaphor that would encapsulate the person they just spent time with. Give them time to rehearse a two-minute presentation about the other person based on the theme of their metaphor.

Review
Once all the participants have presented their partner, ask:

- What did they learn from this exercise?
- How can they use it in the workplace?
- What did they learn about communication skills and about each other?
- How has this exercise helped to lower the surface of the water?

The art of storytelling

People love to hear stories. They tend to remember them and to repeat them. Storytelling through the ages has proven to be an inexpensive way of communicating memorable messages – whether through community storytellers, dramatic arts like plays and pantomimes, or the movies.

Storytelling is a timeless art that can be used in performance development to drive home difficult or complex points about leadership, team work, vision, goals or client relationships. The art of storytelling relies very much upon language, voice, pitch, pace, tone and timing. Here are a few exercises you can use in your training and facilitation to enforce important messages and help participants develop not just the art of storytelling, but linguistic and mental agility.

Collecting stories (30 minutes)
This is a great way to generate stories. At the beginning of this session, have all participants share one story topic with the group. Rather than writing down the story, ask a scribe to note key points to summarize it on a flip chart or acetate. Give a title to each story, write the title of each story on slips of paper, ask each participant to draw one out of a hat. Allow 30 minutes for the entire exercise.

Working in groups of five to six, each person has two minutes to use that topic to tell a story with a beginning, middle and an end. I usually give them a couple of guidelines: include laughter, dialogue, modulate their voice, or use sounds, visual images and feelings to enliven the story.

Sometimes I ask them to invent a few new words or a new language to use when telling their story. Tell your storytellers you want to see a room full of engaged faces, and to hear voices that are excited about the story they are telling, and the one they are hearing!

Variety: the spice of a story (30 minutes)

Variety in voice makes a story. Thinking about the voice work you engaged in earlier, ask the participants to vary the pitch, pace, tone and volume of their voices to illustrate their story more dramatically. To be effective, just like trainers, storytellers need to capture and hold the attention of their audience.

Ask your storytellers to engage their voices, hands, body, and breathing for the exercise. The five listeners sit in a semicircle, and the storyteller stands in the middle to relate the story. As facilitator, call time after five minutes; the next person stands to tell his or her story. Ask the audience to be involved, supportive and enthusiastic to help the storyteller.

Creative storytelling (1 hour)

This is an exercise I use when training trainers and facilitators. Ask individuals to write down a performance issue they need to work on. Some examples are designing interactive exercises, presentation skills, designing course-evaluation forms, using music in a learning session, structuring a workshop or designing a role play exercise. Allow one hour in total.

Collect the topics and shuffle them like a deck of cards. Have each participant choose one. If anyone chooses his/her own topic, have him/her decide whether to keep it or not. Give the participants five minutes to think of a story to illustrate a key learning point for that training topic. Ask them to think about their own experience and how that can be used to highlight the learning point. It isn't necessary for them to elaborate extensively on the topic, only to tell a story that illustrates a key learning for the group.

Ask delegates to draw a memory map that complements their story on a piece of flipchart paper. Depending on the size of the group, break it into small groups of five; participants then deliver their stories to the smaller group. If your group is no larger than 12, ask individuals to present their stories to the larger group.

Trainers take on Hollywood!

Our most entertaining storytellers are moviemakers. Films have been used in education and training for decades to drive home a point, make a powerful learning statement or make analogies to complex problems. Think about what films, or film extracts, are relevant to your topic. It may be useful to set an evening project for participants to watch selected pieces, or an entire film.

Films cover a vast array of performance-development topics: from creative problem solving to handling diversity, managing conflict, team building, client care and organizational change.

A powerful tool for change

Because moviemakers are our most prolific storytellers, facilitators have infinite choice in films to drive home difficult points about leadership, vision, motivation, creativity, team work, conflict, customer service and change. As a performance coach, I am always looking for films that act as metaphors or illustrate messages we wish to discuss in our workshops.

I consistently set films for delegates and clients to watch – no matter what you are trying to teach, they will always take away more than that. If you are at a loss as to which films to choose, spend a few hours searching the film sites and reviews on the Internet. Just reading the reviews will give you many ideas for interactive group exercises to suit any theme. Here's a summary of how you can use movies as a powerful development tool for change.

Remember the Titans (Walt Disney, 2000)

Remember the Titans is the powerful true story of a football team's determination to win, bringing together a town torn apart by racial prejudice and intolerance. The town, divided by resentment, friction and mistrust, eventually comes together in triumph and harmony. The year is 1971. After leading his team to 15 winning seasons, football coach Bill Yoast (Will Patton) is demoted and replaced by Herman Boone (Denzel Washington.) Boone is tough, opinionated – and black, as different from the town's beloved Yoast as he could be. How these two men overcome their differences and turn a group of hostile young men into champions is played out in a remarkable story full of soul and spirit.

- Compare Coach Boone's appointment with the changes in your organization or team. Discuss such consequences as resentment, disorientation, loss of team members and fear of the future.
- Discuss the coach's comment to the team, 'Football is about controlling that anger', and one team mate's retort to the captain, 'Attitude reflects leadership, Cap'n.' How does this relate to teaching leadership on and off the field, in and out of the workplace? What does it teach us about conflict?
- Discuss the importance of motivation and the ability to forge a team when dealing with change and adversity. Brainstorm some obstacles that you may encounter in the workplace when fellow team members refuse to come along. What can you do to ensure that the team succeeds?
- How can setting meaningful goals and aligning them with individual and organizational values bring the team together when facing sudden change at work?

The Legend of Bagger Vance (Robert Redford, 2000)

Set during the depression in Savannah, Georgia, local golf hero and First World War veteran Rannulph Junuh (Matt Damon) is suffering from post-traumatic stress syndrome and a major dose of survivor guilt. Junuh escapes a battlefield massacre by chance and as a result has lost his golf swing. How he gets back into the swing is the theme of the film. The disillusioned Junuh has gone into seclusion, distancing himself from those who knew and loved him. His former flame, Adele Invergordon (Charlize Theron), is fighting to make money to pay off the grand golf course her recently deceased father built, while Junuh sits drinking and gambling his life away.

To save her course, Adele decides to pit the two most prominent American golfers together for a cash prize – but needs a local for the townspeople to go along with it. A young lad named Hardy (J Michael Moncrief, meant to be a younger version of the narrator, played by Jack Lemmon) brings Junuh into play – along with Bagger Vance, who appears mystically out of nowhere. The genial golf caddy Bagger Vance (Will Smith) is not unlike the Lord Krishna in the Hindu scripture (Bhagavad Gita), assuming human form to instruct a warrior.

The golf tournament pits Junuh against two golf legends, the decent Bobby Jones (Joel Gretsch) and the hedonist Walter Hagen (Bruce McGill). This story of a young man's fall from and return to grace is slightly larger than life. Although somewhat predictable, and the narration by Jack Lemmon a bit corny, it's an elegant film that holds the sport of golf up high.

- Discuss Bagger Vance's line, 'Inside each and every one of us is our true authentic swing. Something we were born with. Something that's ours and ours alone. Something that can't be learnt. Something that's got to be remembered.' What does he mean, and how can we use this individually, and together, in the workplace?
- Remember what Bagger Vance said: 'I play for the moment yet to come, looking for my place in the field.' What's the field? How did Junuh find his field? How can you get there? Why would you want to?
- Why did Hagen ask Junuh to go on tour with him? What can we learn from this?
- How is this concept useful to us in the workplace: 'The game can't be won, it can only be played?'

Finding Forrester (Gus Van Sant, 2000)

A moving story of a unique relationship between a reclusive one-time prize-winning novelist and a young, black, amazingly gifted scholar-athlete. The film explores the struggle of this underprivileged inner-city kid named Jamal Wallace (Rob Brown), who is a talented urban basketball player, but one who also reads everything he can get his hands on. He scribbles prose and poetry in secret, until the reclusive William Forrester (Sean Connery) begins to mentor him. Forrester's debut novel, *Avalon Rising*, took the world by storm 50 years before. As the friendship and film unfold, we discover why Forrester shuts himself up inside his Bronx apartment watching the basketball court below where Jamal hangs out. A compelling film with insights into the heart and soul of a dedicated writer.

- Jamal says to Forrester, 'I can't get past the first 10 pages of *Avalon Rising*.' Forrester replies, 'I took quite awhile to get past those 10 pages myself.' Discuss how we can overcome obstacles that seem to block the way ahead, whether it's to do with change at work, new relationships or new tasks that we need to grapple with.
- Forrester says to Jamal, 'If I ask you not to say anything to anybody (about working with me), can I trust you?' Jamal nearly loses his place at school and an important competition because he keeps his word. It is only at the last moment that Forrester steps in to help him. What can we learn from this about trust and integrity in personal relationships at work? Why can it be difficult to keep our word?
- Forrester tells Jamal that the key to writing is 'to write'. How can we apply this to work? What is the key to tackling a new task, a daunting new project, a new relationship?
- What is a 'soup question'? How can it help us to realize our dreams?

Field of Dreams (Kevin Costner, 1989)

This is a film about vision and idealistic dreaming. It is also a celebration of baseball. Standing in the middle of a cornfield, Iowa farmer Ray Kinsella (Kevin Costner) hears the words of 'Shoeless' Joe Jackson (Ray Liotta), a member of the infamous 1919 Chicago Black Sox baseball team that threw the World Series: 'Build it and they will come.'

With this vision, Kinsella builds a baseball field with bleachers and floodlights right in the middle of his cornfield. The ghosts of 'Shoeless' Joe and the other Sox players, disgraced in the 1919 scandal, appear for a few games with Ray. The voice appears again, telling him to 'ease his pain'. Ray travels to Boston to see the controversial 1960s writer, a disillusioned Terence Mann (James Earl Jones), to try to understand the meaning behind the voices and the purpose of the field.

Mann tells him, in a memorable speech, how baseball once reflected the best of America: 'The one constant through all the years, Ray, has been baseball ... This field, this game, is a part of our past, Ray. It reminds us of all that once was good, and that could be again. Oh, people will come, Ray. People will most definitely come.'

Kinsella meets with small-town doctor 'Moonlight' Graham (Burt Lancaster), whose pro-baseball career was limited to only one inning. The baseball field signifies a place where people who have sacrificed parts of their lives for others are given a second chance. The film climaxes with Ray's reconciliation scene with his dead father.

- Ray Kinsella has a dream, a vision. When he first shares it with his community he is laughed at, taken for a mad man. How can we ensure that we reach for the stars, reach for the dreams that are possible at work, in our careers and in our personal lives – and not be daunted by the sceptics?
- In the organizational world, there is much talk about 'shared vision' and 'shared goals'. Discuss how in your teams, in your departments, in your organizations you can motivate and inspire everyone to take part in future goals, a future dream, a future vision.
- Kinsella travels from Iowa to Boston to seek out someone to help him understand the meaning of the voices he hears and the real purpose for the field. What does this teach us about listening to our intuition? What else does it teach us about sharing vision in our teams?

Other films to consider for exercises

- Leadership and management: *Thirteen Days, Braveheart, Crimson Tide, Air Force One, The Godfather, Space Cowboys.*
- Managing conflict: *West Side Story, The Turning Point, Chocolat, Traffic, The Contender, Crouching Tiger Hidden Dragon, Crimson Tide.*
- Team building, motivation and vision: *Stand and Deliver, Billy Elliott, The Full Monty, Bridget Jones's Diary, The Wizard of Oz, Tin Cup, The Commitments, The Dirty Dozen.*
- Communication: *The Prince of Tides, The Big Chill, Children of a Lesser God, Grey Owl.*
- Creativity and problem solving: *Apollo 13, Fly Away Home, The Flight of the Phoenix, The Magnificent Seven.*
- Managing diversity: *Trading Places, Pay It Forward, Do The Right Thing.*
- Managing change: *Grey Owl, The Wizard of Oz, The River Wild.*
- Humour: *Meet The Parents, The First Wives Club, Saving Grace, Chicken Run.*

Choosing the right film (20 minutes)

Have your larger group break up into smaller ones. Each small group brainstorms up to 10 favourite films that illustrate key training topics (change, creativity, diversity, team work, leadership). Compile a list of each group's selected films and you have your list to choose from!

In conclusion

Storytelling is a useful technique to:

- capture the attention of your participants;
- communicate key messages that your participants will remember;
- establish rapport with your audience;
- build credibility as a performance coach;
- develop the talents and skills of your team;
- develop a stronger, more motivated team.

As facilitator, the key is to tell a story and help your learners personalize the message and identify with the meaning.

The richest source for your stories is your own life experience and that of your participants. Stories based on experience can be told with passion, authenticity and memorability. Encourage your team to draw on their most compelling experiences and to share and apply their stories to the workplace.

Remember: when working with theatre-based exercises, introduce a topic, integrate it with an experiential exercise and perhaps use a true story to provide anecdotal evidence. Then review what has been learnt through open discussion. This keeps it alive and relevant, makes it fun and ensures delegates discover their own answers. Most important, involve your participants in their own learning; allow time to reflect and integrate the learning.

The grand finale

Theatre based activities go beyond the theatre. They nurture skills, attitudes and behaviour that are crucial to lifelong learning. By being exposed to their own creative possibilities, participants learn to share what they know and to become more responsive to each other.

Theatre-based exercises help learners develop performance skills, learn the basic rules of storytelling and transform ordinary reality into extraordinary reality. Finally, learning to project themselves in unfamiliar situations, they develop imagination and intuition.

Where to go for more

Many acting schools today run training seminars for the corporate, legal and educational worlds. Some will come into the learning environment and tailor-make a programme to suit your objectives. To find an acting course in your area, ring a local theatre or drama school and ask for help. It's a good idea to allow at least one to two full days for participants to have time to put their new skills into practice, and to reflect overnight on what they have learnt.

Books

Chancellor Press (1982) *The Illustrated Stratford Shakespeare,* Chancellor Press, London

Johnson, Spencer (1998) *Who Moved My Cheese?* Vermilion, London

Kermode, Frank (ed) (1987) *Shakespeare's The Tempest,* Methuen, London and New York

Lazarus, Joan (1986) *Theatre Arts Discoveries: A leader's guide to informal drama activities,* University of Wisconsin, Madison, Wisconsin

Marriott, Alice (1947) *Winter Telling Stories,* William Sloane, New York

Rittenberg, Mark and Dufala, Joyce (1984) *Active Communicating Survival Kit,* Corporate Scenes, Berkeley, California

Spolin, Viola (1986) *Theatre Games For The Classroom: A teacher's handbook,* Northwestern University Press, Chicago

Films

Finding films, news and reviews:

http://movieweb.com

http://psc.disney.go.com

http://www.filmomh.com

http://www.filmsite.org

http://www.filmtracks.com

http://www.rottentomatoes.com

http://www.tvguide.com/movies

http://www.upcomingmovies.com

Journals

Carley, Mark S (1999) Training goes to the movies, *Training and Development* (July) pp 15–18

Feinglass, Art (2000) Tips from the acting world, *Training and Development* (August) p 20

Flacks, Niki (1994) Don't go out there alone, performance tips for trainers, *Training and Development* (June) pp 19–27

Hicks, Sabrina (2000) Leadership through storytelling, *Training and Development* (November) p 63

Pitcher, Patricia (1999) Artists, craftsmen and technocrats, *Training and Development* (July) pp 30–33

Reynolds, Paul and Reynolds, Peter (2000) Make mine a double, *Training and Development* (May) pp 48–49 (importance of storytelling)
Wild, Russell (2000) On a role, *Working Woman* (July/August) pp 79–80

Training, acting classes and drama schools

Search engines (www.yahoo.com or http://directory.google.com)
Search for: Acting Workshops + City or Theatre Workshops + City

Australia
Act 5, Perth (Web site: www.geocities.com or act5mail@yahoo.com)
Playspace, Physical Theatre Studio, Sydney (Web site: http:www.artmedia.com.au)

Canada
Second City Theatres (Training Centres: Chicago, Toronto, Las Vegas, Detroit) (Web site: www.secondcity.com)
Women's Theatre and Creativity Centre, Halifax, Nova Scotia (Web site: www.chebucto.ns.ca/ Culture/WTCC/WTCC-home.html)

UK
Central School of Speech and Drama, London (Web site: www.cssd.ac.uk)
Express Training (Web site: ww.expresstrainingcc.com)
Guildhall School of Music and Drama, London (Web site: www.gsmd.ac.uk)
RADA, The Royal Academy of Dramatic Art, London (Web site: www.rada.org/)
Rita Morris Associates, Leeds (So To Speak) (Web site; www.ritamorris.com)

France
Hart Theatre Company, France (Web site: www.perso.wanadoo)
Training in Voice and Active Communicating (Web site: www.perso.wanadoo.fr)

South Africa
Express Training (Web site; www.expresstrainingcc.com)
Market Theatre, Johannesburg (Web site; www.theatrechannel.com)
UCT Theatre School (The Baxter Theatre) Cape Town (Web site: www.uct.ac.za)

USA
Access Communications, New York (Web site: www.access-comm.com/who.htm)
Brave New Workshop, Minneapolis (Web site; www.bravenewworkshop.com)
Burn Manhattan, New York (tel (212) 502 0868)
Corporate Scenes, Berkeley, Calif (Web site: www.corporatescenes.com)
Groundlings Theatre, Los Angeles (Web site: www.groundlings.com)
Improvisational Theatre Groups (USA) (Web site; www.improvcomedy.org)
Los Angeles acting classes/seminars (Web site: www.at-la.com)
Second City Theatres (Chicago, Toronto, Las Vegas, Detroit) (Web site: www.secondcity.com)

Theatre Lab Workshops, Washington, DC (Web site: www.theatrelab.org)
Theatre city search (Web site: www.geocities.com)
Theatre schools nationwide (Web site: dmoz.org)
Training in the Round (Web site: www.trainingintheround.com)

5

Brain fitness: your mental tool kit

'The brain's interconnections far exceed the Internet's!'

Several years ago, my UK business partner, Jenny Greenwood and I were trying to encapsulate the work we did with people and organizations. We wanted to find a term that would convey the use of brain-based learning to accelerate and improve performance – fast-tracking individuals and organizations to success. We also wanted to convey how much fun it is: hence, brain fitness.

Our unique combination of accelerated learning, neuro-linguistic psychology, theatre-based learning and emotional competencies has evolved into a mental tool kit for performance consultants and learners. That's what this chapter is about: how your brain works and how you can use that knowledge to enhance your workshops.

We found that the development programmes that work best use multiple-intelligence learning. This includes music, drama, drawing, debate and discussion. But intelligence without emotional savvy doesn't get the best results. In other words, if we engage our brains and our emotions, our ability to reach peak performance is intensified.

For many years, cognitive thinking has taken centre stage; emotion has been banished offstage. Yet brain research shows that emotions and thought are deeply connected. Developing emotional intelligence, harmonizing emotion and thought, is what makes the difference between a performer and a top performer.

As developers of people, we need to merge cognitive and emotional learning. This improves self-confidence, motivates people to change and enhances learning.

Building mental muscle

The brain and innovative learning

The 1990s were dubbed 'The Decade of the Brain' by the then US President, George Bush. During the last three decades, scientists have been exploring how we process information, patterns, emotions and memory to determine exactly how we learn.

I use tools from the brain-fitness toolbox in every one of my workshops and coaching sessions. It's a mental kit that transforms performance. The really fascinating thing I find in all of my sessions is that most participants are astonished to learn about how their brain works – and how this knowledge can work for them. This transforms their ability to achieve.

In a recent brain-fitness workshop, the managing director of an engineering firm came up to me in great excitement. He said he had been looking for years for new techniques to help build performance and creativity. He had used Edward de Bono's six hats with great ingenuity. But now, armed with an array of new brain-fitness techniques, he felt he could begin to build even greater motivation, self-esteem and creativity in his staff.

How does your brain work?

Our brains are a dense web of interconnecting synapses. They constantly make new connections – hence our ability to learn new things. Your brain has approximately 100 billion nerve cells (or neurons). Each neuron can make up to 10,000 synaptic connections to other neurons. In other words, every neuron acts like a messenger. Each cell processes information, which it sends to other neurons across tiny gaps called synapses.

This electrochemical process is the basis of all human behaviour. Every time we breathe, think, move or speak, communication takes place between hundreds of thousands of neurons. All the incoming information that your learners are processing is through the brain's vast number of interdependent networks. Whatever information has been stored previously influences how new information is processed and learnt.

This is important to us as performance developers because it can have a profound effect on how we put together our programmes. As learners are exposed to new experiences and new information, nerve cells grow new branches or dendrites. These dendrites are the major receiver of new information: the more you use your brain, the more you grow new dendrites or brain branches. Throughout your lifetime, your brain can continue to create new branches.

Hence the importance not just for new learning, but for innovative learning and thinking. This increases the brain's patterns and networks exponentially. My mother-in-law is an amazing example. She was a stage actress in Britain and South Africa prior to the last World War. To this day, nearing her nineties, she still learns a new poem everyday. She constantly amazes us by pulling out of her memory bag poems or speeches from Shakespeare plays.

In your sessions, if you creatively use movement, voice, dialogue, music, story-telling and interaction you will enhance learning and performance.

The cerebral cortex: conscious brain

The brain is divided into two hemispheres, each specializing in certain functions. These two hemispheres are linked together and are called the cerebral cortex. The cerebral cortex is known as the conscious-thinking centre. This 'thinking brain' is responsible for seeing, hearing, talking, thinking and creating – all your higher intelligences.

The two hemispheres are separated by the corpus callosum: a band of tissue that connects the two halves, right and left. Effectively the two halves act as one, sending information back and forth with incredible speed. Apart from the pineal gland, every brain module is duplicated in both hemispheres. Each receives infor-mation from the opposite side of the body, which it also controls.

Right-brain thinking

'Right-brain' thinking is a popular metaphor in the training and business world. It has become synonymous with creative and lateral thinking – and thinking

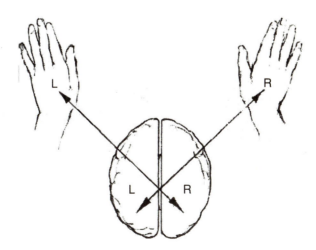

Figure 5.1 Right and left hemispheres

'outside the box'. In fact, the two hemispheres of the brain work together. The right hemisphere has become known as the unconscious, non-verbal part of the brain. It is associated with creative, innovative thinking, as well as activities such as brainstorming, memory mapping, visualization and intuitive thinking. There is some misunderstanding of right-brain thinking, because brainstorming and memory mapping are actually whole-brain activities.

The left hemisphere is associated with the conscious, verbal part of the brain. This is known as the objective, logical, mathematical and linguistic side of the brain. It is often associated with careers such as accountancy, law, statistics and investment broking. 'Right-brain' careers include graphic design, art, writing and music.

It has become very popular in the fields of education and performance development to say that we need more 'right-brain' thinking. What we actually need is more 'whole-brain' thinking: a combination of left and right brain. Although each hemisphere is responsible for certain functions, both sides are involved in most thinking that we do.

Whole-brain exercise (30 minutes)

I use this simple exercise to encourage learners to think about how they can develop their brain power. Learners start to think not only about their role at work, but the tasks they perform. To develop whole-brain thinking, integrate a variety of right- and left-brain tasks.

Ask your learners to think about all the activities they perform in their daily working lives. Using the lists below, identify whether they engage more in right-brain or left-brain activities. Once they have determined which is their more dominant thinking style, left or right, have them think about what activities would help them to develop the other side of the brain. Allow 30 minutes for the exercise.

For example, a graphic designer would use pictures, and more visual, creative and imaginative types of activities to design a Web site, advertisement or promotional material – all right-brain activities. A lawyer would most likely use words, facts, statistics, linear and linguistic skills to draft wills, draw up contracts and deal with administration – left-brain tasks. Yet a lawyer could use creative thinking when negotiating a contract in a difficult divorce case.

An accountant would use maths, computers, lists, facts, analysis and sequential numbering – left-brain activities. But an accountant could use right-brain, global, visual thinking to draft a strategic overview of a merger or acquisition.

Left-brain thinking	Right-brain thinking
Objective	Subjective
Conscious	Unconscious
Speech/verbal	Spatial/musical
Words	Pictures
Logical	Intuitive
Facts	General
Controlled	Emotional
Sequential	Simultaneous
Structured	Spontaneous
Analytic	Synthetic, gestalt
Logical, mathematical	Global, strategic
Intellectual	Creative
Numbers	Drawings
Computer	Daydreaming
Linear	Imaginative
List maker	Brainstorm map
Regularity	Rhythm and movement
Worldly	Spiritual

Exercise review

To evaluate this exercise, have your participants discuss what they learnt about themselves and each other, and what they can do to build their less-preferred thinking skills.

The limbic cortex: unconscious brain

Although the right-brain/left-brain model has become popularized in recent years, it excludes the important limbic system, now recognized as playing a vital role in processing emotions. All interactive exercises in my workshops incorporate some kind of personal connection; I look at how to bring in all of the person. The reason is that emotions have a strong impact on learning. Here's why.

Beneath the corpus callosum is the area called the limbic system. The limbic system is small and divided into two interconnected halves. It is virtually hidden from view underneath the cerebral cortices. Neural and synaptic, the limbic brain is divided into two hemispheres, and is capable of thinking in a similar way to its cerebral neighbour.

However, the limbic brain relates to the unconscious and affects our experience. Its main job is to feed information to the conscious-thinking brain. Emotions are generated in the limbic system, along with other urges that direct our behaviour. The limbic system has a central role in processing short-term memory, transforming that into long-term memory. This gives it a significant link to learning.

Whole-brain metaphor

Most delegates are fascinated by the brain, and want to learn how to build their brain power, fast. Ned Herrmann's 'four thinking styles' is a classic metaphor for 'whole-brain' thinking. It opens the door to creative thinking, enhanced learning and performance.

Herrmann has combined left- and right-brain (with its cerebral and limbic counterparts) to create the whole-brain model. In his *Whole Brain Business Book*, Herrmann divides the brain into four quarters. Each is identified with a specific thinking style: rational, experimental, organized and feeling. The cerebral (northern) hemisphere is cognitive and pragmatic; the limbic (southern) is intuitive and instinctual.

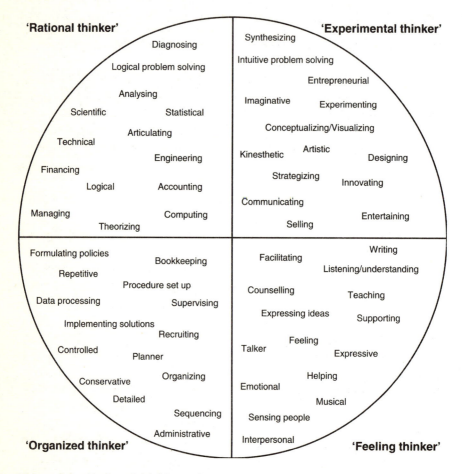

Figure 5.2   Preferred thinking styles

These four styles interact with each other to create a network of thinking patterns. This useful metaphor helps us understand how adults take in information, how they think and what activities they prefer in the workplace. Our ultimate goal as performance consultants is to help learners apply whole-brain thinking, and ultimately to create whole-brain teams in the workplace.

Whole-brain thinking tools (45 minutes)

When designing a seminar, think about how to incorporate activities from all four thinking styles to satisfy the learning, thinking and doing styles of each of your participants.

The next exercise helps individuals determine their preferred thinking style, and how they can build mental prowess by including activities from the other styles. Exercise two outlines a group activity to help each group determine the main thinking styles employed in their work.

Exercise 1: Individual whole-brain exercise (10 minutes)

Look at your own preferred style of thinking. How you can incorporate all four thinking modes into your daily work and play? First, circle the typical activities you undertake (at work and home) in each thinking style. In a second colour, identify what's missing. Circle activities you could engage in to develop more brain power. Think of activities to stretch and challenge yourself, pushing you beyond your preferred thinking styles.

The more you use different parts of the brain, the more fit and flexible you are mentally. Also, the more you grow your brain! It is estimated that Einstein probably used 4 per cent of his brain, and that most of us use less than 1 per cent. Here is a start to developing greater mental and creative flexibility by incorporating all four thinking styles into your entire life's activities.

Exercise 2: Group thinking-styles exercise (20 minutes)

Divide delegates into small groups. Ask them to brainstorm the key activities in each department of their organization (or each of their job roles within the group). Using Figure 5.2, list each activity under the four relevant thinking styles. Ask delegates to determine which activities are a combination of thinking styles. If groups begin to integrate more whole-brain thinking into their teams, they will become more creative, effective, self-sustaining, risk-taking and solution-seeking. It's important to be aware that your workplace style may be different to that used in your personal life.

Exercise review (15 minutes)

Discuss what participants gained from this exercise and how it can be applied in the workplace. One key discovery: there are many approaches to solving a problem. It is important to incorporate as many thinking styles as possible into a team or group. A whole-brain problem-solving team greatly increases the chances of developing breakthrough solutions to solve both major and minor problems.

Brain-based learning

Brain-based learning is learning in a way your brain prefers, and in a way your brain would naturally learn. Brain-based learning also helps learners make connections between their new learning and what they already know. Hence the popularity of using brainstorming, memory maps and creative thinking to generate new ideas in the learning environment and at work.

The brain continually makes new patterns. This is what participants do with new learning. They interpret the new information in the context of what they know, make a generalization – and work out how to apply the new learning to their circumstances. Context is important; it is the physical, emotional and intellectual environment that makes up each learning experience and gives it meaning.

Thought and emotions are deeply connected. When we bring appropriate feelings and emotion to learning, we harness the limbic system, and learning is much more effective and powerful.

In low-stress learning situations, we can reflect and think analytically. When highly stressed, we feel helpless and fatigued. Our brain responds by stopping us from using our more complex thinking skills. This is why a relaxed, comfortable environment is much more conducive to developing people and performance.

How do adults learn?

Adults learn exactly as children do, using all of their senses. Learning mostly comes through experience. Have you ever asked yourself, 'How do I like to learn?' At work, most of us learn in an informal setting: through personal experience, group collaboration, personal mentoring, even by making mistakes. Everyone has a favourite teacher, parental figure, boss or colleague who has coached them at some point in their lives. So how do we bring that into the learning environment?

Trainers can fall down by trying to put all learning into a formal 'classroom'. Many of us have come to performance development thinking we can teach, rather than thinking about how to help our learners learn. As most of us have discovered, talking to our participants from the front of a classroom just repeats an experience learners hoped to have left behind once they entered the workplace.

Exercise: Positive and negative learning (10 minutes)

Think of a positive learning experience you had in school when you were younger. How did you learn this new skill? Perhaps it was a maths lesson, a drawing class, a music lesson, or out on the sports field.

- What was positive and memorable about that experience?
- Did you have a chance to try out something new?
- Which of your senses did you use?
- Did you have recognition and support from an adult or other classmates?

Example

I loved my French language classes. Able to learn by listening, hearing, speaking, creating imaginary conversations (auditory), writing (visual) and acting out speaking parts (kinesthetic), I found learning languages fun and easy. My teachers were always supportive, enthusiastic and helped when we had difficulties.

Compare your positive experience to a negative learning experience at school. Think about why it was difficult to learn this new topic or skill.

- What were you not allowed to do?
- What kind of feedback did you receive?
- What actually stopped you from learning?

Example

My example is a high school chemistry class. I loved the idea of what we were learning, but had no support, advice or help from the chemistry teacher. He did not know how to help us 'actualize' the experiments, so couldn't brief us properly. He also did not know how to recognize a job well done. Unable to use all of our senses and intelligences, and without support or recognition, most of us who performed well in other subjects did not do well in that class!

The principles of learning

The key principles to remember are that adults learn only if they:

- want and/or need to learn;
- can relate the learning to past, present or future experience;
- feel comfortable in a non-threatening learning environment;
- can practise the new learning in a realistic setting;

- have a high level of self-esteem;
- receive information in a way that suits them (ie have rapport with the facilitator and other participants);
- have the opportunity to discuss and create personal relevance;
- can measure their progress and receive coaching.

Here are some of the key aspects to consider when helping adults to learn. How can these help you to produce more effective, fun and dynamic workshops?

Learning-oriented	What do your participants actually want to learn?
Motivation	What motivated them to attend?
Goals	How does the programme relate to their learning goals?
Values	What are their personal values and the organization's?
Experiential	What participative activities will enhance learning?
Context	How can you reduce delegate anxiety and make learning fun?
Application	How can learners apply new skills in the workplace?
Reflection	How can you build in group analysis and discussion?
Mentoring	How can you use mentoring to address individual needs (in the training room and in the workplace)?
Group interaction	Use small groups to encourage collaboration, support and sharing of experiences
Team training	Use other facilitators to coach, team-teach and reinforce learning
Follow-up	Provide follow-up sessions to evaluate how learning is applied in the workplace

Train your brain

The more we use our brains, the more we grow them. We've all heard the phrase 'Use it or lose it'. With new learning, we grow new branches within the brain. Without learning, we lose those important networks that influence memory, learning and motivation.

So how do we do it? We can work with visual, auditory and kinesthetic learning. These are just three of the nine intelligences people can use to build up brain connections.

Preferred learning styles

Using a wide range of learning styles simultaneously engages the whole person and makes your programmes livelier, more interesting and fun.

The use of visuals such as flipcharts, notes, acetates and slides with graphics, animation and colour appeals to those who learn best by seeing. The use of aids with sound such as video, films, tapes, CDs, music, dialogue and discussion appeals to those who prefer auditory learning. Kinesthetic learners are happiest when involved in participatory activities such as puzzles, games, role plays, case studies, brainstorming, storytelling and computer-generated exercises.

Preferred learning-styles questionnaire

Here's a quick, fun exercise to help your delegates understand their preferred style of learning. Ask them to circle the answer most like them, making a total of the three scores at the end. If they insist that two representation systems are equally important in one or two questions, have them circle two.

1. When you're annoyed, do you:
   V   silently seethe inside?
   A   shout and scream?
   K   tense your muscles, suck in your breath, shout, fume?

2. When you are congratulated, do you prefer to:
   V   receive it in writing?
   A   hear it said out loud?
   K   be given a handshake, pat on the back or a hug?

3. When you forget, do you:
   V   forget names but remember places?
   A   forget faces but remember names?
   K   remember best where, when and what you did?

4. When you learn, do you prefer:
   V   the written word, pictures and colours?
   A   to listen to a lecture or be given instructions?
   K   to participate in activities?

5. When you read, do you:
   V   enjoy reading descriptions and creating pictures in your mind?
   A   hear the characters' voices?
   K   like to act out the roles?

6. When you're really concentrating, are you distracted by:
   V   a messy room?
   A   unwelcome noise?
   K   sudden movement?

7. When you relax, do you:
   V   watch TV, read, see a play?
   A   listen to music, the radio, enjoy conversation?
   K   play sports or games?

8. When you remember specific incidents, do you:
   V   see well-focused, coloured pictures?
   A   hear voices and sounds?
   K   see pictures with movement in them?

9. When you spell, do you:
    V   see the word?
    A   sound the word out?
    K   write the word down and make sure it feels right?

10. When you speak, do you:
    V   speak little and mostly listen?
    A   like to listen and to speak as well?
    K   use your hands and face to express yourself?

Total: V =
A =
K =

Match teaching and learning styles

As a performance coach, incorporate all three preferences when presenting new information or material. It's easy and fun to do. It may be simply a matter of adding one or two aids or activities to highlight your message – such as story-telling, colour, music, brainstorming or interactive games.

It's vital to adapt to people's preferred learning styles. Let's take a look at how we can teach to visual, auditory and kinesthetic preferences.

V = Visual learners like:

- animation;
- colour/graphics;
- diagrams/key words;
- memory maps;
- overhead transparencies;
- pictures/films/videos;
- posters/flipcharts;
- visualization techniques.

What to do:

- Use highlighters, colour, shapes, graphics, charts.
- Look at pictures, films and videos.
- Use memory maps, overhead acetates, slides, diagrams, flipcharts, posters.
- Do visualization exercises, and take participants through a visualization.

A = Auditory learners like:

- analogies/metaphors/anecdotes;
- audio and videotapes;
- music/singing;
- storytelling/looping stories (telling a story within a story);
- teaching others;
- to read aloud;
- to be read to aloud.

What to do:

- Use storytelling, anecdotes, metaphors.
- Make and use audiotapes.
- Use music during exercises and breaks.
- Have participants teach the information to someone else.

K = Kinesthetic learners like:

- acting it out/pantomime/role plays;
- brainstorming;
- debate/discussion;
- experiential exercises in pairs/small groups;
- games/puzzles;
- making and using memory maps;
- writing/taking notes/making notes in margins.

What to do:

- Do experiential exercises, memory mapping.
- Case studies, writing, journal keeping.
- Act it out, use music, sing, invent songs, dance.

Using multiple intelligences

We take in information through our senses, but we process it through our intelligences. Howard Gardner, author of *Multiple Intelligences*, identified our intelligences as:

- linguistic;
- logical mathematical;

- visual/spatial;
- auditory;
- kinesthetic/physical;
- interpersonal;
- intrapersonal;
- naturalistic;
- existential.

In *Frames of Mind*, Gardner challenges the practice of using only the accepted primary intelligences (linguistic, mathematical/logical and visual/spatial) in academic performance. He suggests that we achieve success by using a combination of intelligences and a variety of skills to solve different kinds of problems.

Knowing what we now know about the brain and its network of patterns, it's easy to understand that the intelligences work together in elaborate ways. In life and in work we tend to gravitate towards activities that suit our strongest intelligences, often ignoring the least developed. Are you using your strongest intelligences in the workplace?

I remember a young teenager who worked for me in the sales and promotion department of a daily newspaper in the south of England. One of my line managers came to me, very insistent that this lad was wasted working in distribution, as he had great potential in the field of computers. The keen observation of my line manager meant this young man moved into an area of work where he not only had a strong intelligence, but was able to gain the confidence and self-esteem he would never have developed in his previous department. It was to be the making of him.

Think about how to enhance your performance-development sessions using a different combination of intelligences. Many quizzes and questionnaires are available to help determine which intelligences are most developed in an organization, team or individuals. Try one yourself to see if you are working with your preferred intelligences, and what others you need to develop to grow your brain power. Which combination of intelligences would be useful and enhance your training sessions?

Learning and emotion

Daniel Goleman in *Emotional Intelligence* tells us that emotional intelligence is separate from technical skill and cognitive ability. In learning a new computer software program, or how to structure a marketing plan, we can use association and the higher-thinking skills. For purely cognitive learning, we engage that part of the brain we learnt to use in school, the neocortex.

1. Linguistic/verbal

Skills:	Listening, speaking, reading and writing
Characteristics:	Likes to write
	Has the gift of the gab
	Talks face to face or at a distance
	Reads to get information
	Listens to others to get information
	Tells jokes, stories
	Enjoys reading
	Good memory for trivia
	Appreciates work games
	Spells accurately
	Uses language to achieve results
	Good at debate
Key question:	How can you use the spoken or written word, dialogue, debate and discussion during training?
Learning strategies:	Lectures, discussion groups, brainstorming
	Word games, stories, metaphors, analogies
	Learner presentations, dialogue and speeches
	Writing activities

2. Mathematical/logical/scientific

Skills:	Ability to understand numbers and think logically
Characteristics:	Talent with maths, logic, systems
	Likes to compute numbers
	Enjoys applying math skills
	Enjoys technological and scientific problems
	Thinks in abstract concepts
	Measures, categorizes and analyses situations
	Looks for rational explanations
	Appreciates logic games
Key question:	How can you use numbers, calculations, logic, classifications or critical-thinking skills?
Learning strategies:	Logical problem-solving exercises
	Classifications and categorizations
	Quantifications and calculations
	Logical-sequential presentation of subject matter
	Scientific demonstrations

3. Visual/spatial

Skills:	Sensitivity, awareness and appreciation or use of colour, line, form
	Ability to visualize how things will look
Characteristics:	Can visualize clear images
	Sensitive to visual information such as texture
	Likes colour, design, drawing
	Likes to use graphs, blueprints, diagrams
	Enjoys using cameras/video recorders
	Good with directions, navigation
	Enjoys geometry

Appreciates illustrated reading materials
Likes puzzles

Key question: How can you use visual aids, visualization, colour, graphics, animation and art in your sessions?

Learning strategies: Charts, graphs, diagrams and maps
Visualization
Videos, slides, movies
3-D activities
Painting, drawing and creating collages
Using memory maps and visual organizers
Computer-assisted design software

4. Auditory

Skills: Ability to listen, understand rhythm, beat, pitch as well as sensitivity to those elements as they relate to recognition, interpretation or response to sounds from the natural or physical environment

Characteristics: An expressive speaker
Enjoys learning languages
Sensitive to natural sounds in the environment
Knows when music is in or out of tune
Sings well
Enjoys radio, CDs and tapes
Plays an instrument
Knows the melodies of songs
Sings or hums while working

Key question: How can you bring in speaking, audiotapes, music, environmental sounds, or set key points in a rhythmic or melodic framework?

Learning strategies: Playing background music
Setting sound or music anchors
Group singing
Rhythms, songs, raps and chants
Linking tunes or songs to concepts
Music software

5. Kinesthetic/motor

Skills: Uses the body to gain information or solve problems
Talent with movement

Characteristics: Wants to relate things to own experience
Relies on agility, strength, endurance
Likes to play sports, exercise or dance
Interested in health and physiology
Likes working with hands
Uses gestures to emphasize a point
Is well-coordinated
Learns or expresses by touching
Can build or construct things

Key question: How can you involve the whole body, movement or use hands-on activities?

Learning strategies:	Creative movement
	Study trips (field trips)
	Mime and pantomime
	Hands-on activities
	Theatre-based exercises
	Tactile materials and exercises
	Virtual reality software

6. Interpersonal

Skills:	The ability to perceive accurately and respond appropriately to other people's needs and feelings
Characteristics:	Known for giving advice and counsel
	Acknowledges the needs of others
	Responds well to others' needs
	Enjoys group sports
	Seeks advice of others
	Has close friends
	Enjoys groups and crowds
	A good leader
	Likes interacting with friends and family
	Enjoys conversation and dialogue
Key question:	How can you engage participants in sharing and group learning?
Learning strategies:	Group activities
	Peer training, coaching and mentoring
	Board games
	Brainstorming
	Simulations
	Interactive software

7. Intrapersonal

Skills:	Inner control and focus
	Ability to self-analyse
	Can understand and satisfy own needs and desires
Characteristics:	Spends time alone
	Likes to set own agenda
	Can set own initiative
	Thinks about goals
	Independent-minded
	Keeps a journal
	Enjoys personal projects/hobbies
	Seeks personal growth
Key question:	How can you elicit personal feelings and give learners choices?
Learning strategies:	Independent learning
	Self-paced learning
	Choices in learning
	Journal keeping
	Personal goal-setting activities
	Reflective exercises

8. Naturalistic

Skills: Can observe, relate to and respond to nature in a complex way
Characteristics: Enjoys nature and conservation
                     Promotes environmental practices
                     Would enjoy being on safari or a marine dive
                     Likes to walk the dog, groom pets
                     Learns best when experiencing nature
                     Likes an appropriate, pleasant setting
                     Understands and responds to nature
Key question: How can you bring the natural environment into your training
                     situation or create a natural environment?
Learning strategies: Sounds of the natural environment
                     Exercises set in the outdoors
                     Describe their experiences to others metaphorically

9. Philosophical/ethical/existential

Skills: Examines the meaning of life and forms a rationale for what one does
Characteristics: Likes to reflect on life
                     Wants to create a more just society
                     Works towards a better world
                     Enjoys learning related to philosophy, values or justice
                     Engages in philosophic discussion, reading or meditating
                     Likes to develop a rationale for beliefs
                     Interested in value systems and belief systems
                     Likes to relate the task to larger goals
                     Engaged by integrity, morality and ethics
Key question: How can you bring values, beliefs, different points of view and
                     developing a rationale into performance development?
Learning strategies: Exercises in understanding other points of view
                     Debate and discussion
                     Setting goals to individual and organizational values

More complex activities that demand motivation, changing behaviour, inter-personal dynamics and achieving goals require the emotional brain. Goleman has identified the importance of emotional intelligence to enhance learner competencies of self-confidence, empathy, achieving results, continual improvement, influence and team work. We need to engage emotional intelligence to ensure that training is transferred from the training environment to the workplace.

How do we link emotion and learning?

First, find out why your participants are with you. What motivates them to learn? Perhaps this new learning will ensure a promotion, or enhance their career in some way. It might ensure that they stay at the top of their profession, or enable them to do their job more effectively and efficiently.

If they are required to learn new skills or new information, their desire to learn will engage them emotionally. Spend the time needed to find out what is driving them and what they want. You can then make the connection between what they need and want with what they will gain.

Linking learning goals to personal values

Whether working with groups or an individual, one of the first things I do is to link learning goals to personal and organizational values. It is crucial for individuals to understand themselves – what makes them tick and what drives them. In order to set goals, we need first to understand our values: they have a direct link to our motivators. To find out what drives someone at work requires several questions. Here is an exercise to help you discover someone's personal values.

Personal-values exercise (10 minutes)

- What is important to you about work?
- What is important about that…?
- What else is important to you?

Dig deeper than surface level. You are helping the learner uncover the intangibles that drive them. So if the individual says 'money', ask 'What is important to you about money?' The answers usually fall within the parameters of safety, security, financial security and freedom to do what you want. Those are values that underlie a goal of making money.

Often, instead of values, individuals list goals. Your job is to ask, 'What is important about…?' to help uncover the value behind the goal. At the end of the exercise, you will have a list of intangibles that represent their values. Some examples from my clients are:

- honesty;
- integrity;
- balance;
- freedom to choose;
- support;
- doing something of value;
- giving something back;
- helping others;
- teaching.

Organizational values exercise (10 minutes)

Once you've uncovered their personal values, the next step is to discover how they link their values with those of the organization.

- What is important to the organization about the work they do/the products they manufacture/ the services they offer?
- Why is that important?
- What does it do for them?

Often the answers you receive will relate more to end-goals, such as to make money, build up a client base, be the best in the marketplace. Ask what is important about each of those points to uncover answers such as:

- being unique;
- offering something no one else does;
- taking care of client needs;
- understanding our customer;
- giving customers what they want;
- professionalism;
- being innovative;
- being creative.

These are a few intangibles that drive an organization. If personal and organizational values don't match, individuals may be stressed or demotivated at work. They will find it difficult to pursue targets and goals that are in conflict with their own underlying needs. If they are not stressed, the challenge is how you as a performance developer deal with these individuals.

For example, I have a very good friend who was head of training and development for an international organization. As she moved into her third year with the organization, she began to realize that her values were in direct conflict with the way the organization managed people. She realized that her talents were marketable elsewhere. She had confidence in her own ability, an integral part of emotional intelligence and competence. So she left the organization and set out on a quest to seek a position more suited to her values.

Engage feelings

Creating a 'feel good' ambiance from the very beginning of a session is important. Motivated learners engage with their feelings. This is why, when setting goals, it's important to understand what motivates and drives our learners.

Artists, craftsmen, technocrats

Patricia Pitcher talks about the need for artists, craftsmen and technocrats in the workplace. The 'artist' brings in such qualities as warmth, generosity, humour, interpersonal skills, emotions, inspiration, intuition, unpredictability and visioning skills. 'Craftsmen' are well balanced, trustworthy, reasonable, sensible and realistic. They know what works and what doesn't; they're practical, not theoretical.

Technocrats may be brilliant analytically, but they can make bad judgements about people, situations and the marketplace. They don't learn from their mistakes, because they don't think they make any! They don't feel much emotion, except possibly anger if contradicted. Pitcher is saying that we need a balance – and in fact, it's a whole-brain balance – between the intuition, visioning, playful, emotional right brain and the practical, pragmatic, theoretical, analytical left brain.

We've all grown up with the adage 'Don't let your head rule your heart'. But to learn and to remember a new skill or new information, we need to engage the emotions. Think about those events in your life that you remember most – it is because there is some kind of emotional attachment to them. If you engage the emotions of your learners, they are more likely to pay attention, and to remember.

Improving confidence

One way to involve learners emotionally is to engage their confidence. Begin with what they already know, and make a link between this and the new skills and information they will learn with you. If people perceive learning as threatening, their emotional response will ensure they put up a barrier. If you create an atmosphere of safety, security and comfort, emotionally they will feel able to move into uncharted waters. They will be willing to take the risk and challenge of working with new concepts and ideas.

Creating security, well-being and confidence

I start from the moment delegates enter the training environment. I play music conducive to warmth and comfort. I try to be there before anyone else to welcome individuals prior to starting the session. By helping them to feel secure in a strange environment, giving them a sense of well-being through the ambiance of the room, and making them feel comfortable, you're off to a good start. Introductions and icebreakers are the second component to create a sense of security, comfort and confidence that this is where they should be.

Emotional competencies

One of the major questions about performance development in organizations I have worked in has been, 'How can you ensure training will be applied back in the workplace, and not just create a feel-good factor that lasts a few days?'

In *Working with Emotional Intelligence*, Daniel Goleman suggests that emotional intelligence creates competencies that help transfer training to on-the-job performance. Goleman has divided emotional intelligence into social and personal competencies that include:

- self-confidence;
- empathy;
- the need to get results;
- constant improvement;
- influence;
- team work.

Early on in my training career, I discovered that no matter what the subject matter, learners needed to be confident in order to learn. Once confident, they could develop other emotional competencies: creating empathy with others, achieving results, understanding the need for continual learning, how to work within a team and how to influence others in the workplace.

To develop emotional competence:

- Engage learners in participative, experiential learning.
- Find out what learners want and need.
- Link learning goals to both personal and organizational values.
- Provide constructive, tactical feedback.
- Engage learners' passion and motivation for learning.
- Develop a realistic action plan linked to goals.
- Encourage a culture in the workplace that supports continual learning.
- Create an environment for learning that engenders comfort, security and the ability to take risks.
- Help participants to tailor performance development to their own needs.

CASE STUDY: CAPACITY-BUILDING FOR TEACHERS

Recently, for an impoverished school in the small valley where I live not far from Cape Town, we set up an appeal to raise money. The aim was to rebuild a primary school to satisfy the needs of poor children living in a rapidly growing community.

Part of the process has been the capacity-building of the teachers, who had been disengaged from the parents of the children they teach for historical reasons, and who didn't feel empowered to take part in the rebuilding of the school. Part of the capacity-building has been to help the teachers take charge of their own training programme, and to be committed to the building project.

Encouraged to talk directly with funders about their needs, they drew up their own development plan, complementing the needs of the school building project. The teachers have begun to participate in the project committees and to manage their role in a properly elected governing body. The process has taken nearly three years, because it was important to first build the confidence, self-esteem, team work and capability of the teachers. They have begun to support and trust each other and to develop the confidence to take part in what they now see as 'their' school.

We used the following emotional competencies to understand the teachers' training needs (see Goleman's *Working with Emotional Intelligence* and Jennifer Salopek's article *Train Your Brain*).

Social competence – empathy:

- The ability to handle relationships.
- Developing an awareness of others' feelings, needs and concerns.
- Cultivating the opportunities presented by their diverse community.

Social competence – social skills:

- Learning how to produce desirable responses in others.
- Managing conflict successfully and resolving disagreements.
- Learning how to collaborate and work towards shared goals.

Personal competence – self-awareness:

- Learning how to manage themselves.
- Recognizing their own emotions and the effects of those emotions on others.
- Beginning to believe in their own self-worth and capabilities.

Personal competence – self-management:

- Developing self-control and managing their own emotions and impulses.
- Taking responsibility for their own performance.
- Becoming more adaptable, with flexibility in how to do things.

Personal competence – motivation:

- Developing the will to achieve and meet their own standards of excellence.
- Becoming committed – aligning their personal goals with those of the school.
- Remaining optimistic in the face of conflict, difficulties and setbacks.

In workshops with the teachers, we began the slow process of building their self-esteem, helping them to take the initiative, to take responsibility for their own capacity-building. As a result, they have increased their social and personal competencies and have developed the ability to manage a unique, diverse school with complex challenges in their rapidly changing society.

Building self-esteem (20 minutes)

Self-esteem is the key to lifelong self-motivation. We can be motivated by others to perform but that is often through fear.

First, think about the characteristics and behaviour of people you know who have high self-esteem.

- How do they manage change?
- How do they communicate with others?
- What are their levels of performance?
- What motivates them?

Think now about someone you know who has low self-esteem. What characteristics and behaviour does he or she display that lets you know he/she lacks self-esteem?

- How does the person's behaviour show his/her lack of confidence?
- Where does he/she fall down in communicating with others?
- Who does he/she look to for motivation?
- What are his/her performance levels?

If you could coach this person, how would you help that individual to develop higher self-esteem – to believe in him- or herself and begin to understand what his/her self-motivators are, positive and negative? Think about identifying positive values and beliefs. Look at when the person has performed with excellence. How can they model their own excellence? How can they learn from their mistakes?

Remember to learn from failure. Failure is feedback and allows for reflection and new learning. How can you help people to bring that into their belief system? Think about what they have accomplished in the past. How can they call on those resources?

Turning point

As performance development focuses more on technology and technical competencies, it remains to be seen whether organizations will embrace the need for emotional as well as cognitive competencies. If we have technical competence without the ability to lead, motivate and communicate with our teams and our clients, people will become only the cost of doing business – rather than the heart of business.

For example, I work with a young entrepreneurial firm that couldn't figure out where it was going wrong in terms of motivation. The CEO decided to undergo coaching himself. At the end of this process, he realized that his team was relying on him for motivation. He was trying to motivate them with his vision. But it wasn't their vision, or their goals.

To engage his team more 'emotionally', and to understand its underlying motivators, we went through a series of coaching sessions. All the staff members were encouraged to clarify personal values, their driving passion in staying with the firm, and what would empower them. The overriding response was the need to participate more in overall strategic decisions. They wanted to have their skills, knowledge and expertise acknowledged. The team now has the driving motivation it needed, having understood that emotional involvement and recognition complement technical competence and the achievement of bottom-line goals. The organization is moving from strength to strength.

Emotional intelligence uses a different part of the brain from cognitive intelligence, which uses the neocortex, or thinking brain. Emotional intelligence comes from the limbic brain. It learns differently and requires lots and lots of practice to learn. If you are training people in new skills, but you don't give them the chance to practise, or to develop confidence as they begin to achieve, you're losing the value that performance development brings to an organization.

I spoke one afternoon to a group of young women lawyers of a South African legal firm who wanted to share their ideas and discuss how to develop their mental performance. The managing partner said to me: 'We don't need any training here; we had one day's training two years ago and that will do.' Quite a thought!

This senior managing partner did not realize that cognitive and technical skills alone were not enough to create a successful legal partnership. All of his partners needed to develop their emotional competencies in order to manage people effectively, handle clients, market their skills and cope with high-pressure jobs. But without the support of their male partners, the only recourse for those women lawyers was to create their own separate, professional development plans.

Together we care

When I was working with UK Holiday Inn hotels in the early 1980s, we discovered that business was not increasing substantially enough to warrant the number of new hotels that had been built. After a good deal of research, we found that the hotel chain was associated with nice rooms and a clean spacious environment, but the perception was an ambiance that was 'soulless'. A new marketing campaign was initiated to get across the message of a friendly, helpful, supportive environment that would take care of customer needs, whether for business during the week or for the family at the weekend.

That was the start of the weekend break – and the dual emphasis on leisure and business. What had been lacking before was the sense of 'How will the customer feel after a night at a Holiday Inn?' We put the emphasis on customer care with a difference. A programme was put together called 'Together We Care'. The company began training its hotel staff in emotional competencies – in the skills that were needed to bring customers in again and again.

Putting emotion back into the equation

Positive feelings such as fun, enjoyment and collaboration with others have a powerful effect on learning. Strong emotions (positive and negative) tend to mean something is usually well remembered. The brain's centre for emotional memory is the amygdala. It monitors the 'fight or flight' response. This, once engaged, will ensure learning cannot easily take place because negative emotions, like stress or fear, prevent new information getting through to the thinking brain.

Remember your favourite birthday party? Your first kiss, or the day you got married? Compare that with a traumatic event in your life – we usually want more of the first! Thus for real learning to take place, we need to create an environment of safety, comfort and security in the learning environment.

This primitive part of our brain needs to be well managed, which means that emotional intelligence competencies need to be learnt. Emotional intelligence, because it can be learnt, improves throughout life.

Basic emotional intelligence skills are:

● team work;
● sharing information;
● supporting others;
● empathy;
● adaptability.

Emotional intelligence is teachable. It is a comprehensive profile of self-awareness: managing feelings, motivation, empathy, social skills and personal competence.

How to go about it

Identify the strengths and weaknesses in your team, group or organization in social and personal competencies. Look at self-esteem, self-confidence, motivation, goal setting or performance in the workplace.

In social competence, look at the ability to handle relationships, empathize with team mates, or to develop social skills such as team work, collaborating, cooperating, working towards shared goals and managing conflict well.

Where personal competencies are concerned, identify strengths and weaknesses in self-awareness, self-management and motivation. Help individuals to build self-confidence, believe in their own self worth, recognize their own emotions and the effect they have on others. Help them to develop behavioural flexibility, honesty and integrity. Look at their will to achieve. How are they meeting their own standards of excellence? Evaluate their ability to take the initiative.

Intuitive intelligence

Intuitive discovery

Heard the story about Einstein lying on a hill looking at the sky? He was allowing imagination, intuition, vision and dream to take over. The result? His intuitive discovery of the theory $e=mc^2$. Developing intuitive intelligence allows you to make decisions based on hunch, emotions, values and beliefs: a right-brain approach.

Intuition, often aligned to common sense, is in essence more akin to emotional intelligence. Intuition is a right-brain activity, involving a wide variety of skills: the ability to observe, listen, reflect back emotion and fact, think creatively and combine perceptive interpersonal skills with an understanding of oneself and others. According to *Webster's Dictionary*, intuition is the direct perception of truth or fact, independent of any reasoning process.

Ten-minute exercise
At the end of a workshop, evaluate what worked and what didn't. Write down what you did consciously. Then write down what you did intuitively. What made you take an intuitive decision?

Have you ever planned a talk or training session, then upon arrival done something completely different? This is due to information you perceived on arrival (delegate attitude, situation, venue, timing). You intuitively understood something different was needed from what you planned. Perhaps your brief did not take into account underlying needs, conflicts, worries or lack of skills. Spend time with the client beforehand to avoid this. But it can happen, even so.

Intuitive intelligence is what we know in our gut: an emotional reaction. Often, we don't pay attention to this information – and sometimes discover the session didn't go well as a result. To avoid this happening, I usually begin a session by drawing up a wish list: what do the participants want individually from the session and for the team? Create an action plan of the high priority items to fit into the time allowed, and how you plan to accomplish them.

Relaxation and visualization

I teach relaxation and visualization skills to individual clients who come to me for coaching. I recommend they meditate or relax 20 minutes each day, perhaps listening to music or a relaxation tape. I encourage them to develop their intuitive intelligence, their powers of perception independent of rational reasoning. I recommend the same if you manage any kind of group process.

Learn to listen to your internal voice; watch for those physiological reactions in your audience. Listen reflectively, mirroring back content and emotion. Create an environment of trust and safety that engenders listening and respect. Observation is as important as the ability to deliver and present information, so observe people and allow time for reflection and discussion. That is often where intuitive intelligence comes into play. It's in the quiet moments that the greatest learning can be experienced.

Memory and recall

We now know that emotions and thought are deeply connected, and that good learning engages feelings. If learners buy in to performance development emotionally, learning can take place.

What is memory, if not the ability to remember something or to repeat an act? This is why modelling your own excellence is an important tool for learning. Once you have worked out how you achieved excellence – whether it's on the golf course, speaking in public or solving a problem – you can copy it ad infinitum for excellent results.

Think about your own excellence

What did you do to keep the distractions to a minimum on the golf course? What did you do to calm your nerves that day you spoke so eloquently in public? How did you use lateral thinking to solve that problem last week in the workplace? It's useful to think of your strategy in terms of visual, auditory and kinesthetic. How did you use VAK to achieve your success?

Memory is not like a computer that keeps things handy in a file. To transfer memorable learning from workshop to workplace, learning must be relevant. Memory relies on what is linked, outstanding and relevant to the learners – and practised. But repetition is the least effective method of recall if used on its own. Hence the importance of seeing, hearing, doing and practising to create recall. Most of the exercises I design for my workshops use as many of the senses as possible – and require some practical application, using various intelligences to generate recall. Information not perceived to be relevant won't be remembered.

Eric Jensen, author of *Teaching with the Brain in Mind*, says that learning and memory are two sides of the same coin. The more we access information that is stored in our preconscious (or short-term) memory, the stronger connections we make between neurons, creating stronger memories. That is where quizzes, questionnaires, presentations, summaries and skits to show what has been learnt are all excellent memory devices.

Recall techniques

We recall that which is linked, outstanding and has a personal, emotional connection – and that which is practised or repeated. If new information has little emotional connection for learners, they will have to repeat it or have it represented at least four times. To make your training aids outstanding, add colour, graphics and arrows, making connections between key words to show their relationship.

We store sensory memories in different places; thus if we create a strong visual memory, we stimulate learners to reaccess it visually. To help memory and recall, use 'hooks'. Hooks can be anything from visual, auditory and kinesthetic images to musical anchors, repetitive graphics, themes, visual aids and experiential exercises. The more hooks you use, the more you remember. To recall information we need to connect, link and associate it with things we already know.

Memory mapping

Memory mapping is a very useful recall and learning tool. Tony Buzan, in *Use Your Memory*, suggests several ways to build powers of memory. Use:

- as many of the senses as possible (vision, hearing, smell, taste, touch, kinesthetic or body movement);
- rhythm and movement in your mental images;
- linking and associating one image with another;
- humour and fun;
- imagination and vivid images;
- numbers for order and sequence;
- symbols that give meaning (eg traffic lights, happy face);
- colour – bringing in the full range of primary and secondary colours;
- sequences and order (little to big, a to z);
- pleasant memories or images (negative images can be blocked by memory);
- exaggerated size, shape and sound.

Buzan suggests linking things together by placing them, weaving them and wrapping them together. Use exaggeration, making inanimate objects move, dance or sing. Think how memorable are cartoon-type films that use animated characters and real voices. We explore how to use musical anchors in Chapter 7.

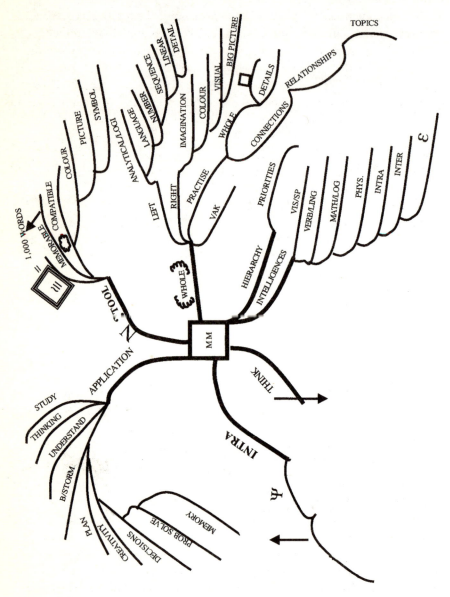

Figure 5.3 Memory map by Jenny Greenwood

Tony Buzan coined the term 'mind mapping', calling it 'radiant thinking'. Memory maps, learning maps and brainstorming maps: are all terms for mind maps. They work because they take into account whole-brain activities. A left-brain activity, they incorporate sequential planning, structuring and analysing. They are also right-brain, applying a network of patterns and associations in the same way the brain makes connections.

Memory maps can be used to take notes, plan speeches or structure reports and training sessions. Once you've used them, you'll never return to linear note taking. Memory maps use colour, graphics, symbols and patterns – crucial information-processing signals for the brain. They are an excellent learning tool; I use colourful, graphic maps for slides and flipcharts. They're visual, attractive and fun to look at.

Learning maps are the fastest way to think creatively. They are a natural function of the mind. By jotting down ideas as fast as they come, linking ideas, words and symbols, you create a powerful thinking picture easily assimilated by the brain. A learning map allows you to record ideas on branches and sub-branches that radiate from a central image in the middle of the page. By recording information in this way, you visually show the relationships between ideas and concepts. This gives you the associated big picture.

Learning or memory maps use your brain's natural associative function to connect and remember information. Complement any learning with as many senses as possible, using learning maps, visuals, sound, music and experiential exercises. This type of whole-brain thinking will help you to learn and to remember.

Thinking, language and behaviour

I should talk a little about NLP. Known as neuro-linguistic programming or neuro-linguistic psychology, NLP provides psychological skills for understanding the mental processes and patterns we use to achieve results. NLP addresses how we use our senses to think, how language relates to thought, and how our thinking strategies control our experience and achievements.

NLP provides a practical understanding of how the brain works: how people think, learn and motivate themselves to change. It is essentially about how we process information, and how this manifests itself in behaviour. It is how we use the language of the mind to achieve specific, desired goals. Like many learning tools, NLP refers to how you organize your mental life: the basis of all learning.

NLP is another metaphor for whole-brain thinking. It taps into our conscious, and unconscious, ways of seeing and interpreting the world. Here's a small exercise in understanding how you organize, and how you can change, your mental processes.

Understand how you think (10 minutes)

This 10-minute exercise powerfully illustrates how you think. Using your sensory skills can change the power of a memory.

1. Colourful memory

Take a pleasant memory from your past. Literally make the colours stronger and more intense. How does having a more colourful past change the intensity of your response to that memory? If you don't notice a difference in your feelings when you make your memory more colourful, try to see that memory in black and white. As the image loses its colour, typically your feeling response will be less intense.

2. Adding light to your life

Do you remember the character Tinkerbell in *Peter Pan*? Whenever she appeared, all you saw were little points of sparkling light. Remembering that image of light, think of another pleasant experience. Literally sprinkle your image of it with 'twinkle dust'. Notice how that affects your feeling response. Those of you in advertising and marketing will have used this type of effect to enhance and brighten an image.

3. Letting your past go

This is useful for unpleasant events, or something you prefer not to remember. Think of a memory that still makes you unhappy, and notice where you see it in relation to your body. How far away is the picture? Undoubtedly it's quite close to you. Try to put a border around that picture and move it, physically, as far in front of you as you can. Let it keep moving away from you until you can hardly see it. Finally, let that picture lie flat, and imagine there is a rocket charger underneath it. Let the rocket charger shoot it into space, far away and gone forever. How does that change your experience of that memory?

Eye-patterning exercises

Eye-patterning exercises are another simple memory tool. In NLP they are called eye-accessing cues. By moving your eyes up, down, left or right, you can access information stored in your memory. This also helps you access dialogue and conversations you wish to recall, feelings you want to remember, or something positive you wish to picture in the future.

Neurological studies show that eye movement is associated with different parts of the brain. By moving our eyes in different directions, we can access pictures, sounds and feelings. This is because we move our eyes in different directions according to what we are thinking, feeling or seeing. It helps you to access information that is visual, kinesthetic or auditory.

Here's how to use eye patterning to help with learning.

To recall images or visual pictures: look up and to the left. What were you doing yesterday? Try to picture yourself. That is how most right-handed people remember images from the past. Although left-handed, I am somewhat ambidextrous, so I look up to the left to recall visual images. If you are very left-handed you may find that you look up to the right.

To construct a visual picture: If you want to think about something you've never seen, or you want to picture yourself succeeding in a future event, move your eyes up and to the right. Think about an event coming up, and picture yourself doing it brilliantly. See yourself with all of the vibrant colour and definition, as if you are already there. You will probably find that you looked up and to the right.

To remember sounds: Such as conversation, dialogue or music from a film, or the distractions that got to you at work yesterday, look across to the left, as if you are looking towards your left ear.

To construct sound: Move your eyes across to the right (towards your right ear). Think of a sound you have not yet heard, plan to hear or want to hear. Perhaps you're thinking of that concert you're going to this week, or that new CD you plan to put on when you return home after work today. Or think about the sound of your partner's voice, or your cell phone ring. You will probably find that you look across to the right.

To access feelings: Your eyes move down and to the right when trying to access feelings. How do you want to feel when you finish that presentation at the end of the day? Or what did you feel like when you accomplished something significant in your life – say learning to ride a bike, the day you got married, or the day your first child was born? Remember these occasions. You'll probably find you look down to the right.

To access your inner voice or internal dialogue: What tone of voice do you use when you scold yourself, or when you congratulate yourself? You'll probably find that your eyes look down to the left. What were you saying to yourself this morning on your way to work? What was it you reminded yourself to remember? Look down to the left to remember.

To visualize: To move into visualization mode, let your eyes stare straight ahead. Don't focus; it's as if they are looking into the distance. This allows you to activate the part of the brain that will help you to visualize.

Developing mental agility

All of the exercises in this chapter will help you to expand and develop your brain power, and to assist others in achieving their potential. When your brain is fit and flexible, you can manage stress more easily. Often at work, vision, imagination and creativity are essential. Think how to use whole-brain thinking and all of your intelligences – not just in the work you do, but in the work you teach. Last of all, we remember:

20 per cent	of what we read
30 per cent	of what we hear
40 per cent	of what we see
50 per cent	of what we say
60 per cent	of what we do
90 per cent	of what we see, hear, say and do

In conclusion

There has been an explosion of brain-based research: many books have been written about whole-brain thinking, accelerated learning, success strategies, boosting motivation, memory and recall. I hope this chapter has given you some practical insights into how to introduce brain-based learning into your development of people and performance.

Pressure in the workplace today includes huge demands on individuals to achieve peak performance, develop 'super-mind' power and achieve memory excellence. Creative thinking, problem solving and developing emotional intelligence: all these forge learning and memory. Remember: when the body is engaged, the mind is also engaged. Exercise, sleep, diet and nutrition are major influences on the health of the brain, reducing stress and boosting mental performance.

The question is: What are you currently doing to increase your brain power and that of your participants? What tools can you take from this chapter to enhance your development sessions – to facilitate recall and ensure the transfer of learning to the workplace?

Above all, remember to have fun doing it!

Where to go for more

Books

Andreas, Steve and Faulkner, Charles (1997) *NLP: the new technology of achievement,* Nicholas Brealey Publishing, London

Antonio, Dr Damasio (2000) *The Feeling Of What Happens: Body and emotion in the making of consciousness,* Harvest Books, Harcourt, New York

Bandler, Richard (ed Andreas, Connirae and Andreas, Steve) (1985) *Using Your Brain – For a change*, Real People Press, Moab, Utah

Buzan, Tony (1977) *Make The Most Of Your Mind*, Colt Books, London

Buzan, Tony (1986) *Use Your Memory*, BBC Books, London

Buzan, Tony (1993) *The Mind Map Book: Radiant thinking*, BBC Books, London

Caine, Renate Numella and Caine, Geoffrey (1997) *Unleashing The Power Of Perceptual Change: The potential of brain-based learning*, ASCD (Association for Supervision and Curriculum Development), Alexandria, Virginia

Carter, Rita and Frith, Christopher D (1999) *Mapping The Mind*, University of California Press, Berkeley, California

Damasio, Antonio (1994) *Descartes' Error: Emotion, reason and the human brain*, Grosset/Putnam, New York

de Bono, Edward (1967) *The Use Of Lateral Thinking*, Penguin, London

de Bono, Edward (1985) *Six Thinking Hats*, Penguin Books, London

Gardner, Howard, (1985) *Frames of Mind: The theory of multiple intelligences*, Basic Books, New York

Gardner, Howard (1993) *Multiple Intelligences: The theory in practice*, Basic Books, New York

Goleman, Daniel (1996) *Emotional Intelligence*, Bloomsbury, London

Goleman, Daniel (1998) *Working with Emotional Intelligence*, Bantam Books, New York

Herrmann, Ned (1996) The *Whole Brain Business Book*, McGraw-Hill, New York. (If you are interested in pursuing Herrmann's concept of four thinking styles, see pages 21, 23, 227 and 272.)

Jensen, Eric (1998) *Teaching with the Brain in Mind*, Brain-Store, San Diego, Calif

Jensen, Eric (2000) *Brain-Based Learning,* Brain-Store, San Diego, Calif

North, Vanda with Tony Buzan (1991) *Get Ahead: Mind map your way to success*, Oakdale, Dorset

O'Connor, Joseph and Seymour, John (1994) *Training With NLP: Skills for managers, trainers and communicators*, HarperCollins, London

Ornstein, Robert (1998) *The Right Mind: Making sense of the hemispheres*, Harvest, Harcourt, New York

Pert, Candace (1997) *Molecules of Emotion: Why you feel the way you feel*, Simon and Schuster, London

Rose, Colin and Nicholl, Malcolm J (1997) *Accelerated Learning for the 21st Century: The six-step plan to unlock your master-mind*, Dell, New York

Stout, Sunny (1993) *Managing Training*, Kogan Page, London

Journals

Bassi, Laurie (1999) Point, counterpoint: interview with Daniel Goleman and Robert B Reich, *Training and Development* (April) pp 26–29

Caudron, Shari (2000) Learners speak out, *Training and Development* (April) pp 52–57

Counterpoint (1999) Working with emotional intelligence, interview with Daniel Goleman and Robert B Reich, *Training and Development* (April) pp 26–31

Durrance, Bonnie (1998) Some Explicit Thoughts on Tacit Learning, *Training and Development* (December) pp 24–29

Fisher, Tom, (1998) High anxiety: preparing trainees to learn, *Training and Development* (December) pp 14–15

Learning, Goals and Emotions (2000) *Training and Development* (June) p 32

Levy, Steven (1994) Dr Edelman's brain, *New Yorker* (2 May) pp 62–73

Martin, Joyce (1999) Live and work by your intelligences, *Training and Development* (October) pp 68–69

Pitcher, Patricia (1999) Artists, craftsmen, and technocrats, *Training and Development* (July) pp 31–33

Salopek, Jennifer (assoc ed) (1998) Train your brain, an interview with Daniel Goleman, *Training and Development* (October) pp 26–33

Weiss, Ruth Palombo (2000) Brain based learning, the wave of the brain, *Training and Development* (July) pp 21–24

Weiss, Ruth Palombo (2000) Emotion and Learning, *Training and Development* (November) pp 45–48

Wolf, Jack (1999) Einstein's theories are relative to training, *Training and Development* (May) pp 21–22

Web sites

ascd.org
brainconnection.com
cainelearning.com
dana.com
ei.haygroup.com (Emotional Intelligences Services, Haygroup)
21learn.org
lern.org
newhorizons.org/blab.html
thebrainstore.com (Eric Jensen's Web site and online bookstore)
renewalatwork.com/books (Renewal At Work)

Audiocassettes

Gelb, Michael (1993) *Mind Mapping: How to liberate your natural genius*, Nightingale Conant, Niles, Illinois

Geller, Uri (1996) *Mind-Power Kit*, Virgin Books, London

Tracy, Brian with Rose, Colin (1995) *Accelerated Learning Techniques*, Nightingale Conant, Niles, Illinois

6

Real magic: motivation and innovation

'If you think creatively, you'll think of it first.'

Creative ideas are born out of individual difference and a diversity of talent in the workplace. People are motivated by what is important to them. They look to work for a balanced life, peace of mind, recognition and a higher purpose. But they must also satisfy organizational goals. By creatively focusing on individual efforts to improve performance and achieve targets, the performance coach can help the group to focus on organizational needs.

Setting creative, well-formed goals allows individual learners to explore what they really want to do. It encourages them to harmonize their aims with the organization's vision and purpose. Performance is thus motivated from inside the organization, capturing people's hopes and dreams.

This is the magic: sparking enthusiasm, generating new ideas and creating the will to achieve. Plug that magic into achieving personal and organizational goals and you'll not only get results – you'll empower people to learn.

Fear takes over when the challenges are overwhelming and support is unforthcoming. Help individuals push beyond their boundaries. Help them set goals that create new horizons for themselves; stretch their competencies and those of the organization. In your workshops, take people outside their ordinary, everyday constraints. Allow them to dream. Help them to think outside the box. Stretch their creative talents. Link goals with personal discovery and professional development. In this way you create imaginative, effective, highly motivated teams, optimize performance and harness organizational excellence.

The desire to achieve

Hopes, dreams and fears

The question needs to be asked: Why is it so difficult to link individual passion to the overall aim of the organization? It always comes back to motivation. People want meaningful, satisfying work. Organizations want highly motivated people to contribute to their success. To marry the two, it's important to align organizational and personal needs. In this way, you create a community with a common purpose and the desire to optimize performance. If organizations drive performance from the inside out, taking into consideration the potential of the individual, it's more likely that people's hopes and dreams won't be lost – and neither will those of the organization.

Individual differences provide a diversity of talent. This is the magic ingredient for creativity and success. People are motivated by what is important to them – and they are looking to work for achievement, recognition, a higher purpose and to satisfy personal needs. That's where organizations must provide opportunities and support.

Creativity and whole-brain thinking

Creativity opens the door to innovation, new ideas and change. Creativity should be rewarded. But too often inspiration and innovation aren't supported, leading to negativity, cynicism and resistance at work. Facilitating the creative process in the learning environment is a start, but this needs to be transferred to the workplace if creative habits are to become part of organizational growth.

There are endless ways for you to pursue an innovative path to learning. Creative people are self-motivated, achieving satisfaction simply from being involved in their work. Creative people are inclined to take risks with new ideas and concepts. But it's vital to establish a climate that supports their creative process. This means allowing for mistakes and encouraging diversity of thinking.

Diverse thinking styles
To encourage creativity, different thinking styles are needed in your team. But not everyone wants to exploit individual creative potential. The right-brain thinker will come up with a new perspective on a problem and the left-brain thinker will want to analyse whether or not it will work.

Diverse thinking styles are needed: rational, organized, feeling and experimental. If everyone conceptualized and created, there would be no one to analyse, organize or bring in the diverse mix of people to make it happen.

A TABLOID APPROACH

In the early 1980s I was working with a large newspaper group on the south coast in England, the Portsmouth and Sunderland Newspaper Group. The newspaper was a broadsheet, but its audience was suited to a more tabloid approach. My boss at the time, Alec Reynolds, was publishing director for seven newspapers. Although very innovative in his own right, he had been allowed very little scope to develop original ideas over his near 40-year history with the newspaper group. It was apparent that his creative potential still burnt underneath a need to meet sales targets, daily deadlines and annual budgets.

We sat down for an entire day, poring over some of the creative ideas my team had devised for a new layout and design of the local newspaper. Alec loved the fresh perspective and set to work thinking about how to bring in the rest of the editorial and advertising team for their ideas and input. Although there was a great deal of resistance to begin with, each department eventually brought in new ideas, and the creative wheels were set in motion.

Innovation involves change, and today change implies downsizing, re-engineering, mergers and acquisitions. In fact it takes creativity to plan performance, bringing in the hopes and dreams of the people that make an organization work. It requires vision and passion to overcome their fears and resistance to taking risks, and to inspire them to deal with new challenges.

Extrinsic and intrinsic motivation

Motivation is what drives us – it is to do with our underlying values, beliefs and feelings. Although motivation can be approached from many points of view, there are two types of motivation to be aware of.

Intrinsic motivation is to do with what an individual wants and needs. Intrinsic motivators are the drive within us. At their roots are an individual's core values and beliefs. Fox, Byrne and Rouault (in their article Performance improvement: what to keep in mind) list the primary motivators for people at work: achievement, a balanced life, peace of mind, recognition, a higher purpose and affiliation. These are intrinsic motivators.

Extrinsic motivation is more to do with someone else trying to convince us to do something, hooking our intrinsic motivators to make us want to do it. We use a comfortable environment, feedback and recognition, salaries, bonuses, benefits, titles, education, performance development and fairness as extrinsic motivators.

Learning, creativity and motivation

Learning and creativity are influenced by intrinsic motivation. We all motivate ourselves in diverse ways. Where managers can encourage this self-motivation is by understanding the job needs and working preferences of their team, providing the climate and support that allow employees to optimize their own performance. Below are tools and techniques to help you.

Learning and motivation are very closely linked – people are motivated by what interests them. The mere pursuit of knowledge and new learning is satisfying to people who are self-motivated. The more they learn, the more they activate their brains. The more they activate their brains, the more they create new associations, think innovatively and improve motivation. Enhance performance in your teams by supporting the creative process with whole-brain thinking. Encourage them to develop alternative solutions to existing problems.

Setting well-formed goals

'If you don't know where you're going, you'll probably end up somewhere else.'
Anon

Setting goals is one way to help people achieve their dreams. It's crucial for any business hoping to achieve its future vision. The process of setting well-formed goals takes individual thinking out of its ordinary, everyday constraints – to think outside the box, to see beyond the borders of today. Aligning goals with personal values is one of the best ways to motivate people to achieve. But personal values need to be aligned to organizational ones to ensure success. That's why so many people today work for themselves. Although a harder route to take, it ensures that organizational and personal values are in sync.

Whenever I work with individuals or groups in setting goals, I first ask them to dream: where do they plan to be in five, 10, 20 years, in the last year of their life? What will they be doing, what will they be thinking? Then we look at short-term goals, linking job and career goals to life goals. Every job you've ever had fits into your overall career structure, and most of us today enjoy several careers during our working lives. This is due to the fast-changing pace of the global workplace, and the mobility of our lifestyles.

Goals outline your route map. What action do you need to take to arrive at your destination? Because goals are closely linked to your internal motivators, it's vital to have a greater understanding of yourself – where you are now, where you are going. Here's a dynamic, two-part exercise to set goals linked to where you are now and where you dream to go.

Exercise 1: Goals and dreams (15 minutes)

This exercise is useful to plan overall goals that balance job, career and personal life. Use this exercise prior to setting 'well-formed' goals – which positively define the primary short- and long-term goals you want to achieve.

- Write down at least three long-term goals for your job, your career and your life. Include one that is a lifelong dream. For example, 10 years before my husband returned to South Africa, he realized it had always been his lifelong dream to return to his own country. Once we wrote it down and included it in our career and life planning, we began to think about how to make it a reality.

- Write down at least three short-term goals for your job, your career and your life. Include one that is something you've been talking about achieving for some time, but because you've never written it down, you haven't achieved it: learning a new language, taking up a new hobby, learning to swim. I had talked about writing a new book for three years, but it wasn't until I wrote down my goals and created a timetable with my publisher that it actually happened.

- Choose one short-term and one long-term goal you plan to work with. You will turn these into practical, well-formed outcomes. For example, one of my nieces came to stay with me upon graduating from university. As we talked about her plans, it became very clear that her next year's plans weren't the right direction for her. We sat down to discuss what she actually wanted, what she was passionate about. She realized her interests had changed during her years at university. She no longer saw herself going into the broadcast media, but rather into the world of marketing and communications – yet linked to a school of journalism. Her short-term goal was to find a job to earn money to finance the right postgraduate diploma. Her long-term goal was to get accepted at the right university to study marketing and communications in the media. We then went on to set well-formed outcomes. Three years later, she is on track to achieve all of those desired goals.

Goals need to be reviewed at least once a year, otherwise you can find yourself going off track in a direction that no longer suits you.

Exercise 2: Setting well-formed outcomes (15 minutes per person)

'If you think you can, you can; if you think you can't, you're right.'
Henry Ford

If you did the previous exercise on your own, you may find it useful to complete this one with a partner. Your partner asks you the questions, and writes down your replies. You have time to think, dream and scheme out loud. Choose one short-term and one long-term goal from the previous exercise. Complete each of the seven questions separately for each goal. This exercise helps you explore every aspect of attaining these goals.

1. *State your goal in the positive.* This helps you to focus on what it is you want to achieve. But you can't move towards it if it isn't stated actively and clearly. What specifically do you want? What will that do for you?
2. *How will you know you've achieved it?* What will tell you that you have achieved your goal? What will you hear, see and feel upon arriving? Sensory experience will let you know you have achieved your outcome.
   - V What will you be seeing when you've got there?
   - A What will you be hearing when you've got there?
   - K What will you be feeling when you've got there?
   - V What will others see you doing when you've got there?
   - A What will others hear you doing when you've got there?
3. *What resources do you need to start and sustain this outcome?* It's important that this outcome is started and sustained by you. Are there any states of mind that will help achieve this outcome? What skills do you need? Do you need any external resources to make it possible? What resources will start you moving towards this outcome? How will you sustain your positive direction?
4. *What will be the context of this outcome?* Where, when and with whom do you want this outcome? When, where and with whom do you not want this outcome? For how long do you want or plan to have this outcome?
5. *What do you want to preserve from now?* What do you get out of your current behaviour that you want to keep while trying to achieve this outcome? Perhaps there are things you currently do that will help you. What are they?
6. *The bigger picture.* For what purpose do you want this outcome? What will you gain or lose if you achieve it? Is it worth the cost of achieving? Is this outcome in keeping with your personal values?
7. *What else do you need?* What do you have now, and what more do you need, to achieve your outcome? Have you ever had or done this before? How can you use those strengths, skills and resources that you've used before?

Using psycho-geometrics: circle, square or squiggle?

Originally designed by Susan Dellinger, psycho-geometrics offers a quick indication of personality styles, and is useful in identifying preferred work styles. It's a fun, practical approach to the diverse work styles in your team. It helps to identify what styles are missing, and how you can develop a flexible approach to people, tasks and problems.

People grow and develop continually; therefore all psychometric tests represent a profile or snapshot in time. The purpose of this exercise is not to put someone into a particular category, but to think more about what other styles are needed to form a more effective, motivated, creative team.

The key principles for a team leader are: know yourself, know your team, be able to communicate, and communicate to motivate. If you're looking to fill a team position, a psycho-geometric profile quickly discerns gaps, identifying the profile needed in a new team member to best complement your existing group.

Dellinger's psycho-geometrics, based on the work of Roger Sperry and Carl Jung, reflects a right-versus left-brain approach. The five profiles are based on five different shapes: box, triangle, rectangle, circle and squiggle.

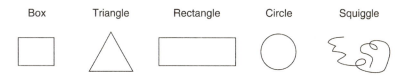

Figure 6.1   Psycho-geometric shapes

Exercise: Synergistic thinking (40 minutes)

This exercise is great fun. I introduce colour and graphics in the shapes, using the exercise to help team members understand different approaches to work. Synergy is created simply by acknowledging and respecting each other's styles.

1. Introduce the different shapes and their characteristics. Ask delegates to think about the following questions for themselves:
   - Which shape most suits you?
   - Are you a combination of shapes?
   - What characteristics do you need to build on to access the characteristics of other shapes?

   Individuals create a memory map of their dominant shapes with the characteristics that fit their own profile (10 minutes).

2. Break up into small groups to share individual shape profiles. Not everyone may agree with what shapes you think you are! That can be a discussion point: how people see you may not be how you see yourself. Ensure that the group contributes positively and constructively. It's meant to be an exercise in working together, not tearing each other apart (10 minutes).

3. Each group draws a shape profile of their team and a profile of the organization's dominant shapes. What are the predominant shapes in both? What is needed to synergize energy and creative thinking in their teams and in the organization overall? (10 minutes)

1. Boxes   **Left-brained**
Characteristics: Good time managers, slow, steady, analytical, determined, neat, organized, need clear instructions, seek accuracy, like routine.
Strengths: Knowledgeable, detail oriented, patient, conservative, loyal, persevering.
Weaknesses: Can be perceived as procrastinators, over cautious, slow, too precise, loners rather than team players.

2. Rectangles   **Right-brained**
Characteristics: Always in transition, inquisitive, searching. Rectangles can be any shape on any day. They are exciting, constantly searching, and need to be understood.
Strengths: Always growing, changing, courageous, looking for options.
Weaknesses: Could be any shape on any day, indecisive, unsure of direction, erratic, disorganized, not good at time management, forgetful.

3. Triangles   **Left-brained**
Characteristics: Fast paced, seek recognition, like telling people what to do, good political players, joke tellers, stylish, tailored, athletic.
Strengths: Linear, logical, focused, decisive, bottom-line-oriented, loyal, work hard, tend to be leaders.
Weaknesses: Impatient, ambitious, competitive, sometimes lack interpersonal skills, like status symbols, tend to step on others on the way up.

4. Circles   **Right-brained**
Characteristics: Relaxed, don't like to be rushed, are people-people. Easygoing, relationship-oriented, need to be appreciated.
Strengths: Cooperative, show empathy, good mediators, persuasive, caretakers, team players, sociable, informal, rapport builders.
Weaknesses: Have trouble making unpopular decisions, can be sloppy.

5. Squiggles   **Right-brained**
Characteristics: Work at a frantic pace, seek freedom, mavericks, theatrical. Need freedom and space, ideas person, tend to be artistic.
Strengths: Conceptual, creative, big-picture thinkers, intuitive, expressive, animated, experimental, willing to take risks, high energy.
Weaknesses: Extreme in personality, challenging, messy, dramatic, prefer to work alone, tend to interrupt others, rebellious.

---

4. Bring the group back together to review and discuss how to apply this back in the workplace (10 minutes).

Synergy and differences

We tend to hire those most like us. For example, an advertising agency may prefer to hire the maverick squiggles and rapport-building circles, as creative thinkers and client handlers are key roles. However, they need accountants and financial expertise, so would also need a few boxes. For a leader, would they want a triangle?

One of my clients in London, a very successful marketing agency, realized they had a tendency to hire similar types of people. The managing director began to look at how to hire different thinking styles – yet keep motivation levels high. She decided to merge with a firm that brought in left-brain energy, to complement her agency's right-brain profile. A balance was created with right-brain squiggles and circles set against the left-brain boxes and triangles ... with a rectangle or two for balance.

Synergy is one of the great contributors to creative thinking in teams. Although different mental approaches can get in the way of mutual understanding, appreciation of diverse styles helps teams to work together. There is no doubt that conflict can be generated by different thinking approaches and personalities, but conflicts are resolved with greater understanding and respect for other approaches. There tend to be six major types of conflicts in teams:

- clashing styles;
- interpersonal differences;
- competition for power, resources and recognition;
- unmet expectations;
- age, gender and ethnicity differences;
- inter-group conflict.

Diversity offers different perspectives and different approaches in a team. Psycho-geometrics represents one way to understand and manage these differences.

Circles may prefer creative thinking in a team, or brainstorming in a group.

Rectangles may prefer role play to resolve problems (according to Dellinger, rectangles can take any shape at any time).

Boxes prefer an analytical, logical approach to a problem.

Triangles want to lead the creative thinking session, focusing on facts at hand to make decisions.

Squiggles want to experiment with more unusual forms of creative thinking: acting it out, using colour, drawing, music, or six-cap thinking to generate spontaneous solutions.

Psycho-geometrics will help your team find new ways to solve problems, generate new ideas and work together.

The power of belief

All behaviour is organized around beliefs. Beliefs are powerful. As long as you can fit a behaviour into people's belief system, you can motivate them to do almost anything.

To create personal change it's important to help your participants to develop powerful positive beliefs, and to change their limiting beliefs into beliefs that empower them. Beliefs help you to tap resources you never knew you had, and open the door to excellence. Beliefs are those powerful forces that help to create internal resourcefulness. Limiting beliefs, on the other hand, can be devastating. They stop us from achieving, from setting goals that move us towards our dreams.

Belief can help in recovery from illness. Many of us know individuals who have experienced such recoveries. Beliefs are your choice: you have control over them. You create them and you can change them.

Beliefs come primarily from:

- your background and environment (home, work, culture, religion, social life);
- specific events (sports, academic, personal);
- knowledge, expertise and wisdom (what you know and what you don't know);
- achievements (personal, academic, job, career, athletic);
- goals (setting well-formed outcomes and planning your route map).

Creating empowering beliefs exercise (20 minutes)

Personal beliefs and values are interconnected. Here's an exercise to design a new, powerful paradigm that will empower you to achieve your goals.

1. Make a list of the negative things that have happened to you in the last year. Think of all of those things that you didn't achieve, and what prevented you from achieving them. List them all.
2. Write down the learning from these events. What can you learn from your non-achievements, and from your justifications about why you didn't achieve? Perhaps you procrastinated, didn't write down your goals, didn't believe you could, somebody else got there first – whatever it might be.
3. Now look at what you have learnt. Use this as a guide to turn those negatives into positives. Write a new statement that positively, actively states what you believe you can do, what you believe you are capable of, what you believe is possible if you set your mind to it.

For example, one of my clients recently wrote:

- not enough time;
- didn't believe I could actually do it;
- not enough money;
- don't know how to start;
- not sure if it's the right thing to do.

Her new positive empowering belief became: 'I know that I can, and I am setting goals that will take me down the road step by step.' She realized her beliefs were negative – they were disabling her. By setting new positive beliefs, she was able to set new goals and to find a new way to move forward. New beliefs become your personal foundation for creating change.

Identifying values

Values are very powerful, and are supported by our belief system. We acquire our values from our life experiences, our family, our friends. Closely linked to our identity, values are the fundamental principles by which we live. Values help us set the right goals – they motivate us and give us direction. But we seldom think about them; they drive us unconsciously. Although we live by them, it's rare that we identify them.

It's become common for organizations to define the values by which they work and participate in the community. Fewer individuals write down their specific values, or think about how their values influence their major decisions. Most of us adopt the values of our organization in order to move up the ladder of success. But if your personal values do not match those of the organization, this can lead to stress, incongruent working behaviour, inner conflict and interpersonal conflict with colleagues. Incongruent values make it difficult to excel in performance, and inevitably lead to personal frustration.

For example, one of my clients, the Whale and Dolphin Society, works around the globe protecting whales and dolphins from over-fishing and disease. It invests in research so that we may learn the habits of these beautiful creatures. The people who work for this organization share similar values:

● wanting to help protect the world's natural resources;
● respect for animals and the natural kingdom;
● respect for the sea and its underwater kingdom;
● wanting to give something back to society;
● wanting to learn from nature.

It would be difficult for someone who did not share these ideals to work with this organization. Their personal and work values would be opposed.

Eliciting values exercise (15 minutes)

Clarifying values is an important exercise to do on your own. Values represent an important part of our style of training or communicating. People are often promoted into positions where they question how they can match their values to the work required of them in the new position. Our values influence our decision-making process. Our values help us make career, management, communication and people decisions.

Try this exercise with your participants prior to setting goals. Ask for positive responses to the following questions.

1. What is important to you (about your work, personal life, social life)?
2. What truly motivates you (at home, in your personal relationships, life in general)?
3. What drives you (to achieve, to get things done, what makes you get up and go to work every day, spend time with your family, friends, do the hobbies that you do)?
4. What has to be true for you to do what you do?

Radical coaching

Coaching has become big business. It is used in organizations to help people achieve peak performance. A broader definition of coaching includes developing self-esteem and building confidence.

Coaching helps individuals to set new goals that will help them (and their organization) to achieve their dreams. It aims to change behaviour, undo limiting beliefs that stop the individual from achieving – and to create new, self-empowering paradigms that ensure goals are achieved. That's radical coaching. In essence it's all about helping individuals to plan their journey, to have a route map that will take them down the road of excellence or peak performance. The coach is a facilitator. The job of a coach is to grow and develop people.

Circle of excellence exercise (30 minutes)

One coaching tool is 'circle of excellence', an excellent change technique. Coaches don't necessarily have all the answers to someone's questions. In fact, the coach may not know much about the individual's business. Coaches need insight, the wisdom of experience, and an understanding of what motivates and drives the individual. A coach is an enabler; a radical coach will take individuals past their personal barriers to visualize as well as achieve their dreams. Here's a creative exercise to do so.

1. Ask your client, 'What resources do you need to move from where you are now to where you want to be'? Ask him or her to lay down an imaginary circle on the floor first; you can even take some tape or ribbon and outline the circle. Let him/her put their circle in the place of his/her choice. The individual stands outside the circle with you.
2. Ask the person to think of a time when he/she achieved his/her goals. The person may wish to pick goals that are of a similar challenge to those he/she has currently outlined.

3. Ask the person to think about what resources (mental, physical, emotional, spiritual) he/she needed back then to achieve those goals. When he/she answers you, repeat back his/her own words. These act as sensors and auditory anchors, helping to put the individual back in that time. They relate to that person's language, not to yours.

4. Ask the individual to think about three situations in the past where he/she used these resources to achieve goals. If he/she cannot think of three situations, think of three resources he/she used to achieve his/her goals.

5. When he/she has identified three resources or situations, invite the individual to step into the circle and to relive the first experience when he/she used some or all of those resources – or to relive the time he/she used the first resource. Have the person visualize it, hear it and really feel it. Get him or her to describe it to you as he/she stands in the circle.

6. At the same time that the individual steps into the circle, step into a circle beside it. This ensures that you stand beside the person, and help him or her to be 'associated', to actually relive it and to imagine he or she is back there, then. Use a very soft voice, asking the person to 'see what you see, hear what you hear, and feel what you feel.'

7. At this point you can ask the individual to fire a physical anchor, such as clasping hands, squeezing an index finger and thumb together on his/her dominant writing hand, or touching his/her face. This becomes a stimulus – it helps the person to reaccess the sounds, the images, the tastes or smells that trigger a reminder of those resources or situations. It may be a snippet of a tune or a song that he/she hums.

8. Have the person step out of his/her circle and you step out of yours. Ask the person to think of the second resource, or the second situation. Then the individual steps back into the circle. Repeat steps 5, 6 and 7 for this situation, and for a third. This will ensure the person anchors and stores these resources for future use. Have the person 'step into the circle and reaccess those resources, or that situation. Visualize it, hear it, feel it – notice what you did to achieve that goal.' Help him or her to really associate with it, as if he/she is actually there.

9. Ask the individual to step outside the circle for the second and third situations. Have him or her think about a future time when he/she will need these resources. 'Imagine yourself in that future situation, and see how these new resources will help you to achieve what you set out to achieve.'

The circle of excellence prepares the individual's psyche to do well, to visualize him or herself achieving what he/she needs to achieve. It's not dissimilar to a situation where you are about to step out onto a stage to give a speech, or to walk into the boardroom to make a presentation. You visualize yourself doing it well, hear your voice sounding confident, and feel yourself physically standing or sitting tall – you imagine in advance how well you do.

Innovative strategies

How many people actually feel creative? Most people have more creative powers than they ever dreamed of – but haven't figured out how to tap into them. Creativity is a skill that can be learnt and practised. It's a matter of looking at it from a new perspective.

Creativity is that spark that sets us apart, from each other and from other organizations. It's that intuitive hunch to go down a different path: to do something in a new way, to see a problem from a new perspective. Without creativity, innovation and intuition, people and organizations cannot grow. How can you encourage it in your learning, in your training and in your organization? Here are some creative thinking strategies to use when training, facilitating new ideas or simply making decisions.

Random thinking

There are a number of random thinking exercises using words or pictures. The first exercise focuses on one word to randomly generate ideas. Be clear what your creative objective is. Is it to solve a problem or to develop a new idea or a new direction? Jot down a few words about your objective on one side of a piece of paper. Put it aside for a moment.

Random word exercise (10 minutes)
Pick up any piece of paper, newspaper, magazine or brochure. Close your eyes; with your index finger, move down the page and stop at a word. Open your eyes; write that word next to your key objective. See what you can do, without being judgmental, to apply that word to your key theme. The purpose of this exercise is to bring in a random word to expand your mental thinking process. It takes your thinking out of its routine, linear approach.

Some people prefer to choose a word relating to their topic; try not to fall into that trap. The success of this technique is choosing a word that seems to bear no relation whatsoever to the task in hand. It ensures you use another part of the brain. Choose a word randomly, and make as many associations as possible with that word, relating it back to your problem. It will give you another perspective.

My UK business partner and I were brainstorming a new business idea a few years ago. We were thrashing around for a suitable name for the company.

Everything we came up with sounded old hat, clichéd or too abstract. We picked up one of our training manuals, ran a finger down the page and landed on the word 'train'. We rapidly began to jot down words related to 'train'. One of them was express. We decided on the name Express Training to put across the idea of acceleration, innovative learning and personal growth.

Random thinking helps you access visual pictures or ideas. The word 'train' gave way to the image of a train, implying movement, fluidity and accelerating speed. We scribbled down words linked to train, and began to draw pictures – which led us to the visual concept for a new logo.

Random reading exercise (15 minutes–2 hours)

Ideally your mind should be able to accept information from any source to help develop ideas. An exercise I do when I want to think creatively about a new talk, new programme or new book is to sit down with lots of journals, magazines and books that I've been meaning to read for a while.

For this exercise, I use different coloured highlighter pens, and keep a blank notebook and coloured Post-it notes by my side. I start reading, making notes in margins and on sticky notes, jotting ideas in my notebook as they come to me. By the time I have come to the end of the one or two hours dedicated to the exercise, I've begun to think in a new way about my topic. I sit for another half an hour to draw memory maps of any ideas I've had about my topic.

Ideally your mind is an open house for any information that creates a link or association to your topic. Even if you are sitting in the doctor's or dentist's office, pick up a magazine and you'll find something of relevance. Use any waiting time for random reading.

Random picture exercise (10 minutes)

Pick up any journal or magazine that has a range of pictures and photographs. Close your eyes, flick through the magazine and stop at a page. Open your eyes and notice the picture on the page. (Keep going until you find a page with a picture or photo.) Use this randomly selected picture to generate ideas. Use your powers of analogy and metaphor to make associations. Write down your associations on a brainstorm map with your key objective in the centre of the page.

Without being judgmental, apply that picture to your key theme, problem or objective. The aim of this exercise is to stimulate ideas with randomly selected pictures. It takes your thinking out of a routine, linear approach. It's also fun.

Contradictory thinking exercise (15 minutes)

This powerful technique asks you to come up with the very opposite of your key theme or objective. Ask a negative question, 'What if people don't do what you want them to do?' or 'What if you don't get the result you want?' or 'What's missing?' In this way, you create a list of negatives or list of problems. Turn that list of negatives into a list of positives; these positives become a list of benefits. You have answered the positive question you really needed to ask. This is an excellent technique when trying to come up with benefits for promotional or selling purposes.

For example, when preparing a career day for one of the International Direct Marketing Fairs in the UK, a colleague and I were having a tough time coming up with a common theme to help us invite the right speakers. We asked the question, 'What haven't we done before?' We mapped all the topics we had never covered. We ended up with a huge list of topics, and we clustered them into groups. Our theme emerged clearly: 'Survival and Succes.' We carried on, asking the question, 'What don't women do to ensure their professional success?' We created a map of all of the negatives; what they don't do. We turned it into positives, creating a list of challenging situations professional women needed to handle well if they were to succeed. We were now in a position to invite the appropriate speakers.

Brainstorming

'A picture is worth a thousand words'. (Chinese saying)

Brainstorming is one of the ways to design learning so that it is creative and exciting. Brainstorming uses the memory map (mind map, learning map) to represent the association between ideas. It works in the same natural way as your brain, and is a graphic way to unlock the potential of the thinking brain.

The way your brain represents its thinking patterns is by branching out from the centre: lines of thought radiate out, forming an infinite number of information points. These networks complement the physical make-up of your brain. Brainstorming accesses this radiant way of thinking: moving in all directions from a given centre point, making associations that proceed from and are connected to the central point.

Associative thinking

Most people don't realize the vast potential of associative thinking. Think about every picture, sound, smell, taste or sensation you've ever had – and all of their potential associations. This is the power of associative thinking. Any key words or images you place in the centre of your brainstorm map radiate outwards into a potentially infinite number of associations.

Calling on the associative nature of the brain benefits problem solving, new-idea generation, running meetings, learning sessions, designing promotional literature. Brainstorming focuses on core issues, improves creativity and recall, creates the big picture and uses all of your skills.

Visionary, organizer, critic

There are three stages to brainstorming. The first is the visioning phase. Tell your participants that they are completely free of restraints. Brainstorming accesses the visionary or dreamer in you – and the creative part of your brain that makes association after association. Don't worry about what is realistic or what problems may ensue. Let your mind wander from idea to idea.

The second stage comes back to organizational thinking. Here you begin to organize your ideas, putting them into categories or clusters. Elaborate on some of them. How can you group them together into coherent themes or clusters? The third phase is that of the critic. Evaluate your clusters and themes. Look at what will work in reality, and how you can make it work.

Brainstorm exercise (15 minutes)

Visioning. Fill in quickly, with printed single keywords on the lines and, without pausing to choose, the first 10 associations that spread out from the centre of the page when you think about the word 'brainstorm'. Put down the first words that come to mind – no matter how silly they seem. It might look something like the map below. Take one minute to do this exercise. Do it with two others to generate ideas and group synergy. Expand each of your 10 keywords with further associations. These become sub-branches to your main branches. Keep adding layers as ideas come.

Organizing. Look at your 10 keywords and try to find words that have a common theme. Redraw your brainstorm map with three or four key categories, linking branches and sub-branches.

Analysing. Evaluate the key branches. Decide which are relevant and explain or define the term 'brainstorming'. Write that out as your final map. You have devised your own definition of brainstorming.

Key guidelines:

- Use a central image or keyword to focus the eye and brain.
- Use images, graphics and colour to stimulate visual and linguistic thinking.
- Use three or more colours for your central image to stimulate memory and creativity.
- Create three dimensions to make things stand out and be remembered.
- Always print words, as they have a definite shape and can be more easily photographed by your brain.
- Combine images using the five senses (sight, sound, hearing, touch, taste, smell).
- Vary size for importance (BIG, Medium, small, tiny.
- Arrange items in hierarchical order for importance.
- Use one keyword per line.
- Print one word per line and make line length equal to word length.
- Connect lines to other lines and major branches to your central image.
- Make your main branches thicker and make them stand out.

Colours can be used to identify themes, topics, different levels of information, to show connections and to make your big picture memorable. If you find the same word or image repeated on your brainstorm map, you have probably discovered another major theme.

If you prefer to work with a computer, there is a wonderful world of graphics and symbols to choose from. If not, create your own small dictionary of symbols based on simple line drawings or recurring themes in your work (a telephone for communication, an elephant to signify memory, a heart for feelings, an eye to represent visualizing, a question mark to indicate questions, an exclamation mark for something outstanding). See Tony Buzan's wonderful book, *Get Ahead*, which offers a pictorial tutorial in drawing mind maps.

Flipside questions exercise (15 minutes)

Asking questions literally means going on a quest; the Latin root for question is *quarere*, to seek or to quest. By asking questions, your brain goes on search and find, a bit like a computer. Asking questions opens up the mind, explores possibilities, makes off-beat discoveries, taps into your imagination. Jot down the question that you need to answer (with your dominant writing hand) on one side of the paper. Write down as many questions as you possibly can to explore the topic. Questions give clarity in defining your issue.

You may write something like:

- How have I handled it before?
- Whom have I approached when I've needed to find solutions before?
- What has worked in the past?
- What hasn't worked?

Put the pen into your other hand, your non-dominant writing hand. Begin to answer the questions using the hand you don't normally write with. By switching hands you activate another part of the brain, opening up your thinking processes. You may come up with some weird and wonderful ideas as you make associations. But they will continue to link new thought patterns – which will help you to solve the problem.

Reframing

Reframing helps you to see your question or problem in another way. It gives you another perspective. Reframing simply asks, 'What does this mean?' or 'What else can we do to accomplish the same thing?' It's a way of opening up your creative curiosity, to help you think more broadly about the issue at hand. A classic example of reframing is seen in changing job titles: waiters and waitresses are called waitrons; trainers have become performance consultants; sales and promotion executives are marketers; PR consultants, publicists; stewardesses, flight attendants; dustmen are waste-disposal operatives!

Reframing takes something out of its normal frame and recasts it in a new context. We see examples of reframing in advertising and on television every day. Serial coffee ads suggest coffee is a romantic way to meet people, not just something to wake you up. Ice cream, instead of a simple treat for children, has become sexualized, and targeted to a sophisticated, young market. Cigarettes, driven from television and radio advertising because of health connotations, are more strongly sponsoring sport (where they can) to link smoking with health and the outdoors.

Reframing is a classic way to redefine something in a new light. Politicians often reinvent themselves. The most successful convince the public that their new frame of reference is as authentic as their new image. Politicians also reframe information: statistics and economic figures are manipulated to tell the story the politician wants the electorate to hear.

The whole point of reframing is to transform meaning. Metaphors are a reframing technique. Fairy tales are excellent examples of reframing. Fairy tales take what seems to be a scary, unlucky or dangerous situation and turn it into a moral tale. People tell jokes and anecdotes to reframe events by putting them into a different context, giving them another meaning altogether.

Ask questions to reframe

To reframe, ask questions. By finding different ways to look at an issue, we find alternative ways to resolve it. Ask as many questions as possible – what's the difference between what you're doing and what you're trying to achieve by doing it?

Say an organization is not known in the local community as socially responsible. Perhaps it is still associated with polluting a local river. What can it do to be seen to be giving something back? What aspect of the business can help develop an image of community support? In South Africa, a big supermarket chain was perceived to develop a caring attitude to its staff by providing health policies for them all.

To turn around the image that training is a costly business, reframe the context in which performance development is seen in your organization. Transform that into something positively affecting the bottom line, client relationships, sales and marketing, production and performance. The term 'investing in people' was a reframe. It showed that investing in people ultimately meant investing in a successful business.

De Bono's six caps

I have always loved the idea of putting on a different colour hat to put a different perspective on a topic. When I use this exercise, I ensure we have different coloured baseball caps to put on. It gives a frame of reference and makes the learning fun. In a recent workshop for a multimedia company, we made our own caps out of brightly coloured paper. It was a creative exercise to get people to associate the six colours with specific thinking styles. Six-cap thinking is a way to generate creative thinking in role play, debate, meetings and problem solving.

The usefulness of six-cap thinking is immense. De Bono argues that the Western habit of using argument and dialectic for thinking misses out on the generative and creative thinking processes. Critical thinking is fine, but it is only one type of thinking. Using six caps is a way of thinking and doing at the same time. As we know with whole-brain thinking, the more of our senses that we use, the more likely we are to be creative and to generate better recall.

I have had some clients who originally thought putting on coloured caps was silly, or using six different colours of paper to hang ideas on the wall was daffy – until they'd done it. In one UK workshop to train lawyers in consultative selling skills, participants thought using colours was perfectly childish. By the end of the two days, not only was each group keen to use colours for generating ideas and thinking on their feet, they began to appreciate the concept of using colour for different thinking perspectives.

The putting on of a coloured cap gives a kind of freedom to the role player. Actors often say they are painfully shy in real life, and taking on a role gives them a sense of freedom. Putting on a coloured cap is taking on a role. A yellow baseball cap gives you permission to think optimistically and positively about a subject. Putting on a black cap gives you permission to voice your criticism and cynicism. Using six-cap thinking is an excellent way to open up your mind; you have six distinct ways to approach and discuss a subject.

Thinking in colour

How can we use six-cap thinking to prepare a speech or presentation? To argue a case or take on different perspectives in debate? To outsmart an opponent in negotiations, to resolve a problem, for role play activities, or to approach any creative activity? There are six colours:

1. White cap: neutral, objective, concerned with facts and figures.
2. Red cap: the emotional view, showing feelings, anger, rage, seeing red.
3. Black cap: negative aspects, why something cannot be done, black and gloomy.
4. Yellow cap: positive, optimistic, sunny point of view, hopeful thinking.
5. Green cap: abundant, fertile, growth, signifies creativity and new ideas.
6. Blue cap: strategic overview, cool-headed, big-picture thinking, concerned with control and organization.

De Bono suggests that a good way to remember the meaning of the six coloured caps is to think of them in pairs:

- white and red: neutral and emotional;
- black and yellow – negative and positive;
- green and blue – creativity and control.

In meetings, I find it useful to ask everyone to put on their white caps when trying to approach an issue from a neutral viewpoint; red caps when thinking about feelings and emotions from a personal or client point of view; black caps when thinking of reasons why something can't be done; yellow caps when looking at the advantages and positives; green caps when generating new ideas; blue caps when taking the helicopter viewpoint – looking at it from above.

Decision-making exercise (30 minutes)

Next time you facilitate a decision, ask every member of the group to wear each of the six caps, one at a time. Have someone stand at the flipchart to write down the contributions made while wearing each of the six caps. This is a bit like brainstorming, but it's important that no switching happens between caps.

Once all six flipcharts are written up, put on the blue cap to look at the overall contributions. See if any more can be added. Put on the black cap to analyse the usefulness of each idea. Circle ideas that may be adopted and draw them on a brainstorming map. Again, put on the black and blue caps to analyse the final decision.

Problem-solving exercise (30 minutes)

This same exercise can be done when analysing a problem. Run through the same scenario, this time with a definition of the problem written up and pinned on a wall for all to see. Have each member of the group use the six thinking colours, one at a time, analysing the problem from each viewpoint. One person writes up possible solutions on the flipchart, ensuring there is a page for each colour.

Once all six flipcharts are written up, everyone puts on the blue cap to look at the overall contributions and the black cap to analyse the usefulness of each idea. Circle solutions that may be adopted. Draw up a memory map with all of the possibilities that could work. Put on the black and blue caps to analyse the final decision.

Steps to creative thinking

Step into the meta mirror

The meta mirror is a powerful facilitation tool. It opens up perspective on inter-personal dynamics where communication has broken down, misunderstandings have occurred or resentment is in place. It helps to give perspective, to stand in the shoes of the other person and to gain the learning that is needed to move on. This exercise is done with the help of a coach or facilitator – but never includes the two parties who are in conflict. It includes only one of the parties, and the facilitator's job is to help that party to see the issue from all perspectives.

How to do it exercise (15 minutes per person)

Stand up with the participant. Ask him or her to describe a specific situation that has caused conflict, misunderstanding or resentment with another person. Ask the participant to pick an actual scene and show you (and the rest of the group if involved) where the two people would stand if they were to repeat that situation. Have the person tell you what happened in the interaction between the two people. Arrange the chairs in such a way that they represent the past situation.

Have the participant (Player A) take his or her seat, or stand facing the imagined Player B. Ask Player A to re-imagine him or herself in that moment: to see, hear and feel it. Ask him/her to replay the conversation with Player B, but this time saying it as he/she really wanted to say it. Ask Player A to speak in present tense as if he or she is really speaking to the other person.

Once Player A has said everything he/she wants to say, he or she should shake him/herself out, hands, head and feet, and return to the sidelines with you – looking at where he/she was just speaking. Ask what he/she sees. What can he/she observe from what just happened? What is the learning for that person in this particular situation?

Now have the same individual step into Player B's shoes. He or she stands or sits where he/she indicated the other player faced him/her. Ask the individual to imagine that he/she is the other person. What would he/she, as Player B, like to say to Player A? Have the person speak in the present tense – what would this other person really like to say? How does this person really feel? Once the player has finished, have him or her stand up once again with you, on the sidelines.

Ask the participant, from the sidelines with you, to look at Player B – where that individual was just sitting. What is the learning to be had about Player B? What can he or she now learn about the dynamic between Players A and B?

Finally, have your participant step back into Player A's shoes. Have him or her sit or stand, and speak once again to Player B. What could the individual say now? What can he/she express in the light of everything he/she has learnt about both players? How can he/she use that learning to express him/herself and to move on?

Ask Player A to step back with you on the sidelines and to shake out.

Ask what needs to happen now to move on. Discuss what action is now needed, if any. Sometimes it is a simple case of forgiveness and moving on, sometimes it is a matter of communication in real life with Player B. It depends on the situation.

For example, one of my clients, a magazine editor, had a very difficult new boss with whom she found communication almost impossible. We literally rearranged my office to mimic her last conversation with this boss, and I walked her through the meta mirror. By the time we had finished, the solution was a very simple one. My client was not representing herself well and needed to adopt a completely different communication style with this one person. She has subsequently gone on from success to success.

Story-telling techniques

The prop and the character exercise (15 minutes)

This is a creative exercise to develop the mental and verbal flexibility of your participants. It helps them to access their own ingenuity.

Ask each individual to think of a character. It can be someone from his/her own personal life (teacher, role model or family member), a fictional character from a film, book or play, or a fictional creation of his/her own making. Give participants 30 seconds to think of this character. If you leave too much time they will go into analytical mode. You want to keep them in the moment.

Work in a circle, sitting or standing, and move round the circle, having the participants ask questions of one character at a time. It's great fun, and asking questions helps to discover a little about the 'essence' of each character. Give each speaker a prop. It helps him or her feel comfortable in front of the group and aids imaginary powers. Props can be anything: a plastic bag, a coffee cup, a cell phone – something small and mundane from everyday life. The entire group then asks open questions of this character, questions that require more than a yes or no answer, such as:

- Who are you?
- What do you do?
- How do you do it?
- Where do you live?
- What is the 'prop' for?
- What do you do with it?
- How important is it?

The group's questions help them to paint a picture of this character, to understand a little bit about who this character is. The participants ask questions; never do they make a statement about the character (such as 'You do this, don't you?). Go round the group in this way, until each character has unfolded. Give about two minutes of questions for each character.

Second-character interaction (15 minutes)

Ask each participant to think of a second character who will meet the first character. Again this can be someone from his/her personal life or a fictional character. Ask everyone to think about a conversation between their two characters that happened one week ago. Ask them to jot down key points or dialogue. Give them no more than five minutes. You'll be surprised how quickly they start scribbling, and they won't want to stop!

Go round the circle, and have participants share in pairs what happened in this 'one week previously' situation with their two characters. Allow two minutes each.

Third character interaction (15 minutes)

Ask each participant to think of a third character who will meet one of the first two. This can be someone from his/her personal life, or a fictional character. Ask everyone to think about a conversation between these two characters that happened one year after the situation imagined above. Ask them to jot down the key points or dialogue. Allow approximately five minutes.

Have the participants work with a different partner this time, sharing the scenario in this 'one year later' situation. Give them about five minutes.

Creative-writing option (20 minutes)

For the second and third characters, another option is to have participants make brainstorm maps of the dialogue or story scenario. They can then share with the larger group, or in pairs, the basic outline of their story.

Review (10 minutes)

Go round the group and ask what they learnt about creative thinking from this exercise. Remember to comment on how quickly they developed their characters and interacted with each other to create stories. Ask how they can use this technique, or even the impact of storytelling, back in the workplace. It is particularly useful in demonstrating any kind of interpersonal dynamic where learning needs to take place.

Metaphoric thinking

Using metaphors is the art of making creative associations. Metaphors help discover a new perspective, a new way of thinking. Metaphors give a big picture association to clarify confusing issues, discover new possibilitie and stimulate fresh thoughts, communicating ideas across teams or disciplines.

Problem solving metaphors (20 minutes)

Try this exercise with three or more people in a group. Have the group jot down the problem or issue to be tackled, then put it aside. Ask them to brainstorm on a flipchart, or large piece of paper, all of the key attributes of that problem. Ask them to think of a metaphor that describes the problem. Make associations with the metaphor (crossing a bridge, designing a house, parachuting from a plane) and the results you are looking to achieve.

Character association exercise (20 minutes)

Do this activity with three or more people in a group. Have the group jot down the problem or issue to be tackled, then put it aside. Ask them to approach the problem from a number of different angles. Have each person fill in five cards with a character (such as warrior, actor, trainer, teacher, car salesman, knight, rock climber, explorer, brain surgeon, judge, Socrates).

Put all of the cards together, and have the group turn over one card at a time. Draw a picture of the character, or put up the word on the flipchart. Brainstorm how that character would tackle the problem. Do this with each of the cards, then jot down on a brainstorm map all of the associations. Analyse each of them to see what solutions you come up with.

Drawing and handwriting

Drawing seems to be a magical activity – particularly to those who 'think' they cannot draw. My advice to anyone who says they cannot draw is, go take a drawing class. Drawing is a learnable skill, in the way that learning a new language is a learnable skill. Kimon Nicolaides, in *The Natural Way To Draw*, says: 'Learning to draw is really a matter of learning to see.'

Drawing is a global, big-picture, whole-brain activity. It is a very useful tool in training or problem solving. Drawing can be used to develop creativity in participants who, in the working world, are predominantly logical, rational thinkers. Drawing develops the perceptual, visual thinking mode. Drawing develops global thinking – yet still calls on the need for detail. Many people, like me, say they can't draw, so please don't ask us to! They may have had an experience as a child that stopped them from seeing, that stopped them from thinking they could draw. I will never forget being six years old, standing at an easel in the back of the room in the first grade. A classmate walked past and said, 'That doesn't look anything like a horse!' I was so embarrassed, I put my paint brush down and never took it up again – until I became a performance consultant and realized the coaching potential of drawing.

Freeing up the creative eye

Drawing is to do with 'seeing'. I began to 'see' the usefulness of drawing when I first started drawing memory maps, and using symbols and graphics instead of words for recall. It is creative, intuitive and visual. The artist uses the brain's visual, perceptual way of thinking. It is also a step-by-step activity, integrating a set of basic skills that are needed to complete a drawing or a picture.

Drawing is not unlike driving. Once you have integrated the various components – how to change gears, keep your hands on the steering wheel, check mirrors, brake, reverse, do a three-point turn – driving becomes an integrated, whole-brain process. Have you ever, upon arrival somewhere, thought: How on earth did I get here? Your mind seemed to be elsewhere. You integrated creative and logical thinking so competently that you were able to see the big picture – the road, how you were going to get there – as well as being able to competently do the detail of driving, unconsciously using hands, feet and eyes.

Developing visual power exercise (10 minutes)

To develop your visual powers, don't think about your drawing ability. Take the word 'work' and draw a pictorial image of it in the centre of the page. Associate with the emotions you feel about your workplace, the job you do, your career. Put a few colours into your image. Don't worry if your picture seems childish or unartistic. The power of the image is to awaken your capacity to visualize.

Everyone can draw; we just draw differently, and some have developed the ability more than others. The aim of this exercise is to give free rein to your enormous powers of visualization. It will also help the memory to recall images, developing your powers of imagination and mental relaxation.

I work with clients individually to help them develop their powers of visualization. One of my clients is a professional golfer. Can you imagine how useful it is for him to visualize driving that ball to within one metre of the hole, or sinking an incredible putt? Visualization exercises call on different cortical thinking skills, and help you achieve, and repeat, potential excellence.

The brain's duality

In learning to draw, we need to access the intuitive brain's way of thinking at a conscious level. This is particularly hard for us in the Western world, as our education system is geared to the rational way of seeing. We virtually neglect the creative half of the brain – so much so that drawing, art, music and dancing are being excluded more and more from the education curriculum. The dreamer and the artist are not encouraged. When the time comes to move into the working world, the creative brain's ability to be innovative, dream and visualize has been greatly reduced.

Visualization exercise (10 minutes)

Learning to draw, participants move into a more intuitive, subjective, global, time-free zone. To encourage this state, take participants into a visualization, using words that call on the visual, auditory and kinesthetic. My favourite exercise is to have them relax, close their eyes – then imagine themselves at the top of a hill looking down a slope towards a white sandy beach and blue waters. As I take them walking down the hill I leave everything to their imagination; even as they step onto the sand, they choose whether to go right or left, walk or sit. I simply ask them to take in the colours, textures, sounds – and what they feel.

This exercise creates a slightly altered state of consciousness, which the artist experiences when painting, drawing or etching. That is the visual brain kicking in, allowing verbal experience to fade into the background. Yet the logical brain is still engaged to allow for sketching of lines, curves, edges and borders.

Putting pencil to paper exercise (10 minutes)

To use drawing in your learning programmes, start with a very simple exercise that helps participants begin to see. Show a picture that can be seen in more than one way (the perception lady or the vase profiles). It's useful to take an optical illusion drawing because it can be seen in more than one way, and can be drawn in more than one way.

Have participants start by drawing only one side of the picture, then have them copy it exactly on the other side. For this exercise use the vase/profiles picture. You only need five to 10 minutes. Ask participants for feedback in what they experienced. They may have experienced some confusion when they switched back and forth between seeing a profile and seeing the outline of a vase. Ask them to share any confusion they felt if they tried to use words to explain to themselves what they were drawing (face, lips or nose).

Betty Edwards calls this the 'mental crunch', making that shift from logical to visual thinking. To make the mental shift from wordy, verbal thinking to non-verbal, spatial thinking, it's important to see drawing quite simply as a perceptual task – one that doesn't involve language in any way.

Figure 6.2   Vase profiles/perception lady

Exercise in visual conflict (30 minutes)

Brainstorming, although whole-brain, is misconstrued as a predominantly left-brain activity. This is because, despite making associations, most people write words instead of drawing symbols, graphics or pictures. Try this exercise. Break participants into groups and have them brainstorm this question: 'How is drawing useful to us?' Ask them to use fewer words on their brainstorm maps. Get them to jot down as many of their ideas as they can in picture form, line drawings, graphics and symbols (using as many colours as possible).

Then have them present their maps, sharing difficulties in trying to stay away from words. One of the conflicts will be making associations with words. It is hard to go between that and writing words down as pictures. A useful way to think in pictures is to use metaphors: an elephant for memory, telephone for communication, cloud for the big picture.

Handwriting and journalling exercise (50 minutes)

Handwriting is also a creative art form. School children are pressured to write beautifully, clearly and with form. In my stress- and problem-solving seminars, I use handwriting and journalling exercises to help participants move from verbal to visual thinking.

Ask participants to write (with their dominant writing hand) everything they can think of to do with the problem they are trying to solve, or the issue that is stressful to them. Then ask them to switch to their non-dominant writing hand. Suggest they begin to write questions about the situation, and keep writing questions until they start to jot down answers in the form of symbols, pictures, metaphors – still using their non-dominant hand.

This part of the exercise needs 25 minutes, as the use of the non-dominant hand is a slow process. Participants (once they stop giggling!) move into a more meditative process that is unaware of time – a state necessary for drawing and innovative thinking.

At the end of 25 minutes, give them five minutes to think of a metaphor that is analogous to their problem and to draw it with either hand. Ask them to take 10 minutes to share their metaphors and possible solutions with a partner. In the larger group, take 10 minutes to review what they learnt from this process.

Writing your name exercise (20 minutes)

Your signature is expressive of you and the culture that you grew up in. Artists use their signatures to identify themselves. My husband has developed a very unique signature, blending his first name and initial of his surname. It expresses how he sees himself, and the informality with which he likes to deal with people. In your workshops, ask your participants to work in a group. Have them print their name five times, and write in script five times (that is, their normal signature). Ask members of the group to pretend they are graphologists, and try to determine from the handwriting samples the personality traits or colours that person would wear. Is he or she expressive, introverted, extroverted, talkative, dramatic, quiet or noisy? What hobbies might he or she like?

Have people work together who don't know each other well. It may be that their interpretations are completely off the wall, but this is an innovative exercise. Each signature is a drawing in itself. Participants are to read the non-verbal expression of each signature, responding to the size, speed and height of the lines, and the perceived feelings in the movement of the letters. There is no moral judgement here, simply an exercise in seeing the world in visual mode.

How you can make the shift

Making the shift to visual thinking involves being unaware of time, not being distracted by sound in the background, being completely absorbed in your task – and it's fun. Help participants to draw on their creative potential. The way forward today is to find new, creative solutions to problems, developing a work force that thinks creatively without restriction.

Drawing and painting, learning a new language, journalling first thing every morning with the non-dominant hand, writing down dreams if you wake up in the middle of the night, meditating, listening to music while you work: all of these activities awaken innovative consciousness, and teach you skills that will release you from 'stereotypical' expression.

My husband, when writing one of his recent plays, invented a language that was not dissimilar in sound to an African language spoken in our part of South Africa. It was so convincing that a friend who was editing his play asked a number of other friends to translate. No one could, but they all thought they recognized the words and argued about which language it was!

In conclusion

To develop creativity is to do tasks the logical brain will turn down, so find ways of helping your participants to see differently. Help them to ease the verbal mode out of the task when trying to think creatively or problem solve. Shifting to visual expression allows them to see in the way that a trained artist sees.

The arch-enemy of innovation is thinking in the same, tired way without inspiration. It isn't so much that the strategies you use are creative in themselves, they just help you to release your own creativity.

Remember: people are motivated by what is important to them. They look to work for achievement, recognition and the chance to develop their personal needs.

By harnessing the needs of the organization to the innovative skills of its individuals, a new energy is achieved. There's the magic.

Where to go for more

Books

Bandler, Richard and Grinder, John (1982) *Reframing*, Real People Press, Moab, Utah

Buzan, Tony (1994) *Use Your Memory*, BBC Books, London

Buzan, Tony (1998) *The Mind Map Book: Radiant thinking*, BBC Books, London (beautiful illustrated examples – note taking, structuring information, enhancing memory)

Clegg, Brian (1999) *Creativity and Innovation for Managers*, Butterworth Heinemann, Oxford

Cook, Peter (1998) *Best Practice Creativity*, Gower, Hampshire, UK (how creativity is being used in organizations; case studies; uses the metaphor of rock'n'roll)

de Bono, Edward (1985) *Six Thinking Hats*, Penguin, London (an easy explanation of the six different thinking styles)

de Bono, Edward, (1998) *Super Mind Pack: Thinking for action*, Dorling Kindersley, London (strategic games and mental exercises)

Dellinger, Susan (1990) *Psycho-Geometrics: Communicating beyond our differences*, Prentice-Hall, Englewood Cliffs, NJ

Epstein, Robert (1995) *Creativity Games For Trainers: A handbook of group activities for jump-starting workplace creativity*, McGraw-Hill, London

North, Vanda with Buzan, Tony (1991) *Get Ahead: Mind map your way to success*, Buzan Centre, Dorset, UK

von Oech, Roger (1996) *A Kick in the Seat of the Pants: Using your explorer, artist, judge and warrior to be more creative,* HarperCollins, New York (guided tour through the roles of the creative process: explorer, artist, judge and warrior)

Books on drawing

Albert, Greg and Wolf, Rachel (eds) (1991) *Basic Drawing Techniques*, North Light Books, Cincinnati, Ohio

Edwards, Betty (2000) *The New Drawing on the Right Side of the Brain*, Souvenir Press, London

Franck, Frederick (1973) *The Zen Of Seeing: Seeing drawing as meditation*, Random House, London and New York

Nicolaides, Kimon (1990) *The Natural Way to Draw: A working plan for art study*, Houghton Mifflin, Boston

Nunn, Janet (2001) *Learn to Draw Animated Cartoons*, HarperCollins, London

Journals

Fox, Derwin, Byrne,Vincent and Rouault, Frank (1999) Performance improvement: what to keep in mind, *Training and Development* (August) pp 38–40
Weiss, Ruth Palombo (2000) Brain-based learning, *Training and Development* (July) pp 21–24

Videos

Psycho-Geometrics: The science of understanding people, and the art of influencing them, CareerTrack, Litho, USA, no C20468 494.

Visual-thinking software

MindManager 2002 Business Edition – To boost team dynamics and productivity. [Online] http://www.mindjet.com

Web sites

http://www.appliedcreativityinc
http://www.creativethink.com, Creative Think (Roger von Oech's site)
http://www.cul.co.uk, Creativity Unleashed Ltd (sections on business creativity)
http://www.drawright.com (Betty Edwards' site for portfolio of drawing materials)

7

Music: the beat goes on

Music is a powerful way to help people remember, and to inspire them to use what they already know. Research shows that music provides an anchor and an emotional connection to improve retention. An anchor is any stimulus that changes our state of being, our state of mind. Music acts as an anchor in the classroom, enhancing our positive feelings, changing a state of anxiety to relaxation, anchoring a piece of music to a positive learning environment.

Research has shown that specific types of music, particularly that of Mozart, stimulate our thinking powers and unlock our creative potential. A whole-brain activity, music is received by the imaginative right brain, and we make sense of the rhythms and words with the logical left brain. Be careful not to overuse music and risk losing its effectiveness.

I use music in a variety of ways in performance development. It complements any number of learning tools. Music is very popular with all participants, from senior managers to line staff. They find it a fun, powerful tool for learning, retention and improving performance.

Singing can have the same effect on recall. Have you ever asked a group of adults which months have only 30 days, the notes of the musical scale, or how to quickly say the alphabet? They recite '30 days hath September', 'Every Good Boy Deserves Favour' and sing the alphabet.

What state of resourcefulness do you wish to create for your learners? Make a list of the music you love that makes you feel good today, and every day. Memory improves when information is attached to an anchor such as music. Music elicits strong emotions, usually positive, which is why advertisers use an incredible array of music in commercials.

Music serves as a memory anchor and an emotional connection to inspire. This chapter will help you select music to motivate, inspire and create those emotional connections essential for learning.

Music as anchor

Creating a resourceful state of mind

Music will help you to build a resourceful state. Any stimulus that changes your physical and mental state is an 'anchor'. Use music and sound as an anchor or positive stimulus to create or change a state of mind. When I attended my first NLP practitioner workshop in London, I noticed the same energetic piece of music announced the beginning of each new session following a break. Using the same music before each session provided an auditory anchor, a trigger to bring participants back into the same learning frame of mind each time.

The music, tailor-made for that workshop, was upbeat and lively, physically and mentally stimulating. When people heard the music, even from downstairs, they began to move, 'jiving' their way back into the learning session. The music was an anchor: signalling a transition, creating an immediate response and stimulating recall in the participants. Use musical anchors to recreate a positive, energetic or relaxing state of mind and body each time it is heard.

The sound of a signature tune, whether for a television ad or favourite childhood programme, triggers memories and a physiological reaction. An old song on the radio can put you back into the past in a flash. I recently attended a primary school play, and couldn't resist singing along to the numerous popular rock'n'roll songs from my teenage years. With each song, floods of memories kept popping into my head, reminding me of people and events long forgotten.

Creating an emotional connection

The first step is to become aware of the musical anchors that put your participants into a resourceful state. As an icebreaker, ask participants to bring a track they like, play it and say something about it. Studies show that memory retention is better when there's an emotional connection. So find out what era your delegates grew up in, and what were the films, the popular music and trends of the time. The next step is to begin to design musical anchors for your workshops, conferences and talks.

Most baby boomers can remember where they were and what they felt on 22 November 1963, the day President John F Kennedy was assassinated. They are personally and emotionally connected to that event. Many will immediately recall the face and voice of Martin Luther King whenever they hear the phrase 'I have a dream'.

Today's generation may even feel tearful when they hear Elton John's *Candle in the Wind*, sung to commemorate Princess Diana at her funeral. For decades, advertisers have very cleverly used hit songs to advertise their goods and services, creating an emotional link between the song and their brand.

We know that music provides an anchor (recreating a state of mind and body) and an emotional connection to trigger memory. We also know that we remember things that are outstanding and linked. With music we can create an outstanding link between our message and the tune, words and meaning of a song.

Auditory donkey bridges

A donkey bridge is a memory aid that links or creates an outstanding mental bridge between two versions of the same information. Songs and music represent strong auditory and rhythmic links that tend to be remembered long past the time of the learning. They can be motivational and inspirational, as well as creating a focus for the message.

Take national anthems, for example. How do we remember them? They stand out in childhood as a personal link to our nation, culture and heritage. At football matches and Olympic Games, national anthems from around the world are used to create an emotional effect and a sense of celebration. The English national anthem, *God Save the Queen*, is always sung by fans at international football matches, and the nationalistic British song *Land of Hope and Glory* at rugby matches. Whenever there is a ritualistic occasion in the States, we hear Americans singing *The Star Spangled Banner*. The new, haunting South African anthem, *Nkosi Sikelel' iAfrica*, conjures up images of the African tradition of communal singing. I use it in South African workshops to create a sense of community in the training room.

Jukebox Learning, an American company that takes rock'n'roll into organizations, has branded the term 'harmogenizing' to mean connecting learning to music. They take classic rock'n'roll tunes and connect them to new concepts to help participants anchor the message. Songs and slogans stay in the mind longer than simple words because they connect right- and left-brain thinking processes.

What music can you play (in meetings, seminars, workshops, conferences) to create a link between the learning and how it is to be applied in the workplace? Here are a few suggestions.

Music as relaxation

Music can determine how we feel and how we see the world. Since ancient times, music has been used to heal, and to create a sense of universal connection. I teach delegates to use music to relax prior to entering a tough negotiation or a conflict situation, to handle stress more effectively, or simply to calm their nerves moments before speaking in public.

	Artist/producer/composer
Teamwork:	
Friends	Bette Midler
I Can Help	Billy Swann
I'll Be There	Jackson Five
Stand By Me	Ben E King
Whenever I Call You Friend	Kenny Loggins
You've Got A Friend	James Taylor
You'll Never Walk Alone	Nina Simone/Rodgers and Hammerstein
Setting goals and visualization:	
All I Have To Do Is Dream	Everly Brothers
Beautiful Vision	Van Morrison
Change Is Gonna Come	Otis Redding
Cool, from *West Side Story*	Bernstein/Sondheim
High Hopes	Frank Sinatra
Higher and Higher	Jackie Wilson
I Wish It So	M Blitzstein/Dawn Upshaw
Just My Imagination	Temptations
River Deep, Mountain High	Ike and Tina Turner
Celebration:	
Brand New Day	Van Morrison
Celebration	Kool and The Gang
Dancing In The Street	Martha and The Vandellas
Entrance of Capulets from *Romeo and Juliet*	Prokofiev
I Just Want To Celebrate	Rare Earth
I'm Into Something Good	Herman's Hermits
It's Gonna Be A Lovely Day	Bill Withers
Mazurka from *Coppelia* (ballet)	Delibes
Oh What A Beautiful Morning from *Oklahoma*	Rodgers and Hammerstein
There Won't Be Trumpets	Sondheim/Dawn Upshaw
Why Don't We Celebrate?	Bruce Cockburn

Relaxation exercise

Used as relaxation, sound and music clear our minds of clutter and give us back our internal sense of well-being. When relaxed, we think clearly. Our performance improves. We handle pressure successfully. Read this exercise first before trying it yourself, or else have a partner read it quietly to you as you experience it.

Close your eyes and imagine the purring of a very contented kitten next to your right ear. Next, imagine someone is softly blowing a trumpet into your right ear, and you only just hear the whispered sensation of the trumpet. It softly becomes the soothing sound of the ocean's waves as they brush the shore, the brushing sound at your right ear. Let the sensations of sound enter your entire body, relaxing every nerve and muscle. Finally, imagine the gospel hymn *Amen* being sung in your left ear, getting softer and softer, until the singing disappears. Taking in a long deep breath, open your eyes. How do you feel?

The healing power of music

Music affects our heartbeat. This is why classical music is used for both relaxation and creative thinking. Classical music has a pulse of about 60 to 85 beats per minute (tempo varies), and is used to slow down breathing and heart rate. The faster the frequency, tempo and volume of music, the faster the heart beats. The slower the pulse of the music, the slower your heart rate – decreasing mental and physical stress, calming mind and body.

If you want to create an ambiance of energy and stimulation, play rock'n'roll music to stimulate breathing and heart rate. If trying to boost productivity in a relaxed environment, put on light classical music such as *The Very Best of the Classic Experience* or *The Most Relaxing Classical Album in the World*. Use baroque music in your workshops to disguise interfering sounds from outside, creating a more private atmosphere where small groups working together can't easily hear what the other groups are saying. The predictability of the form in baroque music is stabilizing. One can feel secure in the knowledge that one is safe from sudden deafening volume changes.

- Peter Kater and R Carlos Nakai's *Enaudi;*
- Jan Gabarek's *Officium;*
- Johann Sebastian Bach's *Air on a G String* from *Suite no 3 in D;*
- Johann Sebastian Bach's *Goldberg Variations;*
- Edvard Grieg's *Morning* from *Peer Gynt;*
- Eric Satie's *Gymnopedies nos 1–3;*
- Wolfgang Amadeus Mozart's *Piano Concerto No. 21 in C (Elvira Madigan), K 467;*
- Gabriel Fauré's *In Paradisum* from *Requiem* Op 48;
- Antonio Vivaldi's *The Four Seasons;*
- Gabriel Fauré's *Pavane;*
- Luigi Boccherini's *Minuet* from *String Quintet in E* Op 13 no 5;
- Ludwig van Beethoven's *Piano Sonata no 14 in C sharp minor (Moonlight);*
- Joaquin Rodrigo's *Concierto de Aranjuez;*
- Ralph Vaughan Williams' *The Lark Ascending;*
- Frederic Chopin's *Nocturne in E flat.*

Smooth, soft jazz

Jazz music is wonderful, although some of it is not perfect or ideal for the learning environment. Playing soft, soothing jazz can be very relaxing for your learners. It creates an ambiance that is conducive for learning and group activities. Jazz also makes a lovely change from classical music. Some of my favourite jazz artists, whose music can be played and enjoyed in the learning environment, are:

- Chet Baker
- George Benson
- Donald Byrd and the Blackbyrds
- Nat King Cole
- John Coltrane (especially *Ballads*)
- Bill Evans
- Stan Getz
- Dexter Gordon
- Jon Hendriks
- Johnny Hodges
- Billie Holliday
- Bobby Hutchinson
- Earl Klugh
- Ramsey Lewis
- Charles Lloyd
- Wynton Marsalis
- Les McCann
- Pat Metheny
- Gerry Mulligan
- Mark Murphy
- Oscar Peterson
- David Sanborn
- Billy Strayhorn
- Jack Teagarden
- Sarah Vaughan

Music to begin and end the day

When delegates first arrive, it's important to set up a comfortable, welcoming ambiance. To complement the music you choose, be available to meet and greet participants, creating an atmosphere that puts people at their ease. Craft your own master list, adding to it as delegates introduce you to their preferred tunes. Music is a delightful way to open a conversation. People love to exchange information about their favourite singers and musicians – or the unfortunate musical taste of their teenage children!

Here are a few of my favourite albums, which I use in that first hour prior to the start of a session and to which I return at the end of the day for reflections or the completion of evaluation forms. There is some exquisite traditional Chinese music that is conducive to soft, reflective moods at the beginning and end of the day. I always recommend trying out any selections for yourself first.

A Beautiful Day Will Come from *Madame Butterfly*	Puccini
A Day Without Rain	Enya
Best Of The Renaissance	Allegri and Tallis by Phillips
Canyon Trilogy: Native American Flute	R Carlos Nakai
Ekhaya	Abdullah Ibrahim
Flight Of The Condor	BBC record of original TV Series
Impressions Of Africa	Various artists
Loon Summer	North Sound
Magical Ring	Clannad
Palestrina Requiem	Cappella Palestrina
Pieces Of Africa	Kronos Quartet
Sacred Planet	Vivaldi et al

Afternoon energy

The afternoon requires a change of pace from your early morning music. These are a few albums that set an upbeat tone after the luncheon break, when people may feel drowsy after eating, and you want to introduce the idea of energy into the afternoon session. Music gets the breath and oxygen flowing, re-activating the brain.

A Baroque Festival	Academy of St Martin in the Fields
African Dawn/African Horns	Abdullah Ibrahim
Born In The USA	Bruce Springsteen
Catch A Fire	The Wailers
Graceland	Paul Simon
Millennia and *Zebra Crossing*	Soweto String Quartet
Moondance	Van Morrison
Motown Music (*Motown Party*)	(any Tamla Motown sampler)
The Star and the Wiseman	Ladysmith Black Mambazo
Women of Africa	Various artists

(Motown samplers will have artists such as Diana Ross and The Supremes, Stevie Wonder, Four Tops, The Temptations, Marvin Gaye, Smokey Robinson and The Miracles and The Jackson Five.)

Mozart makes you smarter

Don Campbell, in his book *The Mozart Effect,* tells us that listening to Mozart 'stimulates and fires the creative and motivational regions of the brain'. Researchers at the University of California (Irvine) have discovered that those who listen to 10 minutes of Mozart's *Sonata in D Major for Two Pianos* before taking an IQ test score higher than those who listen to 10 minutes of relaxation music, or sit in silence.

Some kinds of music stimulate the neural pathways in the brain. Scientists have shown that if you listen to 15 minutes of Mozart, you can improve your abstract and spatial reasoning. The disadvantage is that this improvement is temporary – possibly because listening is a passive activity.

Mozart was an energetic, playful, lightning-quick thinker. The systematic rapidity of his music induces varied emotional responses in us, but his music changes so fast, the mind works to keep up. To boost your brain power, listen to *Mozart for Your Mind*, or choose from: *Mozart In The Morning*, *Mozart At Midnight* and *Mozart For Meditation*.

Thinking creatively with Mozart

Listening to Mozart improves concentration and intuitive thinking. Try it with your delegates. Put on a Mozart concerto when taking them through a visualization exercise, or brainstorming goals and roles for the next year.

Put on one of Mozart's violin concertos as background music when working with small groups or teams – whether they are brainstorming, developing values, vision and mission statements or simply working on a small group activity.

When I am coaching individual clients in my office, Mozart is a favourite to boost imaginative thinking. My favourite recordings are Mozart's complete violin concertos and his complete piano concertos.

Active listening exercise (15 minutes)

Most people think listening is passive, when it should in fact be active. Here is an exercise to develop your 'active' listening skills. Most of us tend to think we're brilliant listeners because we're teachers, trainers, facilitators and coaches: people who work with people. Active listening will help you to expand your 'peripheral' listening skills, becoming fully present for your audience.

This exercise will teach you to develop a more acute 'listening' ear. Try it first yourself. Then incorporate it into your workshops to help learners develop active-listening skills. Make a tape of your own voice, or ask a friend to read it to you, quietly taking you through the exercise.

Close your eyes for 10 minutes and listen to the sounds that surround you. Sense the sounds coming at you from all directions. Start with the nearest sounds, then listen for the most distant ones.

Notice natural sounds such as birds singing, the breeze rustling the leaves of trees, the hum of an air conditioner or refrigerator, the sound of cars passing, the human sounds of clattering dishes or distant voices. Feel every sound integrating itself into your mind and body. Select one sound at a time, filtering out other sounds, gradually beginning to sense and hear them all.

You are now in an attentive and acute state of mind and hearing. For the next 10 minutes, listen to a relaxing piece of music. Choose something like a Gregorian chant, Spanish guitar, Celtic New Age music or a violin concerto. Let thoughts float in and out of your mind, hearing and sensing the music.

After 10 minutes, open your eyes and write down any thoughts that came to you while listening to the music, or any thoughts that come to you now. This can be used as a healing exercise to relieve stress, or to help learners free their mind of clutter and begin a creative-thinking session. Our ability to listen is greatly affected by our state of mind. Listening to classical or relaxing music can create a state of mind that activates the brain and increases attentiveness.

Creating outstanding links to learning

Music complements and exaggerates meaning. The first time I experienced a facilitator effectively playing selected pieces of music to trigger energy, creative thinking and recall was nearly a decade ago in John Townsend's 'Master Trainer Programme' in France. For an entire week, a stream of songs from rock'n'roll to jazz and classical music was used to complement visual messages, exaggerate multi-channel messages, and act as a memory aid during review periods.

The sort of memories that stick are:

- emotional;
- exaggerated;
- symbolic;
- humorous;
- outstanding;
- personally important;
- repeated;
- significant events (political, sports, family);
- unusual.

All leading psychologists, trainers and coaches realize the need to be whole-brained to achieve success in the workplace today. Music will help the logical and imaginative brains work hand in hand, integrating the analytical, sequential, verbal hemisphere with its visual, pictorial, colourful, rhythmic, imaginative counterpart.

Introducing outstanding musical messages, instead of using computer-generated slides, will provide a superb memory link for participants. The learning will be stored in both sides of the brain, ensuring long-lasting memory. Music taken in by the right hemisphere is connected to the information taken in by the left. To create an emotional, unbeatable memory link, play songs that complement your workshop theme. Of primary importance generating a strong link to connect the learning, the workshop and the workplace.

Music to stimulate thinking

Use Mozart or Bach to stimulate learning and recall; natural sounds, classical music or New Age music to create an ambiance to think, work or study; rock-'n'roll music to create energy and action. Rock music is known to increase heart rates, but some rock'n'roll can be rather hard-driving, so is not always appropriate for brainstorming, studying or working.

Rock, country and western, rhythm'n' blues, jazz, pop music – all create a sense of energy, community, action and motivation. Some popular songs will naturally fall into a theme you want to promote within the organization. Bring them into your exercises. Or have the group write their own words to a popular tune. Here are some examples, but feel free to create your own list according to your and your participants' tastes.

Art Of The Fugue	J S Bach
Dance Pieces and *Glassworks*	Philip Glass
Flute Collection	Stephen Preston and Lucy Carolan
Goldberg Variations	J S Bach
Inner Peace For Busy People	Vaughan Williams, Fauré, Vivaldi, Mozart, Albinoni, Chopin, Beethoven
Lake Of Shadows	Phil Coulter
La Mer	Debussy
Middle and Late Quartets	Beethoven
Piano Sonatas Op 111, Op 10 no 1	Beethoven
Solo Piano	Keith Jarrett
String Quartets	Bartok
The Essential Mozart	(Mozart's 15 most popular pieces)
The Trout Quintet	Schubert

Is it all rock 'n' roll?

We are surrounded by music from beginning to end of the day: from radio and television, at work, church and school – to the tune playing in our head. Whether we understand anything about music or not, music and sound have a huge impact on our lives. In every society, music has created a sense of community from generation to generation.

The 1960s' generation used music to create a new identity for themselves, breaking from their parents' mores, values and traditions. From jazz, R&B, rock'n' roll, pop music, funk, jazz rock, hip hop, rap to acid house – music has been used to forge new meaning. Because music influences every aspect of our lives, it is easy to call on to enhance learning, performance and self-discovery.

Jung regarded music as the gateway to the unconscious. Psychologists argue that music is closely linked to emotion. We experience this daily in advertising, films (*Chariots of Fire, Exodus, Sound of Music*), national anthems (*Nkosi Sikel' iAfrica*), classic symphonies (Haydn, Mozart, Beethoven) and contemporary popular music.

Different types of music have different effects on us: alternative rock, blues, gospel, classical, folk, jazz, new age, opera, R&B or soul, hip hop, rock or world music. The list is endless. For performance consultants to use music effectively, it's crucial to understand the influence music has on the emotions, physiology and thinking. So choose carefully, and always listen to a selected piece of music prior to using it in training, coaching or facilitation sessions.

Classical music

There are several styles of classical music to consider, from the 'Vienna classic' of Mozart and Haydn, to the baroque, Renaissance and romantic eras. I use the term 'classical music' to mean formal, European, non-improvised music written before the 1950s. There are different types of composition from which to choose, including chamber music, choral, concerto, opera, orchestral, solo instrumental, symphony and vocal. The most popular for performance consultants is instrumental classical music.

Let me say that this is a very abbreviated introduction to the array of classical music available to you. I am not an expert! I only know what has worked for me, and I therefore recommend that you experiment, and keep a checklist of what music works for you.

Many composers span several periods, because music, like language, is organic in its development. Although I have listed only a few composers within each period, here are some ideas for your learning repertoire – whether you wish to use classical music to energize, inspire, relax or simply to aid listening and communication.

1. *Gregorian chants*: medieval period (c. 550–1450) (Guillaume Dufay, John Dunstable). Gregorian chant, or plainsong, is melodic ritual song that creates a strong sense of relaxation. It moves participants into a meditative state, slowing the breath and heart rate.

2. *Renaissance* (c. 1450–1600) (Allegri, W Byrd, di Lasso, Dowland, Gabrieli, Palestrina, Tallis, Taverner, Victoria (aka Vittoria)). With the rebirth of humanism, cultural achievements and musical innovation came the birth of the 'new music'. Music became more harmonic, although still largely church pieces and secular choral music. Suitable mood-setting pieces for pre-session or mid-morning breaks.

3. *Baroque era* (c. 1600–1750) (Albinoni, J S Bach, Corelli, Gluck (baroque/ classical), Handel, Monteverdi, Pachelbel, Purcell, Scarlatti, Telemann, Vivaldi). Baroque music has vitality, purity and directness of expression. The baroque organ and harpsichord are strongly associated with this period. Music of this era stimulates the brain when studying, writing, reading or working. The fugue is a combination of melodic and mathematical composition, an equal music in which the same theme is played sequentially by voice after voice. It is pleasing to the melodic senses and fascinating to the rational brain because of the intricacy within its development and the miraculous way it solves the problem of hearing all the themes in counterpoint. In this it is much like a successful team pooling ideas, developing them and reaching a harmonious conclusion.

4. *Classicism* (c. 1750–1820) (Mozart, Haydn, Beethoven, Boccherini, Schubert). Revolutionary in its time, music of this period emphasized form, melody, clarity and purity of expression. Improves concentration, memory, visual/spatial awareness and relaxation.

5. *Romantic period* (c. 1820–1910) (Berlioz, Bizet, Brahms, Chopin, Fauré, Grieg, Puccini, Liszt, Mendelssohn, Rossini, Saint-Saëns, Schumann, Richard Strauss, Johann Strauss, Verdi, Wagner, Weber, Tchaikovsky, Rachmaninoff). Mahler was considered a 'classical-romantic'; Elgar an 'English composer', his music choral-orchestral. Vividly depicting an emotional state, the music of this era is imaginative, visionary and romantic – music of grandeur and passion. Choose carefully from piano sonatas, string quartets and symphonies to create an evocative atmosphere.

6. *Impressionistic* (1887–1910) (Debussy and Ravel; closely aligned: Dukas, Florent Schmitt, Roussel, Ibert, Severac). The late period of romanticism culminated in the impressionistic music of Debussy and Ravel. Hinted expression creates a fluid, dreamlike atmosphere with visual power. Good for daydreaming, creative thinking, and unlocking more unconscious, intuitive thinking.

7. *20th and 21st centuries* (c. 1900–present) (Bartok, Britten, Copland, Gershwin, Gorecki, Honegger, Prokofiev, Rachmaninoff, Rodrigo, Vaughan Williams, Satie, Schoenberg, Schumann, Shostakovich, Stravinsky). Including a wide range of styles from neo-classic to neo-romantic, expressionist and atonal. Pieces by Gorecki, Satie and Rodrigo are very suitable for visualization, relaxation and mood setting, or to change an energetic pace to a more reflective state.

8. *Modern* (c. 1945–present) (Babbitt, Boulez, Cage, Glass, Penderecki, Stockhausen) Varied and divergent styles such as serialism, minimalism, chance or electronic music. Choose carefully as it can be difficult for the uninitiated listener. I use selected pieces by Milton Babbitt, Pierre Boulez, Philip Glass, John Cage and Terry Riley for the training room. Explore for yourself first.

Popular music

1. *Rock'n'roll* (from the 1950s onwards) (Elvis Presley, Beach Boys, Beatles, Bob Dylan, Rolling Stones, Grateful Dead, Fleetwood Mac, Credence Clearwater, Joni Mitchell, Dr John, Queen, Bruce Springsteen, Elvis Costello, Dire Straits, Eric Clapton, David Bowie, Van Morrison). Creates energy, stimulates action, relieves tension, but can create tension and a dissonant background if not used wisely! Good for breathing and movement exercises, and for themed workshops and activities.
2. *Top 40 charts* (dance pop, pop rock, soft pop, soft rock) (Elton John, Paul McCartney, Paul Simon, Madonna, Billy Joel, Ricky Martin, Sting, Whitney Houston, Sade, Suzanne Vega, Michael Jackson). Creates energy, movement, takes you out of the moment. Lively break or dance music. A very uplifting CD is *Reflected in Brass*: Evelyn Glennie, the percussionist, playing with The Black Dyke Mills Band.
3. *Blues and jazz* (Louis Armstrong, Dave Brubeck, John Coltrane, Ry Cooder, Miles Davis, Duke Ellington, Bill Evans, Ella Fitzgerald, Herbie Hancock, Billie Holliday, Abdullah Ibrahim, Keith Jarrett, Diana Krall, Charlie Mingus, Thelonious Monk, Oscar Peterson, Bonnie Raitt, Nina Simone, Cassandra Wilson). It's difficult to know where to place Ry Cooder, who spans many styles and is truly a musicologist. Choose from traditional jazz, cool jazz, smooth jazz, New Orleans jazz, bebop and Brazilian and Latin jazz. Inspirational, expressive, releasing emotions of sorrow and happiness, affirming commonality among mankind. Creates ambiance and communality.
4. *World music* (Cuban, Brazilian and Latin jazz, African, reggae, Afro-Caribbean) (King Sunny Ade, Gato Barbieri, Cesaria Evora, Astrud Giberto, Salif Keita, Ladysmith Black Mambazo, Omar Portundo, Flora Purim, Santana, Soweto String Quartet, Cal Tjader). Light orchestral accompaniment to crooning melancholia, smooth Latin jazz and plaintive relaxed romanticism. Wonderfully relaxing, soothing, creating light energy in the background. Excellent for breaks and relaxed synergy in the background.
5. *New Age, Celtic New Age, meditation music* (William Ackerman, Jim Brinkman, Clannad, Phil Coulter, Enigma, Enya, Stephen Halpern, Loreena McKennitt, Mike Rowland, George Winston). Music to enhance well-being and intelligence.

Creates a sense of relaxation in conjunction with a keen mental alertness. Useful background music during group activities.

6. *Spirituals, Gospel* (Clark Sisters, Lorraine Ellison, Aretha Franklin, Mahalia Jackson, Emmylou Harris, Bessie Smith). Creates a sense of peacefulness and awareness of a greater universality or spirituality, taking us beyond our earthly sorrows or pain.

7. *Bluegrass, Country and Western* (Guy Clark, Patsy Cline, Steve Earl, Merle Haggard, George Jones, Alison Krauss and Union Station, Willie Nelson, Dolly Parton, Ricky Skaggs, Gillian Welch, Hank Williams). Stimulates energy, creates a sense of struggle and survival, evokes emotions and the desire to move or dance. Use for stretch breaks.

8. *Folk music* (Contemporary, traditional, British Isles, American folk) (Joan Baez, Robbie Basho, Leonard Cohen, Nanci Griffith, Mary Chapin Carpenter, Pete Seeger). Can be soft, mood-enhancing; useful for themes.

9. *Dance music* (salsa, rumba, soul, pop, rock'n'roll, African percussion, Irish dance). Increases the breathing and heart rate, creates an atmosphere of energy and taking action. *Riverdance* is very good for the lungs!

Although this is only a very small sample of the music available to you, go out and discover a new world of music for yourself. Explore the music that works for your learners. Create a sense of team work, community, motivation, inspiration, vision, creativity, stress reduction and relaxation – and use it.

Legal requirements

Experiment with using music in your seminars and talks, but first check out the legal requirements to use copyrighted material. Any unauthorized rental, public performance, public broadcasting, copying or recording of copyrighted songs and music is an infringement of copyright.

There are three issues: the right to use copyrighted material in seminars, the right to perform previously recorded material and finally, permission to make copies or recordings of CDs, cassettes, records, videos and sheet music.

In most countries there is a special licence agreement for speakers and performance consultants that is cost-effective, providing permission for the use and performance of copyrighted music. Recording rights are usually obtained from the artist's agent.

For more information on what is appropriate for you, speak to a:

● licensing agent for performance consultants and speakers;
● lawyer who specializes in licensing;

- national association for human resources, training and development (ASTD in the USA; CIPD in the UK; IPM in RSA; Australia AHRI; Canada HRDC; Commonwealth IPMA).

Many agents have developed special licences for speakers and training specialists to cover the use and performance of copyrighted music. The Harry Fox Agency (HFA) is a well-known licensing agency in the USA, as are ASCAP (American Society of Composers, Authors and Publishers) and BMI (Broadcast Music, Inc). If you wish to use an existing recording, you'll need to obtain permission from the publisher of the recording. Songfile is a large search agent for CDs, sheet music and tapes. They will also help you to obtain a licence agreement in more than 60 countries.

Singing and learning

Sing your praises

Voice and music can be used very effectively in training, team building and performance development. The use of singing in workshops develops confidence and active communication skills. Think about the sense of community that develops at soccer or rugby matches through the chanting of support for a beloved team. In the working world today, where feelings are relegated to the back-burner, singing touches our emotions, putting emphasis on communication, the ability to listen and the synergy of creative team work.

Success in our organizations is dependent on our communicating creatively with colleagues and customers. Singing is one small tool that we can bring into our learning programmes to tangibly develop personnel. The effects of singing are physical, emotional and psychological. In the training room, singing helps learners to develop confidence and self-esteem. This is also an original way to manage conflict and stress, develop team work and communication skills, problem solve and think creatively.

Singing uses whole-brain thinking. It is the ultimate form of verbal expressiveness available to us. We learn to listen effectively, becoming more aware of the sound and meaning beyond the words themselves. Singing uses the breath fully, exercising the lungs, diaphragm and stomach. Singing is healing for the body and mind, and improves the quality of the speaking voice. Singing creates a sense of community and team spirit with others, bridging the gap between the individual and the organization.

In *Wild Heart Dancing*, Elliot Sobel writes: 'Music is a powerful healer, and no voice is more powerful than the sound of your own voice in song.' Music can provide vision and wisdom for those in leadership. If you are introducing a new product, service or policy, use song to engage the commitment of your workers. In your workshops, have them use song to express themselves, or write new songs that exemplify their new vision, mission or product.

For example, as part of a PR launch when I was working with Holiday Inns, employees from each department created and performed a skit with songs that captured the essence of a new programme, called 'Together We Care'. Songs can shout about new business to clients and customers – and they are a creative way to motivate employees. Song reinforces your message far more effectively than a brochure. Use it in your workshops as a way to involve everyone in creating an ambiance of community and synchronicity.

Music can reinforce an important message at large gatherings. At an annual convention of the National Speakers Association in the USA, a singer listened intently to the keynote speaker's message. He then sang the essence of the message with the piano as accompaniment. At the African Marketing Festival in South Africa, two singers sang tributes to the award winners throughout the entire ceremony. Both events powerfully acknowledged the blood, sweat and tears of those who had made so many corporate dreams come true.

Singing for change

Music is common to every culture and every country. Although we may prefer different types of music, we are all familiar with a wide range. Why not consider using music to cope with organizational change? Change is difficult for everyone in an organization, even the leaders and visionaries of change themselves. It's not often that leaders are given the opportunity to express their thoughts and feelings about the experience of change. Music and song offer an ideal opportunity for individuals to communicate their true feelings and ideas.

Three-songs exercise (2½ hours)

When facilitating a session on organizational change, ask the group to think about what song comes to mind with their current work situation. Ask them to pick a second song to signify the coming transition period, then a third one to depict their ultimate vision – where change is going to take them. Facilitate the group's choice of three songs, exploring how and why these three songs express the feelings, thoughts, opinions, anxieties, hopes and fears of the group as a whole.

A lively and energetic way to perform this exercise is to break the larger group into smaller ones. Give them an hour to brainstorm, to choose their songs and discuss how and why they fit. Give them a second hour to prepare their final presentations to the larger group. Allow time to rehearse and choreograph their act, and decide how they plan to involve the larger group. Another option is to have each group pick one song for one of the three situations: the present, the transitional period, the future.

There is power and energy in allowing music to speak for the group. The results are amazing. People often feel safer expressing themselves through a song, rather than trying to articulate it in their own words. Songs act as metaphors, leaving room for individual interpretation. Songs can move a group from denial of change, into an acceptance of the need to change, and finally to a way of coping with change.

Change: a few selections

Change	Keb Mo
Changes	David Bowie
Changes	Roy Orbison
Changes	Tanya Tucker
Change (Makes You Wanna Hustle)	Donald Byrd
Change My Ways	Duke Ellington
Change of Attitude	Ronnie Dunn
Change of Heart	Diana Ross
Change of Heart	Four Tops
Change of Heart	Huey Lewis and the News
Change of Heart	The Judds
Change What You Can	Marvin Gaye and Tammi Terrell
Change the World	The Graveyard Train
Change Your Mind	Mint Condition
It's Gonna Be Good	Wilson Pickett.

Improvisation exercise (45 minutes)

I developed the idea for this exercise based on a simple improvisation when training with a small Californian company called Corporate Scenes. We were in England, learning basic theatre techniques for trainers with Joyce Dufala and Ivan Midderigh. One of their exercises was to split us into trios, asking us to create new verses for the simple ditty *This Little Light of Mine*.

In subsequent workshops, I introduced the idea of writing new verses to favourite pop songs as a way to celebrate success in the workplace. It worked well in management-development programmes both in the UK with British Telecom, Holiday Inns and Career Track, and in South Africa with the National Union of Mineworkers and the University of Cape Town. The exercise has proven to be fun, inspirational and team building.

Pick a theme the group is working on – anything from leadership, communication, team building, and future vision to sales success and positive thinking.

Work in groups no smaller than four or five, otherwise non-singers feel too self-conscious. This isn't meant to be competitive! Ask them to pick a popular song that gets across the main theme. I suggest they use one verse and the chorus from the song, then add two verses of their own. Ask them to rehearse, then present their show and teach it to the larger group. Great fun, and not to be underestimated as an exercise in creative thinking, motivation and team building.

Vision success exercise (half-day)

Use the metaphor of song to open up a discussion on vision for the organization. When starting the exercise, facilitate the creation of a list of songs to get the group thinking.

Personal songs: ask individuals to work in trios. Have participants in each small group share what song encompasses their personal vision for themselves in the workplace. Ask them to share their three songs and pick one, or create a compilation of the three.

Organizational song: Ask each group to select a separate song to portray their future vision of the company. Each small team's presentation to the larger group will include their two songs, personal and company. In your large group discussion subsequent to the performances, brainstorm how to take their ideas back into the workplace.

This exercise takes three to four hours and is perfect for a half-day session. Here are some examples of the types of songs they may like to choose from.

Motivation:

Motivation	'Angels' (TV theme tune)
Catch A Wave	Beach Boys
That's Motivation	David Bowie
I Shall Sing	Art Garfunkel
We Are The Champions	Queen
Ain't No Mountain High Enough	Diana Ross
You're the Best	Tina Turner

Creativity:

Imagine	John Lennon
Imagination	Al Jarreau
It Must Be Imagination	Kenny Loggins
Imagination	Helen Reddy
You Got Some Imagination	Boz Skaggs
Just My Imagination	Temptations
My Imagination	Bill Withers

Team work:

Good Vibrations	Beach Boys
Celebration	Kool and the Gang
You've Got What It Takes	Marv Johnson
Together	Willie Nelson
Celebrate	Three Dog Night
Together We Stand, Divided We Fall	Tammy Wynette
Together We Stand, Divided We Fall	Marvin Gaye

Leadership:

Stand By Me	Ben E King
Stand By Me	Elvis Presley
Stand By Me	Staples Sisters
Leader Of The Band	Dan Fogelberg
Fearless Leader	Soul Asylum
Follow Me	Odyssey
A Leader Of Men	Ry Cooder

Honouring team spirit

Team-building exercise (45 minutes)

1. *Why this team?* (15 minutes). There's a tremendous energy at the heart of high-performance teams. Songs can be used to build relationships and trust within a team. Facilitate this exercise by sitting in a large circle. Start with a volunteer. Ask participants to speak briefly about why they want to be part of this team, and what they hope to achieve – individually and as a group. Find out what is important to individuals in the group, and how they are connected through the work they do.
2. *Team essence* (10 minutes). Next step, break them into smaller groups (if eight or fewer are in the larger group, have them work as one team). They brainstorm what they feel is the essence of the team: who they are and what they represent.
3. *Rehearsal* (10 minutes). Ask them to choose a song that exemplifies the essence of the team's work together. They can select a specific song, or a tune to which they put their own words.
4. *The show* (10 minutes). After rehearsal, each team performs for the larger group. This exercise can be a ritualistic way to acknowledge each other at the end of the financial year, or even to celebrate their successes at the annual Christmas party.

I worked with a small British Airways team of IT experts at London Heathrow, where several members expressed their desire to make a difference for a company they believed put the customer first. One young man felt he and the team had a chance to further their own growth and development while at the same time contributing to the excellence of the organization. A young female colleague believed that their team work had important consequences for the airline industry, as they worked at the frontline for safety. The song they chose to perform and choreograph was Carole King's *You've Got A Friend*.

A song for success exercise (1 hour)

This is a dynamic exercise for a learning or motivation session. Your group identifies a song that represents success for the organization, its teams and individual employees. The group works out how the song is to be used and where played: in reception, at PR and promotional events, on customer telephone hold, at team building events. Give them time to rehearse, choreograph and perform the song to the larger group. The more you incorporate this song into the working environment, the sooner it will become their success anchor.

Transitions

A quick 'tune-up'

Learning song exercise (20 minutes)

This exercise livens up sessions after breaks, particularly following lunch when all oxygen has left the brain for the digestive tract. In groups of five, participants choose one song that encompasses their learning in the session so far. Give them 10 minutes to quickly practise the portion of the song they have chosen. If they cannot remember the tune or words, let them cheat. Build in five minutes to network with the other groups to discover someone who can fill in what's missing. They quickly trade team members and re-form groups.

Next, ask participants to write the song's words on a visual aid, rehearse, then perform the song to the larger group. It's excellent for inspiration, creativity, memory and recall.

Voice and breath

One of the best ways to develop voice is to work with breathing. There are several easy breathing exercises that will calm the nerves of participants before they teach or perform their songs to each other. Breathing puts oxygen into the brain and the vocal muscles, and gives you back your memory.

I began to work extensively with breathing and movement when, as a hobby, I trained to become a yoga teacher. I wanted to learn the relaxation and breathing exercises that enhance well-being, creating a strong mind–body connection. The yogic philosophy of breath is of incredible benefit to help delegates deal with the stresses and strain of working life.

Breath and belly (5 minutes)

Standing in front of your group, ask them to stand and push away their chairs. Have them put their hands on their belly, letting their chins fall gently down towards the chest, but not letting the chin touch the chest. Ask them to breathe in slowly to the count of four, and breathe out slowly to the count of eight.

Ask them to notice that the belly contracts as they breathe out, and fills up like a balloon as they breathe in. Breathe slowly, otherwise dizziness can occur. Practise this breath three times, then ask them to let their hands fall gradually to their sides, breathe in and lift their heads.

The Ha exhalation (5 minutes)

Let participants move around, chat for a moment, then move into this next exercise. Most people only breathe at the apex of the lungs, and don't take their breath right down into the abdomen. If so, they may experience a feeling of dizziness and instability if they breathe too fast. Have them take it slowly.

Ask participants to put hands on their bellies, lightly bend their knees and lean forward slightly. Ask them to breathe in, then expel their breath with a 'Ha, ha, ha, ha, ha' until there is no more breath to expel. Have them breathe in, stand up, shake their hands, then repeat the exercise twice more. This is a great way to open up the lungs, create energy and bring oxygen back into the brain and circulation.

Do you wanna dance? (40 minutes)

As an energizer after lunch, at a low ebb in the group's energy, or simply as a team builder, combine dance and music. Divide up into smaller teams of three to four. Ask each team to pick a type of dance they were passionate about once in their life, whether it be teenage years, young adult life or today. It could be anything from the lindy hop, mash potato, locomotion, twist, rock'n'roll, rumba and tango to line dancing, bop, swing, waltz, ballroom dancing or square dancing.

Each team has 10 minutes to stand up together and demonstrate to each other their dance choice. The group then chooses one. Give the teams 15 minutes to practise and choreograph their dance. The larger group reconvenes, and each team teaches its dance to the larger group. If you can brief people prior to the day, ask participants to bring an appropriate piece of music for their favourite dance.

Energizer (10 minutes per dance)

These are some other options. As an energizer after lunch, simply have participants choose and practise their dance in their small groups. The next day give them five minutes at some point to practise with the appropriate music. Each team teaches its dance as an energizer after lunch, or as the finale for the workshop. In a five-day Training the Trainer workshop, I have a different team teach its dance each day after the lunch break.

Some of my more creative participants have choreographed their individual dances together to create a compilation, which they teach to the group with their choice of musical accompaniment.

Ideas for dancing music

Here are some ideas to change the pace, to use as energizers or to create your own dance steps.

America (from *West Side Story*)	Bernstein/Sondheim
Blue Suede Shoes/Jailhouse Rock	Elvis Presley
Boogie Woogie Bugle Boy Of Company B	Bette Midler
C'mon Everybody	Eddie Cochran
Diamonds On The Soles Of Her Shoes	Paul Simon
Jumpin' Jack Flash	Rolling Stones
Maggie May	Rod Stewart
Long Tall Sally	Little Richard/Eric Clapton
One (from *A Chorus Line*)	Marvin Hamlisch
Peppermint Twist	Chubby Checker
Red River Rock	Johnny and the Hurricanes
Rock Around The Clock	Bill Haley and the Comets
Take Five	Dave Brubeck
The Lion Sleeps Tonight	Tokens
Willie and the Hand Jive	Eric Clapton.

The final dance

Put on a piece of music. Give your participants two minutes to walk around the room, reflecting on the music, thinking about what they have gained and what they will do differently as a result of your session. Stop the music, and ask everyone to reconvene back in the larger group. Participants share what they have gained personally for themselves and what they will do differently as a result of what they have learnt. Here is a selection of music to help them think reflectively.

Turtle Bay	Herbie Mann
The Missa Luba (A Congolese Mass)	Philips
Canon in D	Pachelbel
Pacific II Jazz Collection	West Coast Jazz Artists
Preludes Op 28	Frederic Chopin
Morning Star	Hubert Laws
Siciliano from the *Second Flute Sonata*	J S Bach

At the very end of your session as delegates walk out the door, handing in their evaluation forms or perhaps stopping to ask you final questions, put on the piece of music you played in the first few moments when they entered your session. That piece of music recreates your initial ambiance of welcome, calm and an atmosphere for learning. It anchors the loop of learning from beginning to end, and is a friendly goodbye.

Search for the music

If you're at a loss as to what music to use in your workshops, play classical. It never sounds dated and is known as the music of the spheres! Classical music can be used to begin and end sessions, during session breaks and as background music during group activities. Use some of the suggestions in this chapter, or go to the classical music section of your favourite music centre and ask for help.

If you want to use rock'n'roll, go to any number of Web sites: Jukebox Learning, Songfile and TimeLife Music. Songfile and Jukebox Learning list hundreds of rock'n'roll songs for use in corporate training. TimeLife Music has created a virtual library of rock'n'roll music since the early 1950s, and also lists compilations of classical music.

Finally, take a morning and rediscover your old record albums, cassettes and CDs, as well as those of your friends. Music is more than just words and harmony. You'll rediscover music that motivates you, moves you and unlocks your feelings, giving you permission to express yourself in song or dance.

Music is fun, practical and creative. We know today that key factors leading to business success are whole-brain thinking, creativity and emotional intelligence. Music and sound develops all three areas, taking organizational and personal development to dizzying new heights.

Music can stir your soul and relax it, too. More than that, it can stimulate thinking, unlock the creative spirit and enhance your mood and the ambiance of the learning environment. Drawing on the latest research into music, expose yourself and your participants to sound, music, and their effect on performance, thinking and creativity. Most of all, have fun doing it.

Where to go for more

Books

Anderson, Yohann (1992) *Songs*, Songs and Creations, San Anselmo, Calif

Campbell, Don (1997) *The Mozart Effect*, Hodder and Stoughton, London

Gaynor, M D and Mitchell, L (1999) *Sounds of Healing*, Random House, New York

Harman, Alec, Mellers, Wilfrid and Milner, Anthony (1964) *Man and His Music*, Barrie and Rockliff, London

Jacobs, Arthur (1965) *A New Dictionary Of Music*, Penguin, London

Jensen, Eric (2000) *Music With the Brain In Mind*, Brain Store, San Diego, Calif

Jourdain, Robert (1997) *Music, The Brain and Ecstasy: How music captures our imagination*, William Morrow, New York

Marcic, Dorothy (1997) *Managing with the Wisdom of Love*, Jossey-Bass, San Francisco

Meyer, Leonard B (1961) *Emotion and Meaning in Music*, University Of Chicago Press, Chicago

Phillips, Maya (1999) *Emotional Intelligence: A practical guide to self-discovery*, Element, Shaftesbury, Dorset, UK

Ostrander, Sheila, Schroeder, Lynn and Ostrander, Nancy (1994) *Superlearning 2000*, Delacorte Press, New York

Scholes, Percy A (1991) *The Oxford Companion To Music*, Oxford University Press, Oxford

Sobel, Elliot (1994) *Wild Heart Dancing*, Simon and Schuster, New York

Journals

Fisher, Tom (1998) High anxiety: preparing trainees to learn, *Training and Development* (December) pp 14–15

Long, Donna M and Lucia, Al (2000) A little bit o' soul, *Training and Development* (July) pp 16–17

Audiocassettes

Campbell, Don (1997) *Music For The Mozart Effect* (vols I, II, III)

Campbell, Don (2000) *Mozart To Go*

Dance steps

Use any search engine on the internet for rock'n'roll + dance steps
StreetSwing's Dance History Archives (Web site: www.StreetSwing.com)

Licensing agents

ASCAP (American Society of Composers, Authors and Publishers) (Web site: www.ascap.com)
BMI (Broadcast Music, Inc) (Web site: www.bmi.com (see licensees/customers))
Harry Fox Agency (Web site: www.nmpa.org)
Jukebox Learning Inc (Web site: www.jukeboxlearning.com)
Songfile (Web site: www.songfile.com) (licensing and search agent)

Songs

Blood, Peter and Patterson, Annie (1992) *Rise Up Singing: The group singing songbook*, Sing Out Publications, Bethlehem, Pa (arranged by category and alphabetically, from ballads to rock'n'roll)

Web sites

Black Coffee Sound Productions: www.blackcoffee.co.uk
The Brainstore: www.thebrainstore.com
Jukebox Learning: www.jukeboxlearning.com
Rock'n'roll Hall of Fame: www.rockhall.com
TimeLife Music: www.timelifemusic.com

8

Doing the dance: rapport and communication or stress?

Getting onto someone else's wavelength is vital in creating rapport. In the first few moments of any workshop or seminar, I try to communicate with all delegates as they enter the room. Welcoming people with a smile, a handshake, introducing myself – asking questions about why they're here, making them feel welcome. I play music to create a friendly, welcoming ambiance, and introduce people to each other.

Rapport is the naturally occurring dance that happens when people communicate. It is a way of harmonizing energies and natural rhythms, such as movement and breathing. Rapport creates a strong sense of acknowledgment – usually outside of conscious awareness.

When people begin to pay attention to how they meet other people, they can refine their rapport skills and enhance their relationships. This is a crucial skill to us as communicators. It requires the ability to use our sensory acuity to see, hear, sense and then match the other person in:

- posture and gestures;
- breathing and energy level;
- speech patterns;
- tonality and rhythm;
- beliefs and values.

In relationships, a lack of rapport creates undue stress. Learning needs to positively engage our emotions, and stress can prevent the assimilation of new information. For the performance coach, rapport is fundamental to effective facilitation and communication. Your participants look to you to lead the way, to set the tone for the day. This chapter looks at specific skills you can develop to enhance rapport with your learners, and to increase your effectiveness as a facilitator.

Doing the dance

Relationships are central to every aspect of our lives, and rapport is central to the success of relationships. You have probably noticed that high achievers naturally make people feel comfortable around them. They genuinely show concern for the other person's values and view of the world. In communication-skills training, rapport is recognized to be the fundamental skill. However, rapport takes place at a level of unconscious awareness, rather than of conscious acknowledgement.

Verbal and non-verbal rapport

Rapport is only one aspect of building a relationship. The American *Webster's Dictionary* defines rapport as a 'harmonious or sympathetic relation' to another person. Building rapport will help you to develop long-lasting relationships, and no matter what field you are in, building relationships is your fundamental skill for success.

Some consultants suggest matching words, body language, clothes, even life interests, to develop rapport with another person. For example, if they love tennis, then you love tennis. But what if you don't play tennis, and what if you really don't like the game? In other words, this approach will only work some of the time. It is possible, even imperative, to build rapport while maintaining your own integrity and sincerity.

To build rapport, it's important to:

- create physical and emotional empathy;
- build relationships based on shared values and goals;
- encourage positive, reflective communication and a feeling of safety;
- be authentic and sincere in your communication.

Building physical rapport

Rapport is something we do naturally. When you observe people with their best friend or life partner, you'll notice they adopt a similar way of speaking and moving. My husband, who is British/South African with an English accent, is often mistaken for an American. Why? Because over the years our phraseology, voice pitch, pace, tone and body language have become so complementary that people assume we are of the same background, despite my strong American accent and his decidedly British one.

Rapport is about reducing our differences and finding common ground upon which to base the relationship. It starts at school when children, particularly teenagers, tend to dress and speak alike. This is carried into the working environment, where people dress to suit their work culture and dress to be accepted or to fit in. We actually start developing rapport skills very early in life.

Rapport is a natural part of communication. We do it easily and unconsciously with those with whom we share common goals and values. It's not so easy with people with whom we feel slightly uncomfortable or ill at ease. To achieve rapport means to be in sync with, to concur simultaneously. If we are out of rapport, we are acting differently from them. For example, if we speak in a loud voice, and they in a soft one, it will be very difficult to create rapport. If they lean forward in excitement and we are so laid back we nearly fall backwards in our chair, it will be tricky to remain on a similar wavelength.

How to be in rapport

To move into rapport, notice how others move, how they sit, how they speak. Begin to slowly adjust your body movements to match theirs. It's important not to mimic their rhythm, just move in accordance with it. Slowly begin to adjust your actions, your voice and your posture to be more in sync with them.

This conscious initiation of rapport will create harmony with others, but at the level of 'unconscious' behaviour. They won't be consciously aware of what you are doing unless you mirror them exactly. Notice how friends, who are naturally in rapport, literally move together, matching words, gestures and tone of voice. It's like watching a dance.

Powerful ways of matching include posture, tone of voice, body and facial expressions, and even your rate of breathing. Notice the rhythm of the other's language, the pitch and pace of their speech. Pay attention to their physical movements. Do they sit still, or express themselves with their hand gestures and facial expressions? To get into physical rapport with each other, begin to align your voice, facial expression, body movement and posture.

Creating emotional rapport

When I was training a newspaper sales team at the *Portsmouth News* in England, one of the keys to understanding customers was to learn how to engage with them emotionally. If clients were upset and angry, the volume and emotional agitation in their voice was a sign of emotional stress. My staff were trained to match their energy, volume of voice (just lower than theirs) and emotional mindset (if they sounded distressed, you matched the distress with voice pitch, pace and tone). This created an immediate sense of acknowledgment, interest and rapport.

Some consultants with a background in psychology advocate the opposite; if the customer is angry, some would argue it's better to show a calm exterior. However, that can make the other person more emotional – your calm front can indicate a lack of interest. If people are stressed emotionally, it is far more effective to match their energy, gradually slowing the pace, lowering the volume of your voice. By matching their energy, you acknowledge their feelings, their point of view and their perception of the issue at hand. This engenders trust, and shows you understand their position. The gap is reduced between the two of you, encouraging a move towards problem solving.

Icebreakers or energizers

Rapport exercises are excellent icebreakers to begin a session, or post-lunch energizers to create renewed energy in the graveyard hour after meals. I incorporate rapport exercises into every one of my workshops. The simple reason is that no matter what you teach, people are constantly meeting other people. Rapport is how to pay attention when meeting another person, whether client, customer, colleague or delegate. Rapport requires sensitivity and acute observation to see, hear, sense and match the other person in:

- posture, gestures and speech patterns;
- breathing, tonality and rhythm;
- energy level;
- pacing, matching and mismatching.

Actors have long known that rapport is fundamental to effective communication. The next exercises will energize your session, stimulating debate and discussion. Introduce them into your workshops to help participants learn specific rapport skills to increase their effectiveness as communicators – no matter what their business or position.

Exercise 1: Walk their walk (15 minutes)

This is a fun, energizing rapport exercise. Use it to alter energy in the room, to introduce people to each other or simply to change pace.

Participants work in pairs. They adopt, exactly, the walking style of their partner. I suggest 10 minutes for this exercise, and tend to demonstrate it first with a volunteer. I'll share a little tip I learnt from one of my colleagues known for his theatre-based training. When he needs a volunteer, Ivan pulls in his breath, stands

Figure 8.1   Copy walk

up tall, smiles and says, 'Thank you, so and so, for volunteering.' It's very rare for a person to say no. Mostly they feel flattered for having been chosen.

Have your group pair up. If the group is an odd number, you as facilitator join one of the pairs. Each pair identifies a 'leader' and a 'follower'. For two minutes, timed by the tutor, the leaders walk in front of the followers, meandering around the room in normal walking style. Have them swing their arms, hips and shoulders naturally, walking at their normal pace.

If you have space, ask the pairs to walk into the corridors, even outside. The leader doesn't turn around to watch his or her partner following behind. The follower walks and moves exactly as the leader moves (shoulders, hips, legs, hands, arms, neck and head). The follower swings arms, moves legs, holds the head and even breathes as the leader breathes.

After two minutes, they switch positions, and the followers become leaders. They repeat the exercise. The leaders walk as normally as possible, swinging arms, moving head and legs in their own inimitable style. The followers walk behind and copy, getting into the moves and 'mental' swing of their partner. At the end of two minutes, ask each pair to share their observations:

● What did they notice about the other person's walk?
● What idiosyncrasies did they notice – such as the way the leader holds his/her head, sweeps his/her feet across the floor, where he/she looks?

- What did it feel like to be the other person?
- What did they learn about the other person?

This reflection is not an analysis of why their partner moves in a particular way. The point is to discuss what was easy, or difficult, about 'walking another's walk', and what they learnt about themselves and each other.

Bring the group back together, asking a participant to flip what the group learnt. What did they learn about rapport? What did they learn about the other person? How will this affect their communication style? Classic answers include:

- They look up; I look down; we see the world differently.
- They walk fast; I walk slow; we perceive life at a different pace.
- I can't move as they move!
- They seem reflective in their motions; I'm more active.

This exercise reminds us that it is sometimes very hard to match others, to get onto their wavelength. If we are able to move as they move, to see the world as they do, we learn more about them and how to communicate effectively with them.

Exercise 2: Behavioural flexibility (15 minutes)

This is a fun and often comical exercise. Participants choose two partners, and position two chairs facing each other. Two individuals sit in the facing chairs, and the third person (acting as observer) sits in a third chair, placed at a 45-degree angle facing the other two chairs.

You may like to demonstrate this with a volunteer. Person A talks; Person B mirrors A's movements exactly, without speaking a word! Explain that this is artificial; in real life we don't mimic another person's movements exactly. However, this exercise is to learn more about rapport. For topics, I often suggest favourite desserts or holidays. Allow 15 minutes, including the review.

Instructions

1. First movement: Person A starts talking. Person B mirrors Person A's body language, and moves exactly as A moves.
   - Get a feel for what it's like to be someone else.
   - Do their dance; mirror their postures and gestures.
   Tutor claps to switch after one minute.
2. Second movement: Repeat the exercise, reversing roles.

The group review is not a session for psychoanalysis! Each pair discusses what it felt like to be mirrored so precisely, and what they learnt about each other. If you have worked with observers, ensure all three in the trio have a chance to work as observer, speaker and mirror. Observers comment on what looked easy, what looked difficult and what happened during the exchange. Once back in the larger group, ask:

- What did they learn about each other?
- How does this help us to create rapport with others?
- How is this useful back in the workplace?

Although artificial, this exercise is informative. It helps us to develop behavioural flexibility. Highlight examples where the group has been in rapport non-verbally during the session: one leg crossed over the other, arms folded, hands on face, scribbling notes, talking at once, leaning forward, leaning back, sitting on the edges of their chairs.

The purpose of this exercise is to show that we can develop rapport with someone simply by adopting their style, moving when they move, adopting their rhythm – but certainly not mimicking or copying. We move as they move, breathe as they breathe, and our communication begins to take on its own rhythm. You often see two people talking, and you can see that they are in sync. They are moving their arms, hands and bodies in harmony with each other. When out of sync, their body language moves in opposition to that of the other person.

Exercise 3: Match, mismatch (15 minutes)
Ask participants to choose other partners, working in pairs or trios. Place two chairs, facing each other at a comfortable distance, with an observer's chair facing both chairs at a 45-degree angle.

You may like to demonstrate this with a volunteer. For a topic, have them choose something they are passionate about. It may be sports, politics, pets, gardening, reading, music, baking, walking. Allow 15 minutes, including the review.

Instructions

1. Person A starts talking.
2. Person B mirrors A's movements exactly (for 30 seconds) but doesn't speak.
3. After 30 seconds, Person B makes a very strange move – ham it up! (Person B may stand up, turn the chair upside down, inspect the bottom, then sit down once again; or Person B may check his/her watch, tap it, take it off, put it to his/her ear, put it back on and resume looking at and mirroring his/her partner.) While Person B mismatches, for about 10 seconds only, Person A tries to keep talking and to keep eye contact with Person B. I've seen some funny

things, with Person A getting down on the floor trying to keep eye contact with Person B who has turned his/her chair upside down to inspect the paint job underneath; or Person A following Person B to the window, trying to keep eye contact as Person B pretends to climb out!

4. Sitting down once again, Person B matches A's body language (as if nothing strange has taken place).
5. The tutor claps to switch after about 60 seconds, making sure each pair has matched, mismatched and matched again. Repeat the exercise, reversing roles.

Before returning to the group circle for the review, ask each pair to chat about what happened – what it felt like when their partner deliberately stopped listening, stopped paying attention. Back in the group, ask:

- What was the effect on the speaker when the listener ceased to listen? (Try to elicit all of their emotions, typically frustration, annoyance, hurt.)
- Do people do this in real life?
- How does this break rapport?
- How does it affect feelings such as trust and comfort with each other?
- What other skills do we need to develop? (For example, patience, active listening skills, non-verbal rapport, concentration, curiosity, focus, reflective listening skills.)

To summarize, explain that we are affected at the level of behaviour (what people say and do), and at the level of identity (who they are, self esteem and self-confidence). Have the group present examples in everyday working life, and ask where they can make changes to improve rapport (with clients, colleagues, their boss).

Behavioural flexibility

The above exercise is artificial, but informative. It helps us to develop behavioural flexibility. If we can move as other people move, if we remain curious about their view of the world, if we set our own egos aside for the moment, we'll be able to connect with each other. How is this is useful in the workplace? How might they use what they have learnt?

We develop rapport with others by simply adapting their style, moving as they move, adopting their rhythm – without mimicking. As we begin to move with them, breathing as they breathe, our communication together takes on its own momentum.

To agree or disagree

We have discussed how to create rapport, how to do the other person's dance, matching body language and voice tone to harmonize with someone else. But what if we don't agree with what the other person is saying? How can we disagree but still respect their point of view and maintain our integrity? Rapport is about matching and mismatching sensitively and respectfully. Try out this exercise to experiment with agreeing and disagreeing.

Exercise 4: Non-verbal match (15 minutes)

Choose new partners. Participants continue to stand, facing each other. You may choose to demonstrate with a volunteer. Participants choose a topic from the flipchart list. Allow 10 minutes with discussion.

Instructions

1. Person A starts talking.
2. Person B matches A's body language and non-verbal movements, but verbally disagrees with Person A's words and ideas.
3. The tutor claps to switch after one minute.
4. Repeat the exercise with roles reversed: Person B starts talking. Person A mismatches verbally, but matches body language.

In the group review, each pair discusses what it was like to have others agree with their gestures and body language but disagree verbally. In the larger group, discuss the following questions.

● What was the effect on the speaker?
● Did it feel more or less sincere than the previous exercise?
● What about rapport between the two?

Try this exercise in reverse: agree with words and disagree with body language.

Research shows that we keep rapport more effectively if we agree with our gestures and body language. There is an unconscious level of rapport created by the congruity and synchronicity of matching body language. As a rule of thumb, you can disagree verbally and still stay in rapport if agreement takes place at the unconscious level of non-verbal communication.

● What did your participants learn from this exercise?
● How can they apply this back in the workplace with clients and colleagues?
● What effect will this have on their relationships at work and home?

Body language

In general, relationships are maintained more through rapport than by agreeing with everything the other person says. It is easier to stay in rapport with someone you like, but our body language gives us away if we are uncomfortable with the other person. Body language sends a message about you: what kind of a listener you are, and whether you are interested in the other person.

Non-verbal communication is often communicated and received at an unconscious level. Research shows that the impact of your message is:

- 55 per cent body language;
- 38 per cent tone of voice;
- 7 per cent words or content.

Some researchers say that anything from 65 per cent to 90 per cent of every conversation is interpreted through body language. That gives us some food for thought! Watch those clicking pens, hands in the pockets, covering your mouth with your hands, folding your arms in front of you, pointing or standing with your hands behind your back. Keep hand gestures above waist level so that the audience looks at your face, and hears the words you are using. Otherwise they will be looking at your feet, or wherever you are gesturing, thus distracting their attention.

Voice tone is a very important part of body language, and by varying your tone of voice you can change the meaning intended. If you take a simple sentence, 'How are you today?', you can ask it in a breezy, optimistic manner, an aggressive way or with sarcasm. You convey your message, not just with the words you use, but with your tone of voice. Add to that your gestures – and you ensure the message you want to convey is the one that is received.

Communication and stress

Inadequate communication skills are one of the largest contributors to stress in the workplace. The inability to get your message across, or to understand another's message, can damage self-esteem and confidence. Most workshops involve some interpersonal connection with others; you as the facilitator are responsible for enabling the communication process.

Rapport is all about communication, and in relationships a lack of rapport creates stress. Hence the number of workshops to develop communication skills – many based on the psychology of communication. As performance development focuses more and more on technology as a medium for training, we are in danger of losing the importance of people, and our people skills.

When you communicate with another person, you respond with your own thoughts and feelings. What you say or do is influenced by your personal thoughts, feelings and kinesthetic reaction. Your behaviour is a result of the internal reaction to what you hear and see. Your internal responses trigger your reactions. In the same way, the other person responds to what you say and do.

We worked with emotional intelligence in Chapter 5, and learnt that our social competencies determine how we handle relationships. Social competence is a combination of empathy (an awareness of the other's feelings, needs and concerns) and social skills (being adept at producing desirable responses in others, and communicating clearly and convincingly). If stressed, we lose our ability to collaborate, cooperate and develop rapport.

The second component of emotional intelligence, personal competence, is how we manage ourselves. This involves emotional awareness (a recognition of our own emotions) and self-control (managing our own disruptive emotions and impulses).

Emotions and physiology

Our emotions have a huge impact on our motivation and performance, and they have a powerful effect on our nervous system. Our nervous system regulates everything from how much insulin is secreted, to our blood-pressure levels. If we perceive communication with someone else as threatening, our nervous system takes us into the fight-or-flight response. This can lead us to an inappropriate response to the other person – mentally, physically, emotionally or behaviourally.

A typical mental response to stress is persistent negative thoughts about the other person, and a loss of concentration when confronted with that person, making rapport even harder to attain. A physical response to stress could be a rapidly beating heart, indigestion or headache. Emotional stress symptoms include anything from lack of self-esteem, poor self-image and anxiety, to a lack of a sense of humour. Behaviourally, we may respond with poor work performance, bad time management, overworking and eating disorders or even withdrawal from relationships – all with serious impact on performance, rapport and communication with others.

Stress busters

Stress and learning

There is a tremendous difference between stress and challenge. If stressed, you feel threatened by new learning experiences. The brain feels under threat, and consequently takes in less information. If you are relaxed and feel positive about the challenge of learning something new, you will learn and remember more easily. Learning needs to engage our emotions positively. Colour, music, visuals, games and activities help to create a calm, positive ambiance for learning.

Exercise: Breathing and relaxation

The best way to handle stress is through positive visualization, exercise, breathing and proper diet. When you wake up in the morning, spend five minutes visualizing how you will handle your day (your projects, your clients and colleagues) positively, confidently and effectively.

Remember to breathe in slowly through the nose, exhaling through the mouth. That brings the greatest amount of oxygen into the brain and body, invigorating and relaxing you at the same time. Proper breathing will enhance your ability to handle stress, as well as rejuvenate the brain. Breathing slowly through your nose helps you think clearly and reduces physical and mental stress. Practise it all day long! Notice how your breathing changes when you are stressed, and notice how your face, shoulders, arms and hands tense up.

Exercise and relaxation are the most direct ways to benefit from proper breathing. Exercise relaxes muscles. It remineralizes your bones and cleanses the bloodstream through oxygenation. Relaxation replenishes the brain and helps to protect it from stress and fatigue.

Exercise gives you the physical energy and brain power needed to think quickly and clearly on your feet. Never underestimate the importance of including some kind of exercise in your working day. It will be the making of you.

Deep-breathing exercise (5 minutes)

Teach your participants this exercise. Sit in a comfortable position with your arms and shoulders relaxed, or lie back on the floor. Inhale, taking your breath in through your teeth, counting to five. Exhale, breathing through your mouth, counting to 10. As you breathe in, gradually fill the belly like a balloon filling with air.

As you exhale, your abdomen contracts and you gently relax your face, jaw, shoulders, arms and legs. Practise breathing for 10 cycles. Practise this exercise every day for five minutes, and you will gradually be able to do it naturally when you need to relax mind and body.

Shoulder-roll exercise (5 minutes)

During the working day, ease out your shoulder muscles by breathing in, lifting both shoulders as high as you can, rolling them backwards five times, then forward five times, letting your elbows roll with them.

Visualization exercise (15 minutes)

1. Play a piece of relaxing music.
2. Close your eyes and begin to breathe slowly, in and out. Draw the breath in for five counts, and release for five counts.
3. Continue counting your breath. Imagine that you are breathing into every part of your body, from the head down to your feet.
4. In your mind's eye, imagine you are walking on the top of a mountain that overlooks a beautiful expanse of ocean.
5. Notice the colours around you and above you.
6. Be aware of the peaceful sounds that surround you – notice the sounds of the birds, trees, breeze and the surf or any distant sounds.
7. Feel yourself relaxing in every part of your body as you walk, breathe and take in your beautiful surroundings.
8. As you relax more and more, visualize yourself achieving whatever you set out to achieve. See it, hear it, feel it.
9. Gradually bring your consciousness back to your breathing, bringing your awareness back into the room where you sit.
10. As you open your eyes, picture in your mind's eye your ability to breathe, relax and achieve your vision.

Presentation excellence

The way adults learn best is not always the way trainers teach. Howard Gardner, in his book *Frames of Mind*, identifies a combination of nine intelligences that contribute to learning. How are you using a combination of these to present information and develop rapport with your audience?

- linguistic: talent with language (listening, speaking, reading, writing);
- mathematical/logical: talent with maths, logic, systems, numbers;
- visual/spatial: ability to visualize, appreciation of colour, line, form;
- auditory/musical: ability to understand rhythm, beat, pitch, sounds, dialogue;
- kinesthetic/physical: talent with movement;
- interpersonal: ability to communicate and interact with people;
- intrapersonal: inner control/focus, objective self-analysis;
- naturalistic: ability to observe, relate and respond to nature;
- philosophical/ethical/existential: examines the meaning of life (ethics, values).

Using appropriate language

What about the words you choose to use? Although they represent only 7 per cent of the message (tone of voice and gestures give meaning to the words), we now know that you can develop rapport with another person by using language in a way that matches the way he/she thinks, speaks and takes in information.

In an ideal world (30 minute exercise)

This is a wonderful exercise to help participants understand the power of language and how it relates to the way they think, use language and behave. It's particularly interesting to discover how their partner uses language, and what effect it has on their ability to communicate and develop rapport.

Ask your participants to do the exercise individually first, referring to the list of visual, sound and feeling predicates for help. Then ask them to share their descriptions with partners. Use this exercise as an icebreaker, a communication skills exercise or to understand how language can be influential in interpersonal dynamics.

I use this exercise as part of any programme to develop flexible thinking and communication skills. Allow 10 minutes to write; 10 minutes to discuss with partners; 10 minutes to review in the larger group.

1 *Describe your ideal day.* Write down what you would see, what you would hear and what you would feel during your ideal day. Try to be as descriptive as you can in terms of pictures, feelings and sounds.
2. *Describe your ideal environment.* Write down what you would see, what you would hear and what you would feel in your ideal environment. Try to describe it in terms of pictures, feelings and sounds.
3. *Share your two descriptions with a partner.* Notice how your partner uses language to describe both situations, and whether the two of you use language similarly or differently in terms of using pictures, feelings or sounds.

Group review

● What did you learn about how the other person uses language to interpret the world around him or her?
● Does your partner prefer visual, auditory or kinesthetic language?
● What did you learn about each other by doing this exercise?
● How will this exercise help you to improve rapport and communication with others?

Visual	Sounds	Feelings
Picture	Tune	Touch
Clear	Note	Handle
Perspective	Ring	Finger
See	Shout	Shock
Flash	Growl	Stir
Bright	Tone	Strike
Outlook	Sing	Impress
Spectacle	Sound	Move
Glimpse	Hear	Hit
Preview	Clear	Grope
Short-sighted	Say	Impact
Discern	Scream	Stroke
Distinguish	Click	Tap
Illustrate	Static	Rub
Delineate	Rattle	Crash
Paint	Ask	Smash
Clarify	Amplify	Tangible
Graphic	Harmonize	Crawl
Show	Muffle	Tickle
Expose	Compose	Grab
Depict	Alarm	Carry
Aim	Hear	Warm
Visualize	Listen	Rough
Watch	Noisy	Soft
Look	Talk	Smooth
Horizon	Shout	Cool
Picture	Clap	Slippery
View	Yell	Tight
Pinpoint	Silence	Unsettled
Scrutinize	Squeal	Lukewarm
Dim	Speechless	Hunch
Watch	Vocal	Stress
Witness	Verbose	Emotional

Listen to other speakers

How often do you attend other speakers' workshops to develop ideas and stretch yourself? It's easy to read books and listen to audiotapes while travelling, but it takes an investment of time and energy to attend someone else's seminar. One of the best ways for performance developers to stretch themselves is to work with another performance consultant, learning new methods and integrating ideas. This also builds your network of contacts and references.

Find associated industries in which you can gain exposure to top presenters. Sit in on their seminars, introduce yourself and model one new technique in your next workshop. Also, listen to audiotapes while you drive, watch videos whenever possible and read at least one new book a month to improve or develop new ideas.

Once in a while learn about something not connected to your area of expertise and draw a parallel with your work. What can you learn from it? The more you stretch yourself, moving outside of your comfort zone, the more you increase your knowledge, expertise and willingness to take risks.

I'll never forget a Fred Pryor speaker whose workshop I decided to attend for fun in London. I chose a presenter working with similar audience sizes to mine. I was completely enthralled by Mary Colletti's dynamism and energy, and when speaking together at the end of the day, realized we had so much to share and learn from each other. She woke up and shook up her audience with tremendous energy and humour. Her unusual metaphor of the rodeo and actually used a lasso throughout her seminar, was courageous in a British culture with little experience of rodeos, but it worked brilliantly. Being unusual, it had tremendous impact.

Modelling excellence

Rapport is about excellence. Model the excellence of other presenters who facilitate in a completely different style to yours. At the African Marketing Festival in Johannesburg recently I was thrilled to see so many speakers dashing in and out of each other's seminars to pick up new ideas – and check out if there was anything different they could beg, borrow or steal!

The Oscar-winning actor Anthony Hopkins credits his success to Richard Burton, who convinced him that he too could become an actor. The fact that another Welshman could make it gave Hopkins hope and courage. President Bill Clinton has spoken many times of his meeting with President Kennedy as an impressionable teenager. We all have a mentor, model or teacher who has influenced us in some way.

To model excellence in others, first discern the sequence of things they say and do that enables them to develop rapport with their audience. Identify what one thing you want to model, and begin to practise it.

- What do they do specifically that connects them to their audience?
- What do they do that you don't do to connect and communicate their ideas?
- What specific qualities do they have that the audience relates to?

Modelling excellence in yourself is best. We often think other people are more talented than we are, or have more natural resources to call on. Nothing is further from the truth. There is no doubt that some people make amazing use of their inner resources and the opportunities they create for themselves. But if you analyse someone's talent to sing, dance, play the guitar, present or deliver training, it all breaks down into images, sounds, feelings and the use of voice and physical motor skills. The secret ingredient is how they put it together.

What do heroes have to do with it?

Heroes and heroines create a sense of possibility. Putting ourselves in their shoes helps us to see with a fresh eye, a new perspective. Who are your heroes? How can you learn from them? Take a look at what your favourite hero or heroine does. See yourself doing things that they do with excellence. They help to remove our self-imposed boundaries, and to understand that each moment is bursting in its potential for learning.

Focusing on heroes and heroines

From the age of 12, I'd admired Clint Eastwood. Not long ago, I put myself in his shoes to solve a problem. In my mind's eye, I pictured myself as Clint, sitting in the saddle, looking out over a land of cattle rustlers (from some film way back in my memory). I took on his screen persona of calm, strength, a slow pace and reflective thinking. The learning for me? To slow down, give myself time out and to remember to take a break. I realized, in that moment, that I was on the road to burn out – and that I needed to cross a week out of my diary to read, relax and rejuvenate.

Exercise (10 minutes)

1. Who are your favourite heroes or heroines?
2. What is it they do that inspires you?
3. Imagine yourself in their shoes. Feel yourself taking on the specific qualities you want to emulate. Feel yourself becoming them. Be inspired the way they are inspired.
4. What can you learn from becoming them?
5. What do they have to teach you?

A celebrity's vision

Think of one of your favourite celebrities. What is it about that person that inspires you? What qualities or characteristics would you like to adopt? Now picture yourself up on a screen in a movie theatre. Run the movie as if you are that celebrity; live out the scene from beginning to end. Brighten the colours, heighten the sounds, enrich the feelings. Now step into the movie and associate into it in every way. Feel yourself becoming all of those qualities that excite you, allowing you to do what you want to do, and achieve your dream. Feel it, hear it, see it: your dream vision.

Tape your sessions

To check that you are on track with the experts, make a video clip of a few hours of your session. Ask one or two colleagues to evaluate it with you. If there's no possibility of making a video, ask a colleague to sit in on one of your sessions and give you constructive feedback. Don't forget about motivational and developmental feedback. Here's a checklist to help your evaluation:

1. Do you lack vitality when communicating with participants?
2. Do you move around too much, or not enough?
3. How do you use your hands when speaking?
4. Do you cover your mouth when speaking?
5. Are your facial gestures, body movements and voice in sync?
6. Do you nod your head so often when listening that you look like a puppet?
7. Are you slouched in your chair at the end of the day?
8. Do you change the furniture for participants and yourself regularly?
9. What idiosyncratic habits could you lose (hands in pockets, scratching an itchy nose, checking your tie, running hands through your hair)?
10. What are you doing to distract learners from your message?

Develop the power of questions

Your job as a performance coach is to ask questions. They function like an electric shock to the brain. As soon as the brain is asked a question, it goes on 'search and find'. Questions stimulate thinking – and are our most useful learning tool.

Ask in-depth, thought-provoking questions. Questions help when coaching, managing, facilitating and training. They keep your participants focused. Whenever a question is asked, someone is compelled to answer. Questions help stimulate thought. They are an aid in persuasion, and help you to regain control when the discussion goes off track. As a coach, that kind of power means you can plan your sessions much more strategically.

Many facilitators feel their job is to tell it like it is. In fact, the more you ask questions, the more your participants search for the answers, the more engaged they are, the more interested they are in learning – and the more they benefit from the session. Questions create attention and rapport as well as participation.

Questions create discovery

Giving a lecture will not engage your participants in learning. When participants disagree with you, instead of becoming defensive, take it that they are curious. Ask the others in the group what they think. Your job isn't to defend your point of view, it's to facilitate thinking, learning and discovery.

People are more committed to learning that they discover for themselves. Because they connect to it on a personal and emotional level, they are far more likely to make a change. Your questions can lead to that 'a-ha' moment when participants get it. Once they've got it, they'll be thirsty for more.

Breathing, nerves and stage fright

Pre-presentation nerves create stress, and can break rapport with your audience. Breathing is the key to handling nerves. I remember when I was first hired as a television presenter for an afternoon women's magazine programme in the UK. I asked the producer if I could hold onto a table as the crew counted down, 'Ten, nine, eight, seven ...'. I held onto the table for dear life, holding my breath, and as the cameraman said 'One', I took a breath. Oxygen flooded back into my brain and my bloodstream, and I started to talk. Breathing is the stuff of life to control your nerves.

Laurence Olivier

A Shakespearean actor once told my husband that as a young man, hired to play a walk-on part at London's National Theatre, he was startled to come across the star of the play, Laurence Olivier, in the wings, making extraordinary facial expressions and uttering nonsense in that famously sonorous voice: 'Be-ba-bo-boo-hoo-ha-hee-hoh-hum...' The greatest actor of his day was calming his nerves and warming up. Try it!

Relaxing is no small matter. Knowing how to relax is an art. Art Feinglass, in his 'Tips from the acting world', explains that 75 per cent of accomplishing your desired results, whether on stage or in life, depends on relaxing before and during a performance. Tension interferes with clear thinking, the function of the brain, the ability to think clearly and the use of your five senses.

Limber, stretch and dance

So: limber up, stretch, breathe and yawn. Tense and release your facial muscles, tense and release your shoulders, arms and hands, legs and feet. Shake out your hands and feet. Then get up and dance to a piece of your favourite music.

Vocal warm-up exercise (5 minutes)

This is a five-minute exercise you can do sitting in a chair or lying on the floor. Place your hands on your belly and close your eyes.

1. *Breathing from the belly.* Breathe in slowly through the nose; breathe out gently through the mouth. Do this exercise five to 10 times as if you are filling a balloon as you inhale. Let the air out of the balloon as you exhale. Notice how different you feel: your face, neck, shoulders, arms, hands, legs and feet are beginning to let go of any tensions.
2. *Massaging your jaw.* Massage your jaw with your fingers to ease out any tension. We keep an enormous amount of stress and tension in these muscles. Let your mouth hang open by applying pressure gently with your fingers along the jawbone.
3. *Alphabet soup.* Inhale deeply, then on one exhalation say the alphabet. Inhale a second time, and slowly on one breath run through the alphabet twice. On a third inhalation, breathe slowly out as you say the alphabet three times. See if you can run through the alphabet four times on the next inhalation, breathing out slowly.

Letting go of mistakes

Letting go allows you to move forward with greater confidence and belief in yourself. If you cannot let go of mistakes, you will focus more on you than on your participants, risking a loss of rapport. The definition of letting go is 'inner surrender as a result of intelligent choice'. To let go of mistakes:

- Recognize what you've done well.
- Look at your mistake – what could you have done differently?
- Let go of the mistake, having gained the learning.

The ability to let go releases you, giving you wisdom, energy and emotional freedom. When you stop obsessing about mistakes you've made, it allows you to focus on the next step.

Developing flexibility

Flexibility is the fundamental skill in learning to let go. Imagine yourself a strong, sturdy tree. Your roots dig deep into the ground; your branches reach up to the sky. Your roots keep you stable and strong, yet your trunk and branches move, bending with the wind. Bend with the learning you gain from your mistakes. Learn to let go:

1. *Mentally:* let go of obsessive thoughts, unrealistic expectations, beliefs and opinions that no longer serve you. Develop new values and beliefs that help you mentally move on.

2. *Emotionally:* let go of guilt, fear and anger. Identify positive emotions that will motivate and challenge you to move towards your vision.
3. *Motivation:* let go of that driving force, of wanting something too much. Identify short and long-term goals with action steps that challenge and stretch you, but are achievable.
4. *Behaviourally:* change any actions that prevent you from letting go. What are you doing that works? What isn't working? Identify how to turn your negative actions into positives.
5. *Physically:* let go by breathing, exercise and relaxation. Where can you make time for yourself in your day? Just do it.

Letting go of criticism

- Adopt a posture of curiosity.
- Be courageous – ask questions to find out more.
- Consider the merit of the criticism.
- What, if anything, can you do differently?
- Ask whether the criticism is valid or invalid.
- If valid, what can you learn?
- If invalid, let it go.

In conclusion

The ability to establish rapport is a fundamental communication skill. Rapport is about reducing our differences and finding common ground upon which to base the relationship. It's an essential skill for trainers, coaches, consultants and managers – any professional who deals with people and manages group processes.

Powerful ways to develop rapport include matching posture, gestures, tone of voice, facial expressions, even breathing. Get into physical rapport with the other person; notice the rhythm of the other's language and movements. Developing emotional rapport reduces the gap between two people and encourages a move towards problem solving.

Actors have long known that rapport is fundamental to communication. Adopting other people's style, the way they move and speak, can be seen as mimicking if we just copy them. Instead, get into their rhythm, try to see their view of the world.

Relationships are not maintained by agreeing with everything the other person says, but through rapport. A lack of rapport can create stress in communicating with others, and stress can threaten new learning experiences. The best way to handle stress is through visualization, exercise, breathing and relaxation. Move towards personal mastery. Model excellence in yourself in others, and develop flexibility by letting go of mistakes.

Where to go for more

Books

Alder, Dr Harry (1996) *NLP For Managers*, Piatkus, London

Brewer, Dr Sarah (2000) *Simply Relax,* Duncan Baird, London

Gardner, Howard, (1985) *Frames of Mind: The theory of multiple intelligences*, Basic Books, New York

Goleman, Daniel (1996) *Emotional Intelligence,* Bloomsbury, London

O'Connor, Joseph and Seymour, John, (1993) *Introducing NLP: Psychological skills for understanding and influencing people*, Aquarian Press, London and San Francisco

O'Connor, Joseph and McDermott, Ian (1996) *Principles Of NLP*, HarperCollins, London and San Francisco, 1996

Sutton, Jan (2000) *How to Thrive On Stress*, How To Books, Oxford

Pease, Allan (1984) *Signals: How to use body language for power, success and love*, Bantam, London

Phillips, Maya (1997) *Emotional Excellence*, Element, Shaftesbury, Dorset

Stout, Sunny (1993) *Managing Training*, Kogan Page, London

Robbins, Anthony (1989) *Unlimited Power*, Simon and Schuster, London

Wainwright, Gordon (2000) *Body Language*, McGraw-Hill, New York

Walters, Lilly (1993) *Secrets Of Successful Speakers: How you can motivate, captivate and persuade,* McGraw-Hill, New York

Tapes and videos

Arapakis, Maria (1994) *Confidence, Composure and Competence*, Career Track, Boulder, Co

Robbins, Anthony (1986) *Unlimited Power*, Nightingale-Conant, Niles, Illinois

Tracy, Brian with Rose, Colin (1995) *Accelerated Learning Techniques*, Nightingale-Conant, Niles, Illinois

Journals

Caudron, Shari (2000) Learners speak out, *Training and Development* (April) pp 52–57

Cruse, Linda and Hoare, Joe (1999) Everyday stress busters, *Training and Development* (November) p 65

Feinglass, Art (2000) Tips from the acting world, *Training and Development* (August) pp 20–21

Warfield, Anne (2001) Do you speak body language? *Training and Development* (April) pp 60–61

Web sites

Body language: www.impressionmanagement.com

It's not what you say: www.peasetraining.com

Rapport training and events: www.rapportsydney.com

So to speak: www.ritamorris.com

9

Facilitation metaskills and deep democracy

Today, facilitation is recognized as one of the most important management skills to effect change, improve performance and achieve organizational goals. But to be a top facilitator requires a broad range of interpersonal and conflict-resolution skills, as well as great insight and awareness of oneself when facilitating a group process.

Facilitation is not training, and the first part of this chapter will share with you the skills required of you as a facilitator. Next, we will discuss the metaskills, or attitudes, you need to bring to the facilitation process. Finally, we will take a look at the principles of deep democracy. This is one of the most powerful tools in your armoury as a facilitator.

Deep democracy is a highly effective way to facilitate group decisions and begin to manage group conflict. It is a revolutionary way of facilitating training, meetings or any group process where decisions need to be reached.

Briefly, the specific intention is inclusion, even of dissenting voices. Deep democracy includes the dissenting voice because it recognizes that it contains a wisdom for the group. It views dissenters as emissaries of a submerged issue that needs to be brought into the open. The basic premise is that the team will be stronger if everyone's voice is heard. This means hearing and including the wisdom of the minority.

I shall try to present a complex process in clear layman's terms. This will inevitably simplify ideas that psychologists and academics have worked on and refined in great detail. You will find this process, however, an extraordinarily profound and powerful one.

Whether you have been asked to facilitate a brainstorming, conflict-resolution or decision-making session, this chapter will set you on the road to becoming a world-class facilitator. The classic tools of facilitation, in combination with process psychology's metaskills and the principles of deep democracy, will take you one step further – into the realm of profound and long-lasting behaviour change at work.

Facilitation versus training

Before launching into the concept of deep democracy, it's important to understand the difference between the roles of facilitator and trainer.

The facilitator's role

The role of the facilitator is to help participants set their objectives. In essence, the facilitator will not decide the content of the meeting. Rather than being a group leader, the facilitator assists the group to find appropriate methods for the issues that arise. The participants set the pace, and the facilitator guides and comments on the group process. The facilitator helps the group become aware of its issues.

The trainer's role

The trainer or teacher's fundamental role is to help participants learn and apply new knowledge, skills and attitudes. In training, the objectives of the meeting are based on the group's learning needs, and it is the trainer who designs and produces the content of the session. A trainer will lead and guide the group through a process of learning, instructing the participants in activities and experiential exercises. Most important, and different from the role of a facilitator, the trainer is goal-, task- and learning-oriented. The facilitator's role, on the other hand, is to create awareness.

Combining roles

Many performance consultants combine the tools of facilitation and training. Deep democracy primarily requires the use of facilitation to guide the group process, helping the group to make a decision, or a number of decisions. If you are training the group in how to use deep democracy, then teaching may be involved to impart the process. This is the beauty of this method: you empower the group by teaching them the process.

By combining the two roles of trainer and facilitator, the participants become less dependent on you. It leaves them with a way to continue once you are no longer there. If you embody both roles, trainer/facilitator, you may be expected to understand something about the subject, but not necessarily be an expert on the subject itself. In most groups, your credibility tends to increase the more knowledge you have about the field or the profession within which you are training or facilitating. It is often a matter of understanding the jargon of the group, rather than the nature of the work itself, that adds to your credibility.

For example, if the participants are marketers, you may not be expected to understand how marketing works, but you will need to understand some marketing terminology, or the difference between direct marketing, advertising, public relations and sales promotion.

If you are facilitating only, you need know nothing about the subject. However, go in without your ego! You are there to bring awareness to the group. It is better if you don't understand their industry or professional language: this allows you to facilitate effectively. When we look at secondary processes (what is not said explicitly by the group), an ignorance of the subject matter helps you to draw that out and create awareness within the group.

Facilitators are not goal-oriented. Your purpose is to give awareness by guiding the group process. Your skill is to draw out and use the expertise and wisdom within the group. They have all the resources they need within themselves. It is your job to facilitate them finding their own solutions – which they own and to which they can be committed.

Managing the group process

Within an organization, facilitation is most often used when people come together to work in teams. This style of management has become more prevalent in organizations today, hence many team leaders require skills as facilitators.

In essence, your role as facilitator is to let the group become responsible for its aims and outcomes, and to manage that group process. However, many of the questioning skills you require as a trainer are also crucial to you as a facilitator.

Reflective listening

Reflective listening is the critical ingredient for effective facilitation. The facilitator uses reflective listening to help the group to see all issues with clarity. This technique is similar to holding up a mirror to reflect back the issues being discussed. Although a seemingly simple technique, reflective listening requires an ability to hear both content and emotion in what is being said. The facilitator reflects back a combination of the two, often slightly amplifying the emotion to create a deeper understanding.

Neutral observer

The facilitator assists the group's efforts towards its objectives. The facilitator is a neutral, impartial observer working to the group's agenda. This requires a range of interpersonal skills such as reflective questioning, active listening, understanding, empathy, compassion and neutrality.

Participant-centred

The facilitator focuses the energy of the group on its task, ensuring the group works well together to achieve its objectives. The facilitator encourages everyone to participate, ensuring that all team members feel able and willing to make a contribution (if they want to). The facilitator's main role is to ensure that outcomes are beneficial to all parties.

Process monitoring

Adding awareness to the group process is a crucial facilitation method. Rather than contributing or evaluating ideas that the group presents, the facilitator adds awareness to the group's discussion, and comments on the content of the meeting.

The facilitator may suggest alternative methods of working, therefore helping the group by offering other ways to problem solve, or to look at a situation. The facilitator also protects individuals and their ideas from attack, acting as a referee in times of conflict, disagreement or tension within the group.

Managing conflict

I mention conflict here because it is an important part of any group facilitation. In deep democracy we work with role theory to protect the individual. We look at issues and roles rather than individuals. The beauty is that the individual is protected and is not scapegoated. Rather than individuals creating difficulty or tension, it is seen that they are playing a role, and voicing something that is in the group. The role is spread beyond the individual. This is important because facilitation is very people-oriented, and it is possible for people to become scapegoats.

Deep democracy recognizes a tenet of Taoist philosophy: that conflict is inevitable. Whatever the issue, there is bound to be conflict between two parts. In gaining resolution, we gain wisdom. It is in the interchange between the parts in conflict that individuals can grow. If there is no conflict, there can be no growth. In Eastern philosophy, we gain awareness through meditation, opening our mind slowly to other views. In deep democracy, we slow the facilitation process down in a similar way to bring awareness and to ensure resolution.

Harness the group's synergy

Facilitators require a high level of interpersonal skills to be able to manage, rather than control, a group. The style and role of a facilitator can fluctuate from that of a motivator to a counsellor or guide, according to the situation at hand. It is your ability to be flexible that may take the longest to acquire. The most important skill of the facilitator is that of neutrality, not needing to be omnipotent.

Trainers and consultants have a depth of knowledge and expertise, and it is important that they acknowledge this to the group. It's important to be transparent, because knowledge gives you rank and power in a group. If you move in with your power and knowledge, you need to also recognize their knowledge and expertise. If you don't, you risk game playing and sabotage of the process if some participants are not there voluntarily.

For example, when I began training educators with the National Union of Mineworkers in South Africa, one of the first things I did was to find out about their experience and background in running workshops and facilitating meetings. Why? It was important to acknowledge their incredible strengths in facilitating and managing conflict. Their skill base was enormous; it just wasn't as comprehensive as they wanted.

As the facilitator, it's important for you to acknowledge that you are not there to hold the 'power' role. Instead, you are there to facilitate the group's process, whatever its agenda, calling on its members' expertise and knowledge. An experienced group facilitator is able to harness the synergy and energy within the group to achieve powerful, lasting learning and change. Capturing the synergy of the group will enhance the cooperative or combined action of all the participants. Most important is to have the wisdom to know when and how to intervene to enhance the group process.

Facilitation styles

There are as many different styles of facilitation as there are facilitators. Be open to different styles: they present learning possibilities for the group. These are some of the styles available to you:

- academic;
- expressive;
- hard–hitting;
- yielding;
- embryonic;
- counselling;
- accommodating;
- precise;
- controlling;
- nurturing;
- respectful;
- decisive;
- approachable.

Facilitation-styles exercise (15 minutes per person)

Here is an exercise to help you recognize your preferred facilitation style, and the opposite style you avoid. The aim of the exercise is to understand how all styles are useful in different situations. You will find this exercise exceptionally valuable if you do it together with another facilitator. Help each other to reflect more deeply. We describe and give names to styles in this exercise to make them conscious; we bring awareness to that which we do unconsciously. Allow 15 minutes for each facilitator.

1. Describe your usual style of facilitating when working with groups. (When I first completed this exercise, I wrote 'interactive' and 'participative'.)
2. Describe this style in detail. Give an example of how you would use this style.
3. Describe your anti-style, or the style that would be the direct opposite of your preferred style.
4. Give a name to this anti-style (I call my anti-style 'controlling').
5. Tell your partner a specific problem you have encountered when facilitating a group. Actually experiment with your partner, and use your preferred style to address the problem.
6. Switch to your anti-style and begin to experiment facilitating in this style. Address the problem using this anti-style.
7. Get feedback from your partner. What was effective and useful about each style?
8. How can you use both of your facilitation styles to enrich your way of working with a group?

CASE STUDY

Working with a group of legal facilitators in London, one group leader explained that her preferred style was to 'dominate' or 'solve the problem'. She was a lawyer by trade, and she named her style 'dominant'. Her anti-style was to be cautious, protective or sensitive. She called her anti-style 'shrinking or holding back'. She indicated that her problem when facilitating a group was 'imbalance'. She felt her participants weren't engaged or involved; she didn't use them as a resource.

By 'flipping' styles, she looked at the part of her that was sensitive and realized she could use that part of the group. She needed to let individuals in her group share more of their thoughts, feelings and expertise. She was so busy trying to solve things, to give them answers, that she wasn't sensitive to their need to discover their own answers, to empower themselves. Her realization as a facilitator was that to create deep changes in people, she needed to create the space for change to happen.

Facilitation skills

The facilitator has a dual role: to let the group become responsible for its own learning outcomes, and to guide the group process. A broad range of skills is required to facilitate adeptly. They are:

- observation and active listening;
- neutrality (a metaskill);
- reflective listening and questioning;
- intuition, perception and insight;
- creating empathy and trust;
- conflict management;
- innovation and creativity;
- summarizing and intervention skills;
- humour, laughter and fun;
- encouragement and praise.

Amplification

Amplification is a reflective listening skill. It requires you to listen for the emotional issues that have weight. The facilitator reflects back the emotion expressed by the speaker, but amplifies that emotion using different words. These words are slightly more charged emotionally. Amplification exaggerates the emotions expressed by the speaker.

It is important to limit yourself to the views expressed by the speaker. The feelings or thoughts of the facilitator only muddy the water. If the facilitator emphasizes the wrong issue or emotion, however, the speaker will bring you back to what he or she is trying to express. Amplification must be carried out with neutrality so the speaker does not feel judged or ridiculed. The purpose of amplification is to mirror what the person actually says or does. There is no interpretation or analysis.

Facilitation metaskills

I have labelled neutrality as a metaskill. In deep democracy, there are a range of metaskills on which the facilitator calls. What is the difference between a skill and a metaskill? A skill can be developed, learnt and practised; it can be taught. For example, you can learn how to use questions skilfully and to listen actively and reflectively.

Attitudes and beliefs

A metaskill, on the other hand, cannot be taught. It is an attitude, and requires a depth of self-awareness on the part of the facilitator. This comes with experience, expertise and practice. Whenever I train facilitators, I explain that they first need to work on themselves, to become self-aware. They need an understanding of their personal triggers and how they respond to conflict and stressful situations. It is through self-awareness that a facilitator begins to effectively use metaskills.

Metaskills are the attitudes and beliefs that a facilitator conveys to a group. Metaskills cannot be learnt in the way we learn technical skills (such as assertiveness or negotiation skills to become better communicators). Metaskills happen at an unconscious level; skills operate at a conscious level. Metaskills are more akin to the processes of the unconscious mind.

Primary process: Conscious

Primary processes are conscious. They represent who we think we are and what we are aware of. They identify where we are now, and what we are familiar with. For example, you can be conscious of what you are saying, that you are listening to a piece of music, that you are impatient, that you want to speak to someone else, and still be thinking of this evening's shopping list.

We consciously identify with phrases such as: 'I am a teacher, I am a trainer, I am such and such a nationality; I am working, I am not working.' When reading, you are conscious of the print of the words on the page, the pictures the words make in your head and the sounds of the words. But there is another, more unconscious process happening at the same time.

Secondary process: Unconscious

Secondary processes operate at the same time as primary processes, but they are unconscious. It is as if they lie just below the surface of the water, like an iceberg, where two-thirds of its mass lies underneath the water and we cannot see it. These take place in our dreams, and are our deeper unconscious processes. They are our emerging identities. They are present within us, but we may not be conscious of them.

These secondary processes are the doorways to the unconscious, and in a group could be represented by laughter, fidgeting, foot wiggling, silences or changes of energy in the room. Bringing secondary processes to consciousness, helping the group to be aware of them, helps to go deeper, gain awareness and learn what they could do differently.

For example, in business, something intangible in the workplace may stop a job from getting done. Or perhaps we cannot solve a problem in a linear, rational, left-brain fashion. It might take a more lateral approach, possibly using intuitive thinking, drawing or brainstorming to generate new ways of looking at a problem.

The facilitator's job is to help these unconscious processes emerge with the group. This will help the group to communicate more effectively, solve a problem, grow and move on.

The iceberg

Deep democracy uses the metaphor of the iceberg. One-third of an iceberg is above the water line; two-thirds of it floats below the surface. In groups, the conscious processes are those things that are said and done at a conscious, or spoken, level. They are above the surface of the water. Those things that are unsaid, implied or understood reside at an unconscious level. They are submerged and need to be brought to the surface. The steps of deep democracy help to bring to the surface any issues needing to be acknowledged.

Those unconscious processes are huge, however. What lies below the surface of the water is so mighty that only aspects relevant to the group, or relevant to that moment, will emerge. The job of the facilitator is to use metaskills to help bring to the surface the ideas, tensions and conflicts that lie submerged below the consciousness of the group.

Incongruence

We communicate with a combination of the spoken word and non-verbal gestures. The words represent what is conscious, what is said. We are usually more conscious of the words being spoken. The unspoken (or unconscious) part of communication, combined with our gestures, may create an incongruence with what we say. That is why when people say they are happy, yet their arms are folded, they are tapping their foot, or they are shaking their head, we know they are not congruent. Their unconscious processes are showing through. Their body and their spoken language are not in sync with each other. That is when mistrust or apprehension can develop within the group. It is the job of the facilitator to observe and bring these underlying issues to the forefront, to consciousness: above the water line.

The metaskills

Your metaskills will enable you to practise the art of facilitation, and to be more successful in moving a group through conflict to growth and learning.

Compassion

Compassion is derived from an individual's life experiences. This may be the most important metaskill. A word that represents the core-root of compassion is 'acceptance'. The first part of compassion is finding compassion towards yourself.

Compassion is neither good nor bad; it exists without judgement. If a facilitator is lacking in compassion, it will be difficult to appreciate all aspects of the group's journey: from noise, disarray, confusion, anger and rage, through quiet, silence, peace and calm, to creativity, originality, imagination, inspiration, inventiveness, vision and resourcefulness.

It's important that the facilitator allows for all mental and physical states to coexist within the group in order to resolve group issues and finally to move the group forward. If a facilitator stays with confusion and anger, and doesn't move the group through the 'fire' or the 'heat', conflicts can remain unresolved. Yet if conflicts aren't allowed to burn, fires can't be put out. An example of the ineffective use of this metaskill would be reflecting back with an attitude of retribution.

I recently saw an example of this in London, working with a group of senior consultants, marketers and trainers. One of the frustrations of the group was that they came together from different organizations, and although they wanted to learn and practise new facilitation skills, some of the conflicts that arose in the group were due to differing needs and a differing range of expertise. Being two facilitators, we were able to stay with the group's frustrations, compassionately helping them to find a voice and finally to choose a menu of topics that could be worked with in a limited two-day workshop.

Neutrality

In order to understand neutrality, it is useful to look at some of its synonyms: impartiality, objectivity, a refusal to take sides, non-aligned status. Neutrality implies that the facilitator lets go of planned programmes, ideas and goals. In order to remain neutral, the facilitator should be receptive to any of the group's unconscious processes trying to emerge from below the surface. As a facilitator, remember what you see in the visible, obvious behaviour of the group is only a part of the whole picture.

Neutrality is one of the most difficult skills to develop. It is useful to have two group facilitators if any difficulties are expected. If one facilitator becomes 'caught', the second stays neutral, giving time to the other facilitator to regain his or her neutrality. Lecturers at Rand Afrikaans University in Johannesburg, with whom I was training in facilitation skills, described the ability to stay objective and non-aligned as 'compassionately inhabiting the neutral zone'.

Detachment or dual awareness

Detachment is being open to all sides in a discussion, allowing for interaction from every side. In working with deep democracy, this is a very difficult skill to acquire. Detachment does not imply indifference. It is a way of staying objective, not getting caught up or drawn into feeling the same emotions as the participants.

Detachment is a kind of disconnectedness. It allows you as facilitator to hover like a helicopter above the fray or the fire. If you get caught, bring an awareness of that into the room or the group. Detachment requires a kind of dual awareness: an ability to stay in the fire and yet be outside of it. The ability to be detached helps you stay 'aware' in the middle of difficult or tense situations. Detachment is difficult because we all want to be liked. Remaining detached, or 'uncaught', by the group's emotions requires an ability to let go of the need to be loved or to be successful. In deep democracy terms, the group may be successful if it disintegrates. This is a difficult concept for most facilitators.

Facilitators who are self-aware, and comfortable with who they are, can more easily develop detachment. They know they are safe, no matter how turbulent the group process becomes. They understand that their objectivity and detachment will help the group to grow, develop and move on.

Because detachment requires a dual awareness – of the group's emotions and of oneself – it is not an easy skill to develop. Be patient with yourself. It comes with practice. The way to gain detachment and neutrality is to work on yourself. Become more aware of your inner processes and triggers. (See the Inner work and Neutrality exercises at the end of the chapter.)

Congruence

To develop congruence, it is important to know yourself. Congruent behaviour is speaking and doing in accordance with your beliefs and values. It requires matching spoken and unspoken thought. To remain congruent as a facilitator, be very aware of your personal intentions when speaking or guiding the group. To be congruent with the group process, it would be your wish for the group to gain greater awareness: conscious and unconscious. To be congruent would require you to be detached with interest.

Earlier, I mentioned that the facilitator is not the central focus of the group. The participants are the central focus. To remain congruent requires an element of letting go of one's ego: letting go of the need to be right, to be the centre of attention, to be heard. It also requires an awareness of the messages conveyed by your words, tone of voice, attitude and gestures. To stay congruent requires compassion, detachment and neutrality.

Patience

Patience is a great skill for all performance consultants. For a facilitator, however, it is crucial. With patience and skilled guidance, the facilitator recognizes that the essence of the group will unfold in its own time. If the facilitator lacks patience, it is usually a sign of being 'caught' in the tangle of the group's emotions.

I think of patience as a combination of serenity, stamina, tolerance and staying power. It is very easy for a facilitator to be impatient with the group's need to explore certain issues at a deeper level. Patience requires an ability to stay in the heat of the 'fire' a little bit longer.

Humility

Humility is sometimes known as having an open mind, or a beginner's mind. It is the opposite of arrogance. It is the ability to learn from the group, and an awareness that learning is crucial to the group's process. It requires letting go: letting go of the need to be an all-knowing guru, letting go of being the one who carries all the knowledge and expertise.

To acquire humility calls for a lessening of ego, an ability to be humble. For trainers, letting go of being 'all-knowledgeable' can be difficult; in facilitation, it is essential. As a facilitator, you are not contributing to content so much as to method. Humility is a skill that takes a lifetime to develop, so don't give up!

The process of deep democracy

Deep democracy is an invaluable tool when facilitating any group process. The concept was developed by Arnold Mindell in the early 1970s. Mindell is also the creator of process-oriented psychology, which combines the insights of Eastern philosophy, modern physics and Jungian psychology to look at human dynamics in a revolutionary new way.

A Jungian analyst, Mindell took the idea that something unconscious is trying to make itself known consciously in relationships, whether between individuals, in groups or in organizations. Deep democracy helps us to gain awareness of conscious processes (experiences we acknowledge) and unconscious processes (which we do not acknowledge) and the edge that separates them. We gain wisdom as we are kissed over the edge, and the unconscious becomes conscious.

I was first introduced to the principles of deep democracy by Bernard le Roux and Myrna Wajsman. Bernard is a legal and education consultant working in Denmark and South Africa. He and I were working primarily with South African educators to help them make sustainable decisions to manage their schools and their classrooms, and to include the parents and the governing body in all decisions. Our work often took place in disadvantaged, poor schools with historically disenfranchised voices.

Myrna Wajsman is a clinical psychologist who teaches the principles of deep democracy as an essential tool for business consultants. Myrna and I have worked together in the UK and South Africa. Although originally trained with Mindell, she has adapted his work over the years.

The principle of inclusion

Deep democracy is an effective way to facilitate group decisions, resolve conflict and include the wisdom of the minority voice. Mindell's theory is based on the greater awareness of a group as it moves to resolve conflict and grow.

Deep democracy differs from majority democracy for one specific reason. Majority democracy favours the majority vote, and can suppress up to 49 per cent of other voices in that population. This means that nearly one-half of the voices involved in the voting, or decision-making process, may not be heard.

If the minority is not taken into account, there is room for possible sabotage of any decisions taken by the majority. Mindell's theory is that the minority voice, if continually not heard, can become an unconscious terrorist process, which may prevent the majority from implementing their decisions. Deep democracy respects the majority voice but includes the wisdom of the minority. To include their voice, we need to explore 'what it would take' for the minority to come along with the majority.

The minority voice often has a knowledge of its own that the majority does not yet know. If this wisdom forms part of the majority decision, it strengthens the implementation of any decisions the team takes. In this way, deep democracy includes both the majority voice and any dissenting voices. That is its strength. This helps to avoid sabotage, terrorism or disruption of the group's overall decision.

Minority, majority or agreement to go along?

The concept of majority voting implies that the majority has all the power. The majority can make the decisions, no matter what the minority vote thinks or feels. However, there are other types of decisions in the workplace.

- *Individual:* here one individual makes a decision for the entire team or organization. This often happens when one person has the rank, power or financial clout to do so. This may happen in a family-managed organization where the senior family member has the final say.
- *Minority:* sometimes the minority voice holds the power. This can happen due to the way votes are counted in democratic systems, or it may be that the minority has the rank, power and will to rule. This can lead to the majority being disenfranchised, as was the case in South Africa under apartheid. It can also be a board of directors who hold the final decision.
- *Majority:* democratic nations use the majority vote to elect their governments and to make the decisions that govern their nations. However, this can disenfranchise those in the minority who feel they are not heard. We see this in

organizational disputes between management and labour, where labour feels its voice is not heard because it is considered a 'minority' decision maker, or in political disagreements when a minority group feel it has no voice.

- *Agreement to go along:* this is the basic premise of deep democracy. All decisions are inclusive not just of the majority voice, but of the wisdom or contribution of those in the minority. In this way, the minority goes along with the majority by adding the wisdom of its voice. It keeps people in relationships, even if they (the minority) are not in total agreement with the decision to be implemented.

In a small way, we see this inclusion of the minority wisdom in parliamentary politics, when a majority government party manages to enact a new law with the condition of several addenda from the political parties or groups not in power.

The steps of deep democracy

1.   Gauge the will of the team

Don't settle for a majority vote. Ask the team members to indicate their choice by voting (this could be as simple as raising hands). This will show you what the group wants. The highest vote gives you an indication of what the team wants to do, but is only part of the final solution. If you stop here, the 'no' vote will not be heard and may subtly or overtly subvert the implementation of any decision.

2.   Search for the 'no'

Those who voted against the decision are obviously expressing their dissent. Those who withdraw do so less obviously. They are not on board. Find out what the 'no' is saying and why. Ask the dissenters what their objection is and assist them in expressing it fully. You may even ask those who have withdrawn to say why they cannot give wholehearted support to the will of the team. The 'no' may, for example, be related to time: 'We don't have a whole day to spend on strategic planning,' or 'I have a meeting in the afternoon that I cannot postpone.'

3.   Spread the 'no'

The question to ask here is: 'Is there anybody else who feels like this?' Usually you will find people in the team, even those who voted for a proposal, who share, even just slightly, the doubt expressed by the 'no' vote. Acknowledge the person who expressed the 'no' as having spoken for others, but also for the team itself. What is the wisdom contained in this dissent? To use the above example: others may also be concerned about the time the strategic planning may take. The wisdom is related to working more effectively or perhaps to honouring an important appointment by a team member in the afternoon.

4.   Include the 'no' in the decision

In the spirit of not wanting to exclude or leave any team member behind, ask the objectors, 'What would it take for you to be able to support the decision of the majority of the group?' It must be clear: the will of the group is not diverted, it is added to. The objectors will state their dissent as a positive condition: 'I'll go along with it if I am sure that it will be over by midday.'

The decision stands, but a time proviso is added: the process must be over by 12.00. The objector may even be asked to play the role of timekeeper and become an integral part of the implementation process. The spoken, or unspoken, invitation of the team to the objector is, 'We want you to come with us, we are a team.'

Facilitating discussion exercise (1 hour)

The following exercise creates debate and discussion on the principles of deep democracy. You can hand this out as a group exercise, whether you are teaching facilitation, want a role-play, negotiation, communication, decision-making activity, or simply wish your group to practise their facilitation skills.

Group exercise

Everyone in the group spends 10 minutes reading the deep democracy steps, writing down comments and any questions they may have. Members of each small group take turns facilitating a 15-minute discussion on a different topic.

Roles: facilitator, observer, timekeeper

Each person in the group will take one of the following as a facilitation topic. Each time your group changes facilitator, please change topic, observer and time-keeper roles. Each facilitator will facilitate for 15 minutes, and is to draw a conclusion or summary of the discussion. You may use the flipchart.

Topics

1. Facilitate a discussion on what happens currently within your department or organization where decisions have to be reached. Facilitate an open discussion about when and where the minority voice is heard, and what happens when it is not and the vote goes with the majority.
2. Facilitate a discussion on the usefulness of this four-step process as a tool for your department and your organization as a whole. Discuss why and why not.
3. Facilitate the usefulness of including the 'no' in any decision making; how including the minority voice can have positive results in procedure and policy making, as well as the style of management within your organization.

4. Facilitate how and where you can include the concept of deep democracy within your working day. How would it be useful for you in workshops, seminars and lectures, and facilitating meetings?

Group review

When the group comes back together as a whole, discuss what happened in their small groups. Allow 20 minutes.

- What was the learning, and how did their discussions go?
- Did their facilitation encapsulate the four steps?
- What did they do to include the minority voice?

How to do it

Deep democracy is a powerful tool to use if you are managing a group process where decisions are to be made, conflicts need to be resolved and the group allowed to grow. I have described the four steps of deep democracy, including the skills needed to move through each step, and have given examples of each step.

It is useful to be trained in the conflict-resolution steps of deep democracy (stage four below) if you plan to incorporate this concept into your development of people. You will find it an exciting new way to approach decision making and conflict resolution in your groups.

Stage 1: Determine the will of the group

- Find all of the issues first.
- Take the majority vote.
- Gauge the will of the team.
- Look for the 'no' or the minority opinion.

In order to gain a sense of the majority view, ask the group or team members to indicate their choice by voting. This may be as simple as raising hands. It may require a discussion to get all the topics chosen onto the flipchart or out in the open. For example, if the group has to make a decision about which issues to discuss, I stand at the flipchart and ask for all the suggested topics.

Once they are all on the flip, each topic needs to be defined; only then can a vote or poll be taken. However, if it is a matter of resolving a conflict, it is important to take a vote on whether the group is willing to resolve the conflict.

Do not stop with the majority or highest vote. This would disregard any knowledge or wisdom available within the minority group. The highest, or majority, vote will be an indication of the topic that the majority of the group wants to work on or discuss. This is only the beginning. If you stop here and go with the majority voice, those who are saying 'no' to this topic will not be heard. This may undermine the implementation of the decision, consciously or unconsciously.

We recognize that some people won't agree. We are trying to get those who don't agree to stay on the bus, to stay with the programme. If we ignore the minority voice at this point, it will emerge at some later stage to disrupt the process. If you don't search for the 'no' (the minority voice) – and it may take time – you may only get part way down the road in your decision-making process (or in gaining awareness for the group). If the minority has not agreed to go along, at some point the group will protect itself by interrupting or stopping the group process.

Do this only when there is a very important issue, and when you are not limited for time. It would not be appropriate, say, for an emergency when decisions need to be taken quickly to resolve a situation.

CASE STUDY

This is a situation I had to deal with recently. We are in the process of building a new primary school in my community for the poorest children who don't have proper education facilities. It has been a long process and is based very much on a partnership between teachers, parents and the community at large. The project committee, which is made up of various representatives from each part of the community, decided to launch the opening of the first four classrooms. Although Nelson Mandela launched the appeal three years ago, this time he was unable to attend. Instead, he sent a representative to read his speech.

The committee invited the Provincial Minister of Education (who is of a different political party from Mandela) to cut the ribbon and to give the keynote speech. Some parents felt deeply unhappy about this. Grumblings of dissent threatened to boil over. Very close, underneath the surface, lurked many historical resentments and great hurt. The meeting with the parents was the time to listen to the 'unheard' voice: to gain the wisdom of their opinion, to gain agreement for them to come along, to be part of the festivities and the launch of their new school. We did, and they came.

This situation, in fact, highlighted a major gap in the building project. Similar issues have continued to recycle during this three-year process, and now is the time to open up discussions between parents, teachers and the community to begin a greater healing process. It is going to take time.

Stage 2: Searching for the 'no'

- Find out what those who voted 'no' are saying.
- Encourage the minority view.
- Give permission to the 'no'.

- Help them to express it.
- Use reflective listening skills.

Those who did not vote at all are also expressing their opposition. Some may withdraw or choose not to vote. Both are subtle forms of dissent: they are still voting 'no'. In this second stage, find out what the 'no' is saying, and why they are saying it. After the group votes, ask those in the minority to describe their objections. Help them to express them. Look for double messages where people say one thing but their gestures say something else. You are looking for incongruence.

Invite people to speak, so that the role of the naysayer begins to come out. It is not the individual's voice you are encouraging: it is a role that is held by a minority in the room. This is quite a difficult concept to grasp, because so often we blame individuals for stopping a process from continuing. As facilitator, it is your job to ensure that people feel safe to express views that may be unpopular.

In order to emphasize the importance of hearing the minority view, ask for examples of when a majority viewpoint did not work, or when an unpopular minority view did contribute to the final decision.

CASE STUDY

For example, this is something I experienced while facilitating a Training the Trainer workshop at a California university. There was a minority view in the group holding onto the principle that people could be categorized into certain types, and that those types were lifelong. This was due to the implementation of a psychometric test that a minority in the group favoured. This minority felt that their very belief system was being questioned by not being able to hang onto the results of this test.

My job as the facilitator was to draw out the minority view, and look at how we could add its wisdom to the majority belief: that all psychometric tests are a snapshot in time, not necessarily lifelong. It sounds like a minor incident, but in fact the minority nearly sabotaged the entire workshop.

The minority felt wounded at the level of identity. 'Who they were' was bound up in this particular belief about what seemed to be a simple test. There was major learning for the facilitator in that session, because I nearly lost neutrality, one of the most crucial metaskills. As I had a fellow trainer working with me, he spoke and I was able to recollect my thoughts, regain neutrality and help the group to move forward.

This stage is not an opportunity for the minority to sabotage or gain tyrannical power over the majority. It simply offers them a platform: for their views, frustrations, anger or even irrationality to be heard. The facilitator will eventually help the group discover what wisdom lies within this minority viewpoint. Spend time at this stage of the proceedings. If everyone is not given a chance to voice their views, their non-involvement could lead to terrorist behaviour later.

Give permission to those who are saying no, and encourage them to express their minority viewpoint. Use open-ended questions, reflective listening and support both sides. However, it is not your job to encourage those who are silent to speak. Acknowledge that people may need to be silent. Give space for the silent naysayer role to come out.

Stage 3: Spreading the role of the 'no'

- Is there anyone else who feels like this?
- Use reflective listening skills.
- Nobody gets scapegoated.

At this stage, spread the role of the dissenting voice. The question to ask is, 'Does anyone else think or feel this way?' You will discover that a few people, even if they voted for the majority, share some of the doubt expressed by the 'no' voters. The facilitator acknowledges that those who have expressed a 'no' vote may have spoken for others within the group who share only part of their doubt.

In deep democracy it is believed that everyone within the group will hold a part of that 'no' within them. The wisdom may not necessarily come from the minority. But it is important to find the 'no', to encourage the naysayers to express their viewpoint. The minority will have a power, and if not recognized may sabotage the process (letting the role of the terrorist emerge).

Encourage the 'no' to come out. The 'no' may not initially be the wisdom, but the wisdom may come out as a result of the minority viewpoint. The wisdom may be the result of asking those naysayers, 'What would it take for you to come along?' That's where the wisdom may lie at a conscious level.

CASE STUDY

In a workshop training educators and curriculum administrators in the Western Cape in South Africa, the process fell apart because of language. It was an important issue to a minority in the group. The language issue had not been addressed, although it had been cycling round the gossip channel for weeks. We had to interrupt the workshop agenda and gain agreement from the group to try to understand what the issues were around language.

The minority view was that it was unfair to speak only in English, when the majority first language in the group was Afrikaans and the second language was Xhosa. The wisdom resided in what it took for the minority to come along. The agreement was to continue in English with interpreters, and that jokes had to be translated in all three languages!

Sometimes a recurring issue is an excuse, or is hiding a real issue. Try to elicit some of the more unconscious processes in the group. These emotional or thinking processes may be linked to deeper emotions or resentments experienced by the group in the past. Use your facilitation skills and techniques: reflective listening, neutrality, compassion and amplification.

For example, in South Africa, language (or the sidelining of certain languages) can still be seen as an index of power, prestige and identity. Thus, not to acknowledge concerns over language in the above instance would have been tantamount to burying some very profound and deeply felt issues.

Do not fall into the trap of making the minority the scapegoats. Encourage everyone in the group to express any part of the minority viewpoint that they may empathize with. This is called 'spreading the no'. The question to eventually ask is: 'What wisdom is contained in the dissenting voice? What can we learn from this?'

Stage 4: Include the 'no' in the decision

At this stage we bring the deeper understanding of the minority view and add that to the majority view.

- Set ground rules.
- What would it take for you to come along?
- Gain agreement on what the minority needs.
- Bring in the deeper understanding of the minority.
- What will it take for the minority to go along?

The minority is asked what it needs to go along with the majority voice. The facilitator explains that the majority will pull it along just as the strength of the tide pulls a swimmer into the shore. However, in hearing the minority voice there will be a wisdom from which all in the group can learn. It needs to be clear that the will of the majority will not be sidetracked, it will be added to. This is a practical way for the minority to contribute its wisdom to the majority voice.

Deep democracy considers the minority to be a positive influence, instead of a negative one. Rather than dissenters being perceived as a divisive element, deep democracy considers that within the dissenting voice a wisdom can be gained for the entire group. This wisdom can be included in the majority voice to gain agreement from the minority to go along.

Ask the objectors to state their dissent as a positive condition. For example, 'I'll go along with it if all can be involved and we finish this topic by the end of the day.' It's useful to ask the dissenter to play the role of timekeeper. Ask the group how to include this concern in the majority decision. The unspoken voice of the dissenter is, 'We want this to be something all of us gain from, not just the ones who can stay here all night.'

CASE STUDY

In this fourth stage, it is important to move beyond the excuses. Be aware of topics that repeat themselves. In a workshop I facilitated for university lecturers in Johannesburg, one of the minority issues that kept cycling around the discussion of what to include in the two-day workshop was 'how to use NLP in our lectures'. I quickly realized this was a topic that, if not included in some way, would reoccur and end up as an unsatisfied need at the end of the two days.

The group had many ideas to explore, share and discuss with each other that were relevant to the variety of courses, seminars and lectures they delivered. By making the 'minority issues' conscious within the group, we were able to understand the needs of everyone. Using deep democracy to gain the wisdom of the minority, the group came to a consensus as to what topics to include.

In another university workshop in the States, training performance consultants, the minority voice was concerned that the exercise to end the day would take the group well past the time allotted. A decision was taken by the group to commence that topic two hours prior to the end-of-the-day review. The majority was happy that an integral training point would be taught and experienced, and the naysayers (with strict deadlines) were relieved they would not miss anything. The role of timekeeper was taken on by one of the dissenters. The overall message was: we're a working group and want to experience any new learning together.

Conflict resolution

- Set ground rules.
- Polarize the roles.
- Throw all the arrows.
- Amplify and recognize double messages.
- Slow the process down.
- Use metaskills.
- Kiss both parties over the edge.

If it is not possible to gain agreement at this stage, it is important to gain overall agreement for the group to go into conflict. As the facilitator, it is your job to be protective of all individuals. You encourage each side to throw all of their arrows, one side at a time. And they must own their own side strongly. This is different from traditional conflict resolution, where both sides present their case and try to negotiate a middle ground.

It is important to set ground rules. Write them up on the flipchart. Ground rules can be things like: Everyone must have their say; No violence; We carry on until we're finished; We can walk out if it gets too heated.

In this stage, the group begins to voice issues that lie just below the surface. These issues have been cycling round and round a group. These issues may not be conscious, but need to be voiced if the group is to carry on. Techniques such as amplification, polarization and metaskills help you to kiss each side over the edge to gain awareness of themselves and others. The most difficult task for you as a facilitator is to stay neutral as you help the group grow.

Throw the arrows

In deep democracy, first one side throws all its arrows. It's as if the people on that side have a quiver on their backs, and they throw arrow after arrow. Each arrow represents something they want to say about how they feel. Those on the other side act as if they heard nothing at all, then they throw all of their arrows. At no time is there any justification of either side. They simply throw their arrows. It is known as owning their own side strongly.

This has nothing to do with being right or wrong. Each side needs to say everything they feel: pain, anger, hurt, ill-feeling. Your job as the facilitator is to ensure that all the arrows are thrown. You amplify the content and emotion of each side, kissing each person over the edge (moving them from unconscious to conscious awareness); helping them to own their own side strongly.

The facilitator needs to ensure that both sides are kissed over the edge, bringing awareness. An edge is a metaphor. It represents the boundary separating the individual, or the group's, conscious and unconscious awareness of an issue, or a feeling.

Kissing over the edge

Kissing a person over the edge is a very complex technique, calling on your reflective listening skills and ability to stay neutral and compassionate. The facilitator recognizes that for the individual, going over the edge may result in an understanding of something that is painful or difficult to acknowledge.

To give you a minor example, one of the directors in a large construction company was determined that everyone on the executive board should be able to handle media interviews. He flew off the handle during a live television interview. During our next training session, which was to make a decision on media strategy, his 'aha' was to become aware that he was not the best person to handle the press.

There were many arrows thrown in that session, and it was a difficult moment for him as he began to gain awareness of his own aggressive behaviour. He was not conscious of his tendency to blow up under pressure. The end result was a greater understanding of when this type of behaviour may be appropriate, inside and outside of the organization.

Including the wisdom in the decision

● Find the grain of truth.
● Bring in the deeper understanding of the minority viewpoint.
● Gain agreement on what the minority needs.
● Summarize the decision.
● Add the information or wisdom to the will of the group.
● Clearly set out the provisos.

This is the point at which the group will be able to grow. Once all the arrows have been thrown, it is important to find a 'grain of truth' in what has been said. It may be a tiny grain of truth, but it will be there. This can be difficult, as extreme and uncomfortable things may have been said. Often, wisdom can be found in something said that caused each individual discomfort. Go round the group asking for the grain of truth from each person. Once everyone has spoken, you will be able to bring in understanding and awareness for the group as a whole.

The final stage in deep democracy is to add that wisdom to the majority decision. The beauty of this process is that all team members participate. It is empowering for those who feel they are often overlooked. Silence is never consent, and may indicate an unwillingness to take part due to low self-esteem, lack of confidence or even feelings of inadequacy.

CASE STUDY

In a workshop for about 50 women managers and administrators at a large project-engineering firm in San Francisco, the voices of women who had rarely spoken up began to be heard as they realized that their opinions, thoughts and feelings were being acknowledged and felt by more than just individual women. The excitement and enthusiasm was palpable as these women voiced the issues they needed to explore for their own self-development.

There were long-overdue resentments that needed to be expressed. There were also very senior directors in the room, to whom the resentments had never been expressed. The grain of truth at the end of the session was that everyone acknowledged the need for further training and development for the organization to grow.

Deep democracy encourages everyone to voice his or her opinion. The facilitator sets the tone, creating a climate of respect, acknowledgement and acceptance for each person in the group. The facilitator's compassion and neutrality encourage participation.

Your best tools

Staying neutral

The most difficult metaskill to practise is neutrality. Issues that arise within a group sometimes have strong implications for the facilitator, as well as the team. But if the facilitator 'gets caught' and is no longer able to remain neutral, it will be tricky for team members to reach any kind of resolution. I watched this take place at a workshop for a group of international facilitators recently. The facilitator became 'caught up' by the group's emotions, and lost his neutrality. He did not take sides; he simply came in with another viewpoint, another side. The good news was that he admitted it, stepped back, and was able to regain his neutral stance.

With neutrality, the facilitator helps the group gain insight and understanding into all sides of the argument, aligned with a greater self-awareness. Through self-awareness, individuals can harness their own personal power. Deep democracy helps individuals express their needs within an organization, and helps to create balance within a team and within the organization.

If the minority proviso is not accepted by the group majority, that needs to be addressed. The question to ask is: What will it take for the majority to accept the wisdom of the minority?

Try it in your next meeting, training or facilitation session. Be sincere in your desire to include all voices, and be aware that the final outcome may be different from what you envisage. If the group functions in a deeply democratic fashion, the attitude of the individuals involved will ensure that all can learn from each other, reaching agreement.

Exercise to develop neutrality (10 minutes)

This 10-minute exercise develops awareness of your triggers: what triggers a strong (hot button) response from you when dealing with other people. When we react strongly to someone, we often have some of 'that' within us. For example, when we say, 'I'm not like that', we marginalize that part of ourselves, placing it onto the other person. We react to 'that' part of ourselves, and reject it. By projecting it on to someone else (jealously, envy, impatience) we cut ourselves off from it.

1. Notice a reaction you have to another person, or even a particular group. You could be reacting to their race, gender, class or specific characteristics that catch you in some way.
2. Observe which characteristics you are attributing to this individual or group. Particularly notice the qualities you react to.

3. Close your eyes for a moment. Picture in your mind's eye that you have become this person, with these qualities and characteristics. As you become this person, imagine how you sit, think, relate, move. Explore the way you would look at others. Notice their deepest or most essential qualities.

4. As you become this person, you may find it uncomfortable or embarrassing. If you are doing this exercise with a partner, that partner should encourage you to continue. What you are showing is 'edge' behaviour. If you carry on you will gain insight into what this behaviour means in your life. The person's behaviour is really your behaviour; there's a message for you. With that message you can gain awareness, to help you regain your neutrality.

5. Now, continue with neutrality.

The soft-shoe shuffle (1–2 hours)

This is a physical walking through the steps of deep democracy. It allows people to have a conversation on their feet. I first learnt an adaptation of the soft-shoe shuffle working jointly with a rich high school (primarily for white middle-class students) and a disadvantaged high school (primarily for poor black students) in South Africa. I have subsequently begun to use this with other clients.

The teachers of the original two schools wanted to work together. Unfortunately, on their own they could find no long-lasting way to move beyond the resentments set up during the years of apartheid. The soft-shoe shuffle offered an ideal solution. The physical expression of deep democracy allowed a tangible way for the two groups to decide how students and teachers could work together on specific projects.

My colleague and I met first with one school, then the next. After several meetings with both, using the soft-shoe shuffle each time, we discovered that the aims and needs of both groups were remarkably similar, almost identical. As a result of the soft-shoe shuffle, both groups made the decision to meet in a public place, the public library. Once again, we used the soft-shoe shuffle to create a way forward.

Creating physical space

The soft-shoe shuffle is a way to physically create space between the different voices, or 'roles', in the group. It is akin to having a conversation on your feet. In effect, it creates a 'physical' discussion. The facilitator asks someone to start, requesting a comment or statement relevant to the point of the meeting. The facilitator asks anyone who is in agreement with, or sympathetic to, that statement to walk over and stand next to that person.

Usually about a third to a half of the group move. It is important to explain to everyone in the group, 'If you want to cheat – walk.' That way, you will be included, even if you are momentarily unsure of where you want to be included.

When the first statement is made, some of the group move to stand next to the first person. A second statement or comment is made in response, and people move again. Some of the group will be next to the first speaker, some next to the second speaker, some will not yet be with one group or another. As facilitator, encourage people to contribute statements, one at a time. In this way individuals within the group continue to move, creating a dialogue on foot.

In the example of the two schools, the final meeting in the public library was astonishing. We used the soft-shoe shuffle, and at the end of about three hours, teachers and principals from the two schools realized that their issues, concerns and fears were shared by the other side. It was definitely an awakening for both groups. The end result was they decided to have a barbecue together, to get to know each other and to decide how they could have the students in their two schools work together, sharing resources and becoming acquainted. This was a major breakthrough.

Role theory

Roles are expressions of ideas, opinions and fundamental behaviour patterns. There is much power and energy behind a role, and these roles can inhibit individuals within a group. Roles are larger than the individual, and individuals carry within them more than one role. For the individual and the group to grow, they need to be able to move with fluidity between many roles. Think of all of the roles you play in your life: son or daughter, sister or brother, mother or father, employee or boss.

Examples of roles that exist within groups are:

- absent role;
- facilitator;
- ghost;
- leader;
- minority;
- majority;
- silent role;
- scapegoat;
- teacher;
- terrorist.

The ghost role

We all have the ability to access a number of different roles. In groups, more than one individual may fill a role, and sometimes a role is not filled. In other words, no one takes it up even though it is referred to time and again. This is the ghost role: the role that is mentioned repeatedly in the group's interactions, but with which no one identifies. However, we typically stereotype and link individuals to that role. Deep democracy unhooks the individual from the role.

To do so, the facilitator may take the part of the ghost role, over-exaggerating that role. This makes the ghost visible and real, giving permission for individuals within the group to disagree. By doing so, they can identify the true nature of the ghost role.

If something is said and the group talks about that role, giving it air time, then it is alive and well in the group. It also means that it is beyond the individual. This allows the individual to step out of the role, feeling free to move to another role.

In a workshop with a group of government employees in an important ministry in the UK, I over-exaggerated the role of those who were 'absent'. The ghost role represented those who had not attended the workshop. There was intense resentment about their absence. Facilitators sometimes experience this with participants who refer to their 'boss' as the one who should be present too. By over-exaggerating comments made about the absent co-workers, I highlighted the 'ghost' workers who were absent. I encouraged other individuals in the group to acknowledge the role played by those not present. We went on to discuss how to bring them into the group once the group returned to the workplace.

The silent role

Frequently, those who are silent have a wisdom of their own to add to the overall voice of the group. They may be silent because they are concerned for their own security or comfort in the group, or they may have a concern for the future. As a facilitator, address the silence in the room by making people conscious of it. Make the group aware of the silence, but not of a silent individual. As facilitator you can adopt the silent role, asking others to move into that space with you.

The terrorist role

The terrorist is just another role and in itself is neither good nor bad. However, in the light of its political connotation, it is important to recognize that this is a term long in use to define a potential saboteur role in any group. A terrorist is often a symptom of a minority position that is not recognized by the majority. It is important that the terrorist be heard; if this role is not heard, there may be resistance to the majority. To integrate the voice of the terrorist, allow for feelings and beliefs to be expressed by individuals within the group or organization, particularly differing opinions and beliefs. Finally, support and allow people to take risks – especially taking the risk of speaking up.

This is important in any group session. If there is a voice that is not being heard, it will present itself in many different ways until it has a chance to be heard. For example, in a workshop in Glasgow of more than 100 women several years ago, there was a group of five women in the front row. They started off quietly disrupting the seminar; by the first coffee break, they were positively sabotaging any possible enjoyment for the rest of the group. What I did was to successfully find a way to hear them out and include them in the different break-out groups. Once they had found a way in, they became a more positive influence in the workshop. They had believed their voices would not be heard, and we found a way to include them.

Polarization

In groups, two opposing roles emerge at the point where conflict begins to emerge. This is known as polarization. If emotions are stifled and the group tries to carry on at a rational, cognitive level, the polarization may increase. The facilitator's job is to make it safe for polarization to occur. In this way, issues can begin to emerge above the surface. If not, sabotage may occur to interrupt the group process.

At a design workshop in Portsmouth for senior managers, various organizations were represented. A definite feeling of them-versus-us emerged in the afternoon. The 'them' were those who wanted to be there, and the 'us' were those who didn't. The 'us' group became a disruptive influence once they started drinking at lunchtime.

Many members of the overall group came up to complain to me about this other group. I put it to the big group: What would you like to do? If you vote a part of the group out, they may not go, or some may remain who are not happy with that decision. We spent the next hour on our feet discussing how people felt. We used a technique akin to the soft-shoe shuffle.

Members of the disruptive group themselves made the suggestion that they should split up and work in separate groups. This was accepted, and although we lost over an hour, we finished the workshop with new learning and most objectives achieved.

Hot spots and edges

Sometimes a group will get caught in a hot moment, or a 'hot spot'. A hot spot indicates an element of conflict, and the group's focus can go off course. If the group goes off track, simply bring it back to the point where there was heat: to the item the group moved away from. You can say, 'Something tells me we're not finished yet.'

A hot spot can indicate that the group is at an edge between what is conscious and what is unconscious. The edge is a protection or barrier for individuals within a group, and the group often gives very negative feedback when at an edge. As the facilitator, you can say, 'Maybe there is an issue here.' They may not acknowledge it, as it may not yet be the time to make the group aware they have gone off the point. Allow them to move off the topic with awareness. You can bring them back, and help them to decide with awareness to leave the topic for now. The decision is theirs, as it may not yet be the time to tackle that hot spot.

Awareness, polarity and amplification will stir the conflict. Amplification makes the conflict apparent, polarity brings out the various viewpoints and awareness slows the process down by making sure people want to be there, in conflict. The group must be in agreement to resolve the conflict, and you as facilitator slow them down.

In a workshop for facilitators in London recently, the majority voices in the group said, 'Let's go on to discuss these topics.' One lonely voice spoke up and said, 'Hey, wait a minute. We've just spent an hour going round the circle hearing from everyone, and I feel we've gone a little bit deeper than one normally does in a workshop. I feel that I'm beginning to understand the essence of what makes some others tick. I'm afraid that if we go on to more mundane things, the group will lose a chance that may not be repeated.'

The group stayed with this for only a moment, then slid back into its original discussion and didn't explore this participant's comment fully. The group had been at an edge: they weren't sure they wanted to explore issues at a deeper level. So they slid back into their original discussion. The facilitators made the group aware of this, and a second person spoke up and voiced similar feelings. We then highlighted this, and the group, now aware, began to discuss how to incorporate these deeper insights into the teaching for the day.

Exercise to work with edges (20 minutes)

Sit with someone and just begin to chat together about any subject. Perhaps talk about your favourite hobby or sport. Notice when you go off the topic, or there is a shift in your discussion. Your partner's job is to help you amplify and explore the point where you went off the topic.

Whenever there is a switch in the conversation, that is edge behaviour. As you work with your partner, help that person to adventure around the edge. Think about how you are using language, and work with edges in visual, auditory and kinesthetic mode. Experiment with going over the edge.

- What are you trying to say?
- What do you shy away from saying?
- What sensory system (VAK) is the most difficult?
- What makes it difficult?

When you have finished, tell your partner what happened at the edge, and what awareness you have gained by 'going over the edge'.

Self-awareness

I have referred to the importance of inner work to allow you to facilitate with neutrality and detachment. Also, the more self-awareness you develop, the more able you are to use the metaskills. It is vital for anyone facilitating group processes to understand themselves well if they are going to sit in the heat of any group to facilitate decisions, resolve conflict or problem solve. Here is an exercise to help you develop more awareness of your own processes.

Inner-work exercise: deep democracy on yourself (20 minutes)

1. Think of a vision you have for your life, your career or your work. Use all of your sensory channels to create this vision. What will it look like, sound like, feel like? How will you know when you are there?
2. What stops you from believing fully in this vision? What stops you from acting on this vision?
3. How can you address the 'door closer' or the 'edge figure' who is preventing you from acting on this?
4. Have a conversation between these two parts of yourself. Switch between both parts and gain the wisdom of what the edge figure is advising you. The edge figure is often your best inner critic. Your greatest ally has a wisdom. Turn the critic into a coach. By acknowledging both parts of yourself, you are beginning to practise deep democracy within yourself, bringing in the wisdom of your minority voice.

In conclusion

In some ways, working with metaskills and the concepts of deep democracy is like going on a journey into the unknown. But groups can go only as far as the skills of the facilitator can guide them. The smaller the group you work with, the more likely your success during your first attempts to work with the principles of deep democracy. Your best tools are:

- your own self-awareness;
- not having a personal agenda;

- being interested to work with any issues that arise;
- trying to achieve greater meaning or understanding.

In essence, it is important to recognize that your own personal growth and that of the group are connected. As a facilitator, be aware of how much fire and emotion both you and the group can handle.

In this chapter I have shared with you my work with metaskills and deep democracy. Although the practice of deep democracy began with Mindell, I have been trained in a variation of his original work. There are many facilitators around the world who are skilled in using these precepts, and I encourage you to learn from them. I have adapted them to my work in performance development to great effect. Learning something new is all about incorporating it into what you already do well, so I encourage you to select one or two items from this chapter to work with. Remember: go slowly, use reflective listening, take time.

Finally, I believe that the concept of deep democracy embodies an extraordinary wisdom that we all can learn from and apply in every aspect of our lives.

Where to go for more

Books

Goodbread, Joseph (1997, 2nd edn) *The Dreambody Toolkit: A practical introduction to the philosophy, goals and practice of process-oriented psychology*, Lao Tse Press, Portland, Oregon

Jung, C G (1965) *Memories, Dreams, Reflections*, Vintage Books, New York

Jung, C G (1969) *The Structure and Dynamics of the Psyche, Collected Works, vol 8*, 2nd edn, Princeton University Press, Princeton

Mindell, Amy (1994 and 2001) *Metaskills: The spiritual art of therapy*, New Falcon Press, Tempe, Arizona/Lao Tse Press, Portland, Oregon

Mindell, Dr Arnold (1992 and 2000) *The Leader As Martial Artist: an introduction to deep democracy, techniques and strategies for resolving conflict,* HarperCollins, San Francisco/Lao Tse Press, Portland, Oregon

Mindell, Dr Arnold (1995) *Sitting in the Fire: Large group transformation using conflict and diversity,* Lao Tse Press, Portland, Oregon

Mindell, Dr Arnold (2000) *The Quantum Mind: Journey to the edge of psychology and physics*, Lao Tse Press, Portland, Oregon

Journals

Wajsman, Myrna and Lewis, Greg (1999) Path to empowerment, *CAmagazine* (January/February) pp 45–51

Journal of Process Oriented Work **7** (2) (1995–6) Lao Tse Press, Portland, Oregon

Web sites and workshops

Dharma Partners, Process Workshops (email: dharma@iafica.com)
Hampton Roads Publishers, North Carolina (Web site: www.hrpub.com)
Journal of Process Oriented Work (a semi-annual journal about process work) [Online]
    http://www.laotse.com
Lao Tse Press, Oregon (Web site: www.lao-tse-press.com)
Parrlamond, Organizational and Individual Change (Web site: www.parrlamond.com)
Process Work Center of Portland, Oregon (Web site: www.processwork.org)

10

Synchronicity: putting it all together

'All's well that ends well'
Shakespeare

As you combine the ideas and techniques in this book, you will begin to facilitate a new kind of performance. The secret is to take one step at a time, adapting these tools to fit your style, to suit your pace and the needs of your participants.

These steps, however, are part of an exciting quest, one that never ends – but in the process of which you aim to become a master of your own craft. Here, in summary, is part of the route you have already travelled. Enjoy the rest of your journey!

- accelerating performance;
- become the architect of your future;
- establish a learning environment;
- learning from Shakespeare;
- train your brain;
- innovate to motivate;
- it's not all rock'n'roll;
- refining rapport skills;
- facilitating with metaskill;
- where to go from here.

Accelerating performance

- Identify what drives you.
- Take risks and learn from mistakes.
- Push beyond your limits.

Accelerating performance is all about learning new ways to deliver, present and structure your workshops. Building performance is all about the courage to take risks, developing positive beliefs and learning from your results. The first step is to identify what drives you, determining your values and aligning your goals to them. Jump-start your creativity with collaboration and cooperation, always being willing to learn from colleagues and your delegates.

Think of yourself as a pioneer, opening up doors to let in the light. Blazing the way for yourself, you will blaze the way for your participants, no matter what role you play: facilitator, trainer, HR manager, coach, manager. If you develop yourself, you will enable your participants to learn. Start with yourself.

We have looked at new ways to enhance performance for yourself, your clients and the people in your organization. We have learnt new ways to design and develop performance workshops, coach team members, manage change and push beyond your own limits. As you master these collected ideas and techniques, you will break through your current boundaries. You will be on your way to developing your own individual magic.

Become the architect of your future

- Drive performance through learning.
- Bungee-jump your skills.
- Embark on a personal renaissance.

Believing in your potential and that of your learners is a must if you are to accelerate performance. Learn all you can, and become an expert in one area at a time. Gradually you will see opportunities to integrate all these methods and techniques into your work. You are on the road to your own renaissance.

Personal mastery is all about learning. To enhance performance, teach an appreciation for constant learning. Learn to control your thinking and to focus on excellence. Never affirm limiting beliefs. Reaffirm positive self-belief. Catch the cynic's voice; have a conversation between your conflicting voices.

Learn to wrestle with your demons: self-doubt and internal conflict. Who will be your professional coach to take you beyond your self-limiting beliefs? Do you have a mentoring programme at work? If not, how can you start one?

Your path to renewal means a renewal of spirit. Using the African spirit hierarchy, what are the dominant energies, cultural values and concerns within the organization? How can you promote the values of integrity, performance, truth, power and innovation?

Embark on a behavioural renaissance in the organization. Advocate open communication, brainstorming, creativity, whole-brain thinking teams. Drive performance through learning, and leap over barriers to performance.

Become a role model for others. Personal mastery takes energy, passion and motivation. Seek through learning. That's the never-ending journey.

Establish a learning environment

- Create a climate of possibility.
- Engage your learners.
- Deal with learner anxiety.

Your job as a performance coach is to open the door – icebreakers offer you opportunities. They welcome everyone to the kingdom of learning. Giving the gift of your name is always the best place to start, establishing the tone of the session.

Creative icebreakers develop trust, engage the learners, bring passion back into the learning environment and align individual goals with organizational aims. Start as you mean to go on. Icebreakers help reinforce concepts and liberate the abilities of your participants. Call on their intelligence and experience, and empower them with questions.

Make sure you collect the concerns of your participants. Ask them to contribute their stories, experiences and feelings. People want to know and understand others – it helps them to understand themselves. This creates synchronicity. Our hopes and fears are often similar.

Establish a relaxed and comfortable atmosphere. Give participants a degree of control. Help them to let go of the fear of having to be perfect. Give them room to make mistakes. Allow them to learn by doing.

Whatever your route, bring their hearts and minds to the learning journey. Remember: icebreakers are not just for introductions. Use them to come full circle. End the day where you started. What did they gain? What will they do differently?

Learning from Shakespeare

- Entertainer or trainer?
- Make the link to the theatre.
- Act it out.

Learners learn by doing. Experiment with storytelling, role playing, dynamic-circle exercises, voice work, music, metaphor and films. Dialogue, experiential exercises, breathing and movement create workshops that are stimulating, motivating and challenging.

Remember: make the link between the theatre world and the theme of your session. Theatre-based learning is participant driven, applying the rules of theatre to the business world.

If you are training speakers, presenters or trainers, voice exercises develop vocal muscles, flexibility and group energy. Bring in the master, Shakespeare himself. Or use fairy tales, poems and short stories to develop the pitch, pace, volume and inflection of the voice.

Take on Hollywood to educate and entertain. Films are a powerful training tool for change because filmmakers are today's most popular storytellers. Introduce films, aligning them with learning points in your sessions.

Communication is the essence of the actor's trade. The art of storytelling will develop the linguistic and mental agility of yourself and your participants. Drive home points about leadership, team work, vision, goals or relationships. Transform learning. Develop imagination, communication skills and mental and behavioural flexibility.

Train your brain

- Principles of brain-based learning
- Emotional intelligence competencies
- Memory and recall techniques

Brain-based learning will set your programmes apart – whether you want to jump-start performance, build mental muscle, or improve confidence, memory and recall. Developing the individual intelligences and emotional competencies of your learners will motivate them to collaborate and achieve.

Developing mental fitness leads to innovative performance and thinking. We need to encourage our teams to become whole-brain thinkers. Help them to think creatively, with an understanding of their own unique thinking styles: rational, experimental, organizing or feeling.

Brain-based learning is to do with taking in and processing information in a way the brain prefers, in a way the individual would naturally learn. We take in information through our senses, but process it through our intelligences. Introduce activities that incorporate as many of the intelligences as possible. This will increase the mental flexibility of your team. Put emotion back into the equation. When we connect feelings and emotion to learning, we activate the limbic or emotional brain. Learning can become much more effective and powerful.

Developing social and personal competencies ensures a balanced workforce; they will be motivated and confident. Self-esteem is the key to lifelong self-motivation. Understanding their own emotions will guide individuals to reach their goals, and to develop the will to achieve. How can they model their own excellence?

Use your memory-mapping tools for brainstorming, learning, creating, analysing, evaluating. To transfer memorable learning to the workplace, ensure learning is linked, outstanding, relevant and practised.

Innovate to motivate

- Link learning, creativity and motivation
- Use psycho-geometrics and contradictory thinking
- Radical coaching, meta mirror and drawing

You can create real magic in learning and performance development with innovative thinking. The use of techniques such as memory mapping, the meta mirror, brainstorming and setting well-formed goals captures the hopes and dreams, and dissolves the fears, of your learners.

People are motivated by what is important to them. Focus on individual efforts. Spark enthusiasm by generating new ideas and creating the will to achieve.

Learning and motivation are very closely linked. Help individuals to achieve their dreams and those of the organization by setting challenging goals that are closely linked to their internal motivators. How can they creatively set out stepping stones to reach their end goals?

Be careful not to hire only those like you. Psycho-geometrics helps us take a close look at the diversity of approaches and thinking styles in a team. Introduce creative-thinking strategies: random thinking, contradictory thinking, brainstorming. Brainstorming is a creative tool that works powerfully in the same way the brain works.

Don't be afraid to introduce drawing techniques, a whole-brain activity that frees up the individual's eye. Drawing is all about learning to see again. Storytelling and metaphoric thinking help individuals understand their innovative potential.

Use six-cap thinking as a decision-making tool to problem solve. Step into the meta mirror to open up the dynamic between two people, or two groups where communication has broken down.

Powerful, positive beliefs help to create personal and organizational change. Introduce activities into your learning group to empower personal beliefs.

It's not all rock'n'roll

- Generate outstanding links to learning.
- Music builds the emotional connection.
- Mozart makes you smarter.

Music stirs the soul. It relaxes and energizes the body, stimulates thinking. Use music to unlock the creative spirit in learners, in your organization.

Introduce music as a learning tool. Music provides an emotional connection to retain new learning. It stimulates thinking powers and unlocks creative potential. Memory improves when information is attached to an anchor such as music. Music motivates, inspires and generates emotional connections for learning, helping to build skills, competencies and confidence.

Use music to trigger memory and anchor learning, to complement and exaggerate meaning. Use it as an auditory aid. Mozart or Bach stimulate learning and recall. Rock'n'roll creates a sense of energy, community and motivation. Popular songs can enhance themes you want to highlight.

Music can heal, relax and create an ambiance ideal for performance development. Begin and end with favourite pieces of classical or rock'n'roll music. Change the pace, generate energy or create a mood for visualization and relaxation.

Find out what music your learners are passionate about. Explore how they want to use music in performance development. Use music to enhance well-being and intelligence, to create relaxation in conjunction with a keen mental alertness. Evoke emotions, the desire to move or dance. Music is memorable. It will create that emotional connection long past the day of learning.

Refining rapport skills

- Develop behavioural flexibility.
- Understand the effects of stress.
- Develop communication excellence.

Rapport is that naturally occurring dance that happens when two people meet. Learn how to match body language and voice tone in order to harmonize with, but not copy, someone else. Learn to match and mismatch with sensitivity and respect. Experiment with ways of agreeing and disagreeing. Relationships can be maintained through rapport, more than by agreeing with everything the other person says.

Emotional intelligence, particularly social competence, is crucial in determining how well we handle relationships. A combination of empathy, an awareness of the other's feelings and needs, and social skills all help produce a desirable response in others – and help us to collaborate, cooperate and develop rapport.

Remember that emotions have a huge impact on motivation and performance. Help participants to understand themselves and the factors that push them past their coping skills. Inadequate communication skills contribute more to stress in the workspace than any other factor.

Use appropriate language; match the communication styles of the other person to powerfully build rapport. Model excellence in others; model excellence in yourself. The more you develop expertise and humility, the greater your skills and resources. Tape your sessions, listen to other speakers. Always be willing to learn and discover something new for yourself. Adopt a posture of curiosity about others by asking questions.

Ultimately, feel free to learn from and let go of mistakes. Flexibility is a fundamental skill in letting go. Learn to let go mentally, emotionally and physically.

Rapport is your number one skill as a facilitator and performance coach. You can never learn enough about effective communication.

Facilitating with metaskill

- Managing the group process.
- The metaskills and deep democracy.
- Principle of inclusion.

In essence, the facilitator's role is to let the group become responsible for its aims and outcomes, and to manage that group process. Develop a broad range of skills and metaskills. Metaskills are the beliefs and attitudes that you bring to the group. Metaskills require considerable depth of self-awareness on the part of the facilitator.

Metaskills cannot be learned in the same way that we learn technical skills. They are more akin to the processes of the unconscious mind. The facilitator uses metaskills to move the group through conflict to growth and learning. Compassion, neutrality, detachment, congruence, patience and humility are your crucial metaskills.

Develop reflective listening skills. Learn to ask questions; reflect back the group's issues with clarity. Developing reflective listening helps the group to see its issues in greater depth.

Deep democracy is a valuable tool to facilitate any group process where decisions are taken. Deep democracy respects the majority voice, but includes the wisdom of the minority. Deep democracy explores what it would take for the minority to come along with the majority. It is a revolutionary way of facilitating any group process where decisions need to be reached.

Where to go from here

Thanks, Michelangelo

I once heard the most delightful story about Michelangelo as he painted the Sistine Chapel. A young assistant, anxious to leave, began descending the scaffolding. He looked up at Michelangelo, just as the painter reached out to put the finishing touches to one of the ceiling paintings. 'Michelangelo,' he asked, 'what are you so worried about? You are at the peak of your career. Just paint up and let's go home. No one, but no one, can see that little detail from down here.'

Michelangelo slowly put down his brush, sat back on the top step of the scaffolding and peered down at the lad sternly. 'Every brush stroke is the most important,' he said. 'Because I learn something new with each stroke. That's what's important, the learning. And I am still learning.' Michelangelo smiled, picked up his brush and started painting again.

If Michelangelo, at the height of his career, at the peak of his fame, was still learning, then we all have hope; for we too have much to learn. So, enjoy it! Remember: the magic is in the learning.

Index